The Shaping of Urban Society

THE SHAPING OF URBAN SOCIETY

A History
of City Forms
and Functions

JANET ROEBUCK

CHARLES SCRIBNER'S SONS
New York

Copyright © 1974 Janet Roebuck

Library of Congress Cataloging in Publication Data

Roebuck, Janet.
    The shaping of urban society.

    Bibliography: p.
    1. Cities and towns.   I. Title.
HT111.R57   301.36   73-18205
ISBN 0-684-13644-9
ISBN 0-684-13700-3 (pbk.)

1 3 5 7 9 11 13 15 17 19 C/C 20 18 16 14 12 10 8 6 4 2
1 3 5 7 9 11 13 15 17 19 C/P 20 18 16 14 12 10 8 6 4 2

Printed in the United States of America

Contents

List of
Illustrations

Preface

To attempt to condense the history of Western cities and their society into one volume is presumptuous. The single-minded specialist who lives at the heart of every historian will cry out against its sweeping generalities, lack of specific focus, and superficial treatment of many new or disputed areas of historical research. Certainly the specialist in my heart had to be quelled many times. Nevertheless, a need for just such a sweeping survey of the development of Western cities exists, for urban problems have aroused the interest of many scholars as well as ordinary citizens. Historians working in this field have been concerned with various aspects of the development of specific cities at different times, and consequently the need on the part of young historians for a general introduction to this area of their discipline has grown. Other specialists involved in urban planning, architecture, and sociology require a general background against which their own work may be set, and ordinary citizens simply interested in how the urbanized West became urbanized may also find a general introduction useful.

This book grew out of a general course in urban history that I introduced at the University of New Mexico, and many thanks are due to the students who took it. Their interest, spirit, and the frequent excellence of their work was helpful and stimulating, especially when my own enthusiasm was inclined to flag. I am also grateful to my colleagues in sociology and especially in architecture for their interest in a historian trampling their fields and for their help. Working with the people at Scribners was a very pleasant experience, and I much appreciate their tolerance and good humor as well as their efforts in producing the book. Thanks are due to Mary Uhl, for whose hours of hard labor spent reworking the manuscript I can express no adequate thanks and who will surely receive great rewards in heaven; to Dorothy Marshall for pointing out inconsistencies and errors and making many helpful suggestions; and to Jo Fairbanks for reading proof. They made it a far better piece of work than I could have done but are in no way responsible for its errors and inadequacies, which are my own.

Janet Roebuck

Albuquerque, New Mexico
August 1973

The Shaping of Urban Society

INTRODUCTION

Some Problems of Definition

Urban settlements are commonly classified as either cities or towns. Since these terms have long been in general use, it might be expected that urban historians would be able to define the two main subjects of their studies with some degree of precision. In fact, neither term has a clear definition that can be applied to all places at all times. Even in the mid-twentieth century no uniformity exists in the way various Western nations apply them. In the United States the census definition of a town is a settlement with twenty-five hundred people; in Canada a town must have a thousand people; in Greece, ten thousand; in Sweden and Denmark a settlement of only two hundred qualifies as a town. Population density, number of buildings, total value of trade, and other statistical yardsticks are similarly useless in forming general definitions.

Definition in terms of function also presents problems. A city could be described as a major manufacturing or trading center, a town a minor one, but many settlements would resist these classifications. Las Vegas, Nevada, manufactures little but empty pockets, and according to this definition would not qualify as a city, while a tiny trading post on an Indian reservation in the wilderness might qualify as a town. The extent of the area of influence of an urban settlement might provide a more reasonable basis for definition. Towns could be defined as urban settlements that have a local impact, while cities have regional or international significance. The problem with this definition is the variable

1

meanings of "local," "regional," and "international." In the past, when transportation was generally slow and difficult, both "local" and "regional" denoted geographical areas much smaller than those meant by the same terms in the nineteenth and twentieth centuries. The meaning of "international" is also subject to interpretation, for international boundary lines have been revised frequently. Moreover, a small settlement on an international border may have a "local" area that officially overlaps two nations, while a city in the center of a large nation may have great impact on a vast region but be of minimal international importance.

Urban historians, census takers, local and regional planners, and many other people have spilled much ink trying to distinguish between towns and cities, and a discussion of the strengths and shortcomings of the various definitions would fill several books. All that is certain is that there is no accepted definition of "town" or "city" that applies on an international scale. There is still less agreement about terms like "suburb," "conurbation," "metropolitan area," or "megalopolis." The only generally workable definitions are so vague as to have little meaning. Towns are urban settlements that are smaller than the cities of their time; cities are urban settlements that are generally recognized by contemporaries as the largest and most important settlements. To impose definitions more precise than these is to force urban areas into forms for which they are not suited. To apply a single, rigid definition to both past and present settlements is to ignore changes in their comparative sizes, forms, functions, and effects across time. In any event, in this general survey of urban development the distinction between towns and cities is not of crucial importance since the general characteristics of the most dynamic urban settlements will be emphasized rather than the categories or labels of specific settlements. "Town" and "city" will therefore be more or less interchangeable.

As the basic terms in urban development do not lend themselves to precise definition, neither does the term "urban history." It is a study of towns and cities, but because these incorporate buildings, roads, and public service structures and systems, the term also includes some elements of architecture and planning. Because urban settlements have economic and political functions, urban history includes some economic and political history. Cities and towns house many individuals and groups, and urban history must therefore incorporate some social history. Since philosophy and social theory have sometimes affected urban history, it occasionally overlaps the history of ideas. Urban history thus encroaches on the boundaries of many of the conventional historical compartments.

Because cities have acted in a way that affects most people in some way or other, urban history might be described as a history of Western society viewed from the civic center.

Of course the generalities of urban history sometimes obscure the specific features of urban development, as is the case in social history. No aristocrat, peasant, or urban worker has shared exactly the same personal or family history with other members of his class, and an overview of society, like all generalities, is inevitably inaccurate in many specific cases. Despite this, social history is exact enough within its limitations to yield useful pictures of social conditions and trends for the broad sweep of society. Urban history is similarly imprecise in detail while accurate enough in general. There is and can be only one Rome, one Paris, one London, one New York, one Los Angeles; each is unique and the details of the development of each city form specific histories. Nevertheless, most major Western cities have exhibited enough characteristics in common to constitute city "types," just as there are social "types." Terms like "medieval city" are equally legitimate and useful as such commonly used terms as "industrial society." It is at the general level that this study of urban development operates.

Each type of city discussed herein is the product of economic, technological, and social forces operating together to give it a characteristic physical form and set of functions that in turn mold urban society. These are described in general terms although no individual city conforms exactly to all the patterns outlined. One of the problems of characterizing city types in this way is that economic, technological, and social forces do not change suddenly, but rather gradually as innovations become established and old social forms become inappropriate and in need of replacement. Specific cities characteristic of one historical period may continue in existence almost unchanged while dynamic city development has moved into another phase. Venice, for example, continued to look and operate like a medieval city long after the Middle Ages, and Manchester has retained its industrial city functions and much of its appearance well into the period dominated by the modern city. Furthermore, not all cities go through all the phases described here, and some have never exhibited certain forms; obviously the vast modern urban complexes along the eastern seaboard of North America have never been medieval cities. Finally, the forces that shape the most dynamic cities during any period are not always active in all geographical areas at the same time. The distinction among city types suggested here is therefore of necessity a schematic convenience.

The Historical Role of the City

Throughout the history of Western man, the city has been a dynamic force in social development and has provided mankind with both the leisure and the labor to stimulate intellectual, artistic, and scientific endeavors. The changing nature of the city has also imposed leadership in developing new social forms on its residents, for as the urban environment and urban functions evolved, human society has had to adapt to new demands. The technological and social changes city people introduced, however, inevitably affected the urban organism in turn and thereby gave rise to new stresses and the need for further social adjustments.

Cities have also had an enormous impact on rural society. Urban needs and products have always been prime factors shaping the life-style of rural people living near cities, but even before modern transport and communications diminished the effective distances between farm and factory, cities had often also revolutionized the lives of people in remote farming lands. The Romans, for example, established towns and cities in primitive agricultural regions, not only as part of their military policy, but also as an expression of their city-oriented way of thinking. In the nineteenth century the need for raw materials for the factories of the industrial cities linked distant farmlands with urban industry in an economic chain that crossed national boundaries, continents, and oceans. Although assembly-line production and mass distribution are urban phenomena, no rural area can escape their influence. Nationwide communications organizations, such as radio and television companies designed to serve the needs of high-density urban areas, reach into scattered farming communities as well as urban households. The picture of the good life and of material wealth that the urbanized West presents to the rest of the world has tempted many non-Western, nonurbanized nations to leap in one bound from rural community to mass urban industrialism.

The city has always been the point at which Western humanity has been in closest contact with its future. The nature of their economic functions allows city people more leisure than is generally available to rural people, and the city offers individuals a wider range of choices in both vocations and avocations than does the farm or village. Largely because of this enlarged scope of activities, city dwellers have proven more dynamic than rural people. The city's prolificacy in generating inventions and innovations in all areas of life exceeds that of every other unit of human social organization. Intellectual, scientific, artistic, techno-logical, and social innovations have, in turn, changed the city itself and thrust it into new stages of development. The very fertility and inventiveness of cities has meant that the urban milieu has rarely been as stable as the rural. City man has not achieved the long periods of harmony with his environment that rural man has enjoyed.

City people, constantly changing and being changed by the urban environment, have always been restless, disruptive elements in the world. The urbanite, even more than the explorer or pioneer, has always been eager to turn his back on the past and the status quo and to rush forward along the frontiers of the future. While the explorer satisfied man's essentially primitive urge to wander and to forage much as his most ancient ancestors had done, and while the pioneer sought to establish an old pattern of life in new lands, city man has constantly moved further from the mode of life of his ancestors as he searches for and invents new ways of life and of making a living. He has had precedents to follow and older systems to borrow from as he chooses, but unlike rural man he has lived in a constantly changing, "unfinished" social setting in which the past is often of little significance. The instability of their material and social environment has forced city people to become the explorers and experimenters of society. The accepted limitations of human capacity and of social organization have been challenges rather than supports, as tradition and custom were. In his attempts to solve old problems, city man has often produced new ones; nevertheless he has pressed constantly, although usually uncertainly, into the future.

FROM COMMUNITY TO EMPIRE 1

The Transition to Community Living

The passage of time and the lack of evidence obscures the exact nature of the earliest human communities as well as most of the activities and institutions of early man. It is probable, however, that man's early ancestors functioned in loose family groups which ensured that the basic functions of life could be carried on. They lived by hunting and by gathering wild fruits, grains, and nuts. Undoubtedly family groups combined, and other people joined them to form a more effective survival unit, a hunting pack or tribe. Hunting large animals was no easy task with primitive weapons and tools, and generally the larger the group of hunters, the better was the chance of both individual and group survival. Early families made use of natural shelters, such as caves, and when they were unavailable, may have undertaken elementary construction, such as piling up stones and logs for windbreaks or stretching animal skins over wooden supports to make simple tents. People did not need permanent shelters, for once game and wild fruits and vegetables were exhausted in one place, they moved along to another area where hunting and gathering were better. In this unsettled, nomadic existence the search for food was constant, particularly since there were few ways of preserving and storing food surpluses for any length of time. Hunting and gathering was an unreliable way of obtaining food that tended to produce wild fluctuations: feast when the hunting was successful or the country bountiful, famine when game was short and gathering poor. There was no guarantee

7

against hunger or starvation in the next season or even in the next few days.

The economic incentives for developing a new way of community life were twofold: first, to facilitate immediate daily survival by combining the food-collecting efforts of several people, and second, to gain future security by producing surpluses or certainties of food for future use. People made a major step in the direction of achieving these goals when they discovered that after they had scattered seeds on the ground, food-bearing plants exactly like the ones that had produced the seeds would grow there. Having food plants in one location near travel routes and camp sites made "harvesting" easier and suggested the possibility of planting over a wide enough area to produce a surplus that could be kept for future use.

The domestication of animals was an equally important step toward the development of the elementary settled community. The scavenging opportunities afforded by the scraps and bones littering human camps attracted dogs, whose presence accustomed people to living in association with animals. After being with people awhile, dogs proved useful for warning of the approach of potential danger to the camp and eventually for assisting in the hunt. These experiences established that animals and humans could form a working relationship; in time this observation extended to other animals as well. If tribes could tame food animals as they had dogs, they could keep them nearby and thus have an assured meat supply as well as other animal food products, such as the milk of goats and cows and the eggs of domesticated birds. The application of these discoveries allowed people to enjoy the pleasure of a full belly over relatively long periods of time and gave them the security of being able to face the immediate future knowing that at least their food needs would be filled.

How mankind first discovered farming and animal husbandry is not known, but it is probable that like most of man's most basic and vital innovations, he developed them by chance and trial and error. It is also probable that in its early stages farming simply supplemented the products of the hunt and of traditional gathering expeditions. For example, a tribe might find a good hunting area with enough game to sustain it for a few months, and the nonhunters, the women and children who stayed in camp when not gathering wild fruits and vegetables, might scratch up a plot of earth, scatter seeds, and reap an elementary harvest before the group moved on. People in another group might scatter the seeds of a favored food plant near an often-used camp site and move on, knowing that when they passed that way again there would be vegetable food conveniently nearby. As time passed, accidental and experimental discoveries promoted the idea that more and better plants resulted from scattering only the best seed in the earth. Similarly, it was found that if the best food animals were collected together, protected from predators, and ensured an adequate supply of water and a good grazing area such as the stubble remaining after a harvest, they would repay the labor involved many times over by yielding larger quantities of food. For many centuries, however, groups of people practiced only intermittent farming and were probably sustained largely by the products of the hunt.

Farming eventually restricted mobility, for any tribe that wanted to enjoy a potentially secure food supply had to settle in one place for at least one or two growing seasons in order to care for their crops, protect them from animals, and harvest them. Fields, however small and elementary, are obviously not mobile, and therein lies one of the major reasons for the earliest human settlements. Domesticated animals are potentially fairly mobile because they can be herded across grasslands, grazing as they go, with no loss of their productive capacity, but any extended scheme of planting inevitably means at least short-term settlement. When a group practiced a "mixed economy," the demands of keeping animals reinforced the immobilizing effects of the fields. When a group kept animals in one area for any length of time, they had to guard them against predators, stop them from straying, and protect the cultivated fields from them. All this involved the production of equipment of a fixed nature, such as wooden or stone stockades, and added to the inertia generated by the static character of the fields.

The people of farming tribes, faced with the certainty of a prolonged stay in one place, also had to provide for their own shelter, protection, and comfort. They had both the incentive and the time to develop something more hospitable than a bare cave. Indeed, fertile land that was ideal for growing crops and grazing cattle generally did not have many rock outcrops equipped with handy caves. Quickly erected, temporary windbreaks that were convenient enough for a night or two clearly would not fill the needs of people settling down to stay in one place for many months or even years. The new economy rendered temporary shelters obsolete; in response to its demands, these people developed more permanent and stable ones. They dug pits in the ground and roofed them over with branches, skins, or turf; they constructed small huts of logs, branches, mud, stone, or whatever building materials were readily available. In short, economic drives combined with developing agricultural skills to produce the earliest form of human semipermanent settlement, the agricultural village.

This rudimentary form of settled or semisettled human community still exists in various remote parts of the world; but as far as the development of Western society is concerned, the Neolithic villages that developed in the Near East about eight thousand years ago are probably the earliest ancestors of the urban community. Initially the rate at which the natural nutriments in the soil were depleted undoubtedly limited the duration of a community. Once the soil was exhausted and began to give smaller yields, the group would move, clear and plant a new area, and work this patch until it, too, was exhausted; then they would move on again. Even in the earliest stages of the development of farming techniques, however, permanent settlement occurred in some areas where seasonal river floods regularly replenished the cleared fields with new soil deposits. In less fortunate areas, permanent settlement was possible only after the discovery that soil could be "artificially" encouraged to renew its fertility. Some groups allowed certain fields to go wild for a season or two; others allowed animals to graze on the stubble fields and fallow so that their droppings would fertilize the ground. There is evidence that some industrious village communities collected both animal and human excrement and spread it on their fields. Once fertility and, hence, stable crop yields could be ensured, a community could become permanent and relatively self-sufficient. Food raised by farming, supplemented by fishing, hunting, and gathering, could sustain its people, while trading with nomadic peoples or other settled communities filled special needs. Few early settlements seem to have been totally self-sufficient. Evidence indicates that even in the earliest times trade took place between communities with different specialties: shore-dwelling people exchanged items such as seashells with inland people who might offer better tools; people in rocky places traded ornamental stones for food with people in fertile places; all communities without salt traded whatever they had to offer for that precious commodity. The members of the stable farming community could thus enjoy an existence that was very secure and comfortable compared with that of their eternally wandering, often hungry ancestors.

The social structures of the family, kin, or religious group that early wanderers had developed to regulate their various activities inevitably became the basic elements in the social life of settled farmers. The new needs and restraints imposed by settlement, however, made it necessary to adapt the old social forms to fit the new conditions of life. For example, speed, strength, and aggression were important personal qualities in a community of people who survived by hunting, and the possessors of these qualities were accorded considerable status. Strength continued to be an important asset in farming communities, but speed was no longer so important and aggression was often a disruptive force to be curbed rather than rewarded. In addition, farming communities needed the skill and knowledge that could only come with the experience of many growing seasons. Hence, the young and strong could not be allowed to dominate the older and weaker, but wiser, members of the community. Social mechanisms that strengthened the position of the experienced and held the young in check had to be reinforced or developed so that both groups could contribute their special qualities to the mutual cause of survival.

The family continued to perform the basic functions of nurturing, socializing, educating, and restraining the young while supporting the old; but the special need of the permanent community for a high degree of social stability made it necessary to enlarge the role of the family. In each community a multitude of customs, most of them involving the direct or indirect regulation of family life by the community, gradually developed to ensure the continuance of an orderly, productive society. All communities developed prohibitions and taboos against various disruptive activities and often further strengthened them with religious sanctions; kinship obligations derived additional strength from community expectations and pressures; both communal and religious sanctions reinforced customs governing marriage in the interests of peace and group survival.

The question of land ownership had not much troubled the wandering hunters, but it was of great importance to the settled community. Groups had to decide, for example, whether the community, families, or individuals owned cultivated land; whether or not a crop was to be shared; and how to transmit land ownership from generation to generation.

In short, in order to survive in the settled village community, people had to look for, experiment with, and eventually establish more sophisticated social organizations to meet the demands imposed by settlement. Unless they could find systems to bind the members of the community together in order and harmony, the permanent village community would be in constant danger of breaking up and forcing its members to return to the older, less secure way of life. Such a reversion was clearly undesirable, and ultimately new social customs evolved and new codes of law developed that solved the problems of settlement and made possible the establishment of enduring communities.

The northern tribes of Europe illustrated the evolution of the new social customs and codes of law. It is not known precisely when this evolution took place, but it had certainly reached an advanced stage of development by the ninth century when Alfred the Great established himself as a leader in England. When the Germanic tribes that settled in England were hunters and nomads, the blood feud, or vendetta, was an accepted method of settling disputes. If a man were murdered, it was the privilege and responsibility of his kinsmen to seek out the murderer and kill him in retribution. This "eye for an eye" system of justice was easily understood and probably worked well enough when life was short, simple, and uncertain in any event. When the wanderers settled and families became more interdependent, however, this system began to pose a positive threat to the survival of settled communities. While all groups were more or less constantly on the move, friction likely to spark murder would not occur very often. When it did, it required some effort on the part of the murdered man's kin to find the culprit because both groups moved so frequently. Friction was more likely to occur in settled communities where people lived closer together and had concrete things such as the ownership of land and cattle about which to quarrel. If a quarrel ended in death, it usually involved people living in the same or adjacent settlements, and the murderer was thus much easier to find.

The mayhem that a protracted blood feud could generate in a region of settled kin groups is easy to imagine. The old nomadic system could quickly destroy a community, or at best, if nothing developed to replace it, the settled community could not long prosper. In addition, as communities acquired more complex and sophisticated rules and customs, new problems arose that threw old traditions into question. For example, if a man punished by the community for breaking one of its rules died, either as a part of his punishment or by accident during the execution of some lesser sentence, which social system were his kin to obey? Should they wage a blood feud against whoever had administered the punishment on behalf of the community, or should they accept community actions as taking precedence over kin rights in such cases? Clearly, the blood feud and the interests of the community were antipathetic and one or the other had to give way; in successful societies it was the old system of justice. The laws of Alfred indicate that by the ninth century the blood feud had been commuted to a sophisticated and complex system of kinship rights and responsibilities developed for the payment and receipt of wergeld, or "man price," for death or injury. In the early stages of development, the payments were assessed in terms of valuable possessions, such as oxen, and later, money. The more important a man was to his kin, the greater the size of his wergeld; as a result, wergeld eventually came to define a man's social status. At this stage the blood feud had completed its transition from a potentially disruptive force to a more or less civilized social convention that presented little threat to the settled community, which by this time had taken over the kin's duty of punishing transgressors.

Having tamed plants and animals and made settlements possible and desirable, people had then to "tame" themselves to live in those settlements. The economic sophistication inherent in the transition from roaming and hunting to settled agriculture paralleled a similar increase in the sophistication of the rules by which people lived. The application of many technical and social innovations transformed nomadic insecurity and simplicity into settled security and complexity. The experience gained in the transformation was invaluable training for the establishment of towns and cities and for the development of social systems sufficiently complex to enable people to live in them.

Ancestors of Modern Western Cities

The most direct ancestors of modern Western urban communities were the cities (as opposed to farming villages) that grew up in Mesopotamia between about 4000 and 3000 B.C. These cities grew up in the Tigris, Euphrates, and Nile valleys and were sustained by the food surpluses these fertile areas were then capable of producing. People who had developed to the farming-village stage of settlement on the surrounding grassy upland areas moved down to cultivate the more fertile soil in these valleys, which were oases of abundance in a semiarid region. Periodic river floods deposited new layers of silt that regularly revitalized the soil. Fruit trees and vines, birds and fish, an abundance of wild animals, and a steady and reliable water supply favored the valleys. The construction of irrigation works that extended the cultivated area both supported a larger population and helped ensure its permanence.

The move to more fertile regions seems to have generated a wider variety of interests and occupations in the people who moved, possibly because they no longer had to devote so much of their time to mere survival. Whatever the reason, by about 3000 B.C. the inhabitants of these river valleys had made many new discoveries and had put into practice the innovations that transformed villages into towns and cities. People learned, for example, that some animals could be used for power as well as for food. With the aid of oxen, farmers could use heavier, more efficient plows and turn over a larger area of ground in a workday. The same number of working people could thus produce a larger surplus of food than they had in the past. Up to this point, cultivation using the digging stick and the hoe had probably been mainly the function of women. With the introduction of oxen and the heavier plow, men began to play the dominant role in farming, and women lost much of the power and prestige naturally attached to the food producers.

The widening range of human interests that accompanied the growth of these permanent settlements led to a more rapid rate of invention and discovery. The wheel, an innovation of tremendous importance, was put to many uses. It improved pottery making, for in the hands of a skilled operator it made possible the production of flat-bottomed, symmetrical pots that were a great improvement on the clumsy vessels of the past, far better for cooking and storing food. The wheel also made possible the production of more pots in one day than one family could use in many days, thus leaving potters with a surplus for exchange or sale. By 3000 B.C. two- and four-wheeled carts were in use, carrying people and goods more easily, conveniently, in greater quantities, and over greater distances than in the past when elementary sleds had been the most advanced form of bulk transportation. New techniques of boat building were also developed during this period. The addition of sails supplemented the power of oarsmen. The result was the expansion of the traveling range and trading capacity of the people living on the banks of the great rivers or beside the sea. New discoveries were also made and innovations introduced in the working of metal, especially copper, making possible a better, more durable, and more useful metal in larger quantities. Metal was no longer a decorative luxury but a useful raw material for making tools of all kinds. A system of pictures and markings used to identify property and various other important objects like the sun and moon was refined to such a high level that symbols could be used to convey information to other people and to set down records for future reference. The advent of writing meant that people could transmit technical achievements and cultural patterns to others and preserve them for future generations; this in turn led to greater stability and continuity.

By 3000 B.C. the people of Mesopotamia had developed the technical capacity to sustain a relatively high volume of trade by land and water, to keep accounts, leave records, and write messages, to produce a larger agricultural surplus than had been possible in the past, and to make an abundance of sophisticated tools and implements of metal and clay. In short, the economic system had become more complex, its parts more sophisticated and diversified, and its influence more wide-ranging. The nonfarming craftsmen needed places to live, merchants needed market centers in which to trade, and farmers needed places where they could be sure of selling their food surpluses. Economic and technical advances made feasible a new kind of community, the city.

Although they did have some things in common with the farming villages that had preceded them, the cities of Mesopotamia were not merely larger versions of villages. They were something entirely new in human experience: not only bigger, but also more complex in form, functions, and products than anything before. The city of Ur, for example, although small by modern standards, was much larger than any previous settlement in the region. Its built-up area covered about one hundred fifty acres, and at its zenith it is estimated to have held up to twenty-four thousand people. Surrounding Ur were fields, pasture lands, and gardens, many of which received their water from an impressively extensive and sophisticated irrigation network. The city, protected by its bank and wall defensive works, contained ziggurats (temples), granaries, workshops of all kinds, and facilities for bakers, spinners, weavers, metalworkers, potters, scribes, priests, and farmers.

The ziggurats indicate something of the complexity of this settlement, a complexity that even the most sophisticated village had not come close to achieving. These churches or temples of the Mesopotamians were man-made hills, made of sun-dried bricks and mud, about thirty-five feet high with sloping sides and a flat top. Steps cut into the sides reached up to the temple structure on top, which was decorated with imported woods, precious stones such as lapis lazuli, and worked metals such as lead and silver. The size of the ziggurats and the amounts of material and labor evidently involved in their construction point to the existence of a large, well-organized, stable trading community that had a surplus of labor and of all kinds of materials, including food. The variety of materials used to ornament the temples indicates a wide-ranging trading system and the presence of skilled craftsmen, while the structures themselves suggest that the people who built them must have had some engineering ability as well as the social organization necessary to coordinate the efforts of so many people.

Primitive people had functioned within social structures in which the survival of the family or tribe in a hunting and gathering situation dictated most of their activities. After people began living in cities, they developed more sophisticated social systems in response to the evolution of an economy that encouraged rapid technological change and higher degrees of specialization. City people would henceforth be in the vanguard of innovators in the arts and sciences, industry, and trade, and in time they developed an awareness of themselves as comparatively superior people living in an unquestionably superior environment. Urban dwellers came to depend on their cities not only for material things and a livelihood, but also for more intellectual and psychological functions. Their world view hinged upon the existence of cities other than their own; their sense of history and human progress sprang from recorded and observed changes in the urban environment; their sense of the worth of other people was based on an evaluation of their cities—on their degree of "civilization."

With the diversification and specialization of the economy in urban settlements came a multiplicity of socioeconomic roles that had to be accommodated within the social structure. For example, even the most tightly knit communities found skilled craftsmen so valuable that they were willing to develop ways of absorbing itinerant specialists into their established social systems. In addition, the expansion of trade meant that communities had to find ways of accommodating, at least on a temporary basis, merchants, traders, and sailors, "foreigners" who did not belong to the community or fit into its social structure but whose activities helped it prosper. Further, people of all backgrounds from many places moved to and settled in cities in which they had no social commitments either to family, tribe, or neighbor. Modification of the structure of the survival groups of hunters or the cooperative groups of farmers would not serve to weld this mixture into a homogeneous group, and new systems of identifying, relating, and organizing people within the community had to be developed. Because the cities were walled, distinct communities standing out in a still-agrarian world, the city itself provided the foundation for a new system of social cohesion. People in any city had more in common with other people in their own city than they had with anyone else. They lived, worked, worshiped, and played in the same community, within the same set of walls. They contributed in a variety of ways to the life of that city and expected in return that the city would give them shelter and that its economy would provide them with the means of making a living. The members of the urban community formed a group that was distinct from groups in other cities and from the majority of people who still lived in the countryside. They identified with their city and with the other citizens who lived in it, not exclusively with a family, tribe, or clan. While social relationships within the city developed around more specific and detailed criteria, the general cohesion of city people was defined by the experience of community residence.

In order to allow the cities to survive, their residents had to perform a variety of complex tasks, including finding new ways of ensuring discipline and forming new methods of organizing the community to perform essential functions. For example, the city needed defense against hungry, less developed people who lived outside its confines and its control; its citizens had to build protective walls and other defensive works. The cities of Mesopotamia needed embankments, channels, irrigation works for the control and use of river water; they also had to provide for the building of religious structures of a size and style suitable for a large community. Protective walls, irrigation and flood control works, and temples represented public works on an unprecedented scale for whose construction labor had to be obtained and organized and raw materials and tools secured. Decisions had to be made about what was to be built, when, where, by whom, and who was to pay. In response to these complex new problems, the traditional community leaders—the wisest, the strongest, the possessors of religious knowledge or magic skills—extended and strengthened their powers to ensure that the work necessary to the survival or prestige of the community was carried out. They formed decision-making bodies, established revenue collection systems, and apportioned responsibilities for labor, materials, and finance. They then had to formulate rules to support the new organizational systems, to keep the community stable and peaceful, and to establish judicial systems to deal with those who did not observe the rules. In other words, community leaders appropriated functions and rule-making powers that made the city resemble a supertribal, supercomplicated, non–blood clan. The city, besides being a community, began to act as a suprapaternal authority in the lives of its citizens, organizing their labor, providing for their welfare and discipline, and allotting them responsibilities.

Religious institutions and religious leaders often dominated the processes of organization and direction of community efforts, combining secular organizations and functions with their religious ones and, in effect, exercising the authority of the city. The large and costly religious and semireligious structures of the early cities suggest that the priests, the custodians of magic and mystery, exerted a great influence on the community. For all the technical advances and relative sophistication of the urban community as a whole, ordinary individuals still found much in life that was incomprehensible. Those who did understand, or who were generally believed to understand, some of the mysteries were therefore in a position to use the respect or fear of their fellows to acquire the power necessary to achieve socially desirable or egotistical ends. In turn, their power within the community and their large and impressive temples enhanced their positions and entrenched them as community leaders.

In precity times, people who drew fine pictures of animals supposedly had a special "magic" relationship with those animals. The other members of their tribe probably accorded them respect and gave them free time to draw pictures and work magic in the interests of better hunting and more food for everyone. When life was short and precarious and notions about procreation were vague, a new life was precious and its origins seemed mysterious. Therefore, those who brought new life— childbearing women and the older women who assisted them—were often thought to have special contact with the awesome and magical forces of life and fertility. By association, these women were supposedly able to exert an influence on the plant and animal fertility upon which human life depended. In addition, people who made generally accurate forecasts about natural phenomena—probably based on conscious or unconscious observations but often represented as supernatural visions— were believed to have special contact with the forces of nature that affected human life; they, too, were accorded power and prestige as the possessors of superhuman knowledge and power. As humanity advanced and began to understand the connection between conception and birth, however, women gradually lost the prestige based on the assumption that they had magical powers of fertility; males, the planters of seed, appropriated these powers and added them to their store of "magic."

The "magicians" who eventually came to dominate large groups of people were more sophisticated than their predecessors who were artists and observers. They differed from region to region in the eastern Mediterranean, but whatever priestly cult won dominance, the community typically awarded it a position of great power and influence. This could be extended and expanded to cover more practical matters. The priests who exerted a special influence over the community could, for example, obtain better food, housing, and more leisure time, declaring that such conditions were necessary for the more effective practice of their special skills. By attaching religious overtones and requirements to such issues as where to hunt and plant, where and how to bury the dead, when and how to accord the young adult status, they could influence community organization.

The greater technical knowledge that made possible the establishment of the early cities did not remove all the imponderables from life, nor did it weaken the position of the priests or wise men. The priests sought to strengthen their traditional privileged position in society by whatever means came to hand. The building of larger and more impressive temples, for example, could enhance the traditional respect given them and their functions. Their mastery of new enigmas, such as writing, and their more precise astronomical observations and calculations that allowed them to forecast times of flood, drought, eclipse, and length of days more accurately and impressively also increased their prestige. They took care to protect and strengthen their privileged social position by selecting and training recruits to their ranks and keeping their skills and secrets to themselves. The value of their skills in such fields as writing and calculation, coupled with the respect or fear of the community, put them in a position in which they were the obvious organizers of society, the "natural leaders" who would issue orders, make decisions, and find new ways of organizing society to cope with the needs and demands of city life.

Those who put technical innovations to practical application often transformed them into new mysteries. For example, the working of metals was a mysterious process to most people, and it involved things many thought to be magic, such as fire and materials dug up from the ground; the making of pots on a wheel was a wonderment and fascination to people who had never tried such a thing. The products of the new skills were useful and were sought by people who did not have them; thus the possessors of these skills became valuable and respected people in their communities. Many of the new craftsmen saw, as the priests had seen, that they could translate special skills into social position and power. People to be trained in these skills were often carefully selected and their numbers restricted to preserve the rarity value of the skill and the exclusivity of its practitioners, while the teaching and learning processes were invested with an air of secrecy that tended to enhance the respect and awe of the uninitiated.

The urban communities needed not only people who would organize the building of walls and public works, but also men who would organize their fellows to fight to protect the community or to extend its control into a disputed area. As the cities of the eastern Mediterranean grew in size and in number, the areas not under the control or influence of one or another of them shrank. Eventually economic hinterlands and "spheres of influence" of cities overlapped in places and created sources of conflict.

Also, there was a growing need to protect well-established, prosperous communities from wandering bands of hungry marauders attracted by rumors of the cities' wealth.

The military leaders of the urban community and the strong man who was chief of his tribe resembled each other in many ways. Just as the priests found they could strengthen their social power by monopolizing writing, some men found they could gain power and influence by monopolizing control of the military and defense functions of the city. The holder of military power had the obvious advantages of being able to crush opponents, whether inside or outside the walls, and to profit by plunder. Some military leaders strengthened their positions by appropriating religious functions, and conversely, some priestly groups extended their control to military operations. As time passed, more and more power accumulated in the hands of priestly or military groups. They were the traditional and experienced leaders of society to whom people naturally turned in a crisis when external danger threatened or an internal emergency arose. When both religious and military forms of influence were concentrated in the same hands, power was considerably enhanced, especially after custom led to general acceptance of authority and institutionalization of its forms. Of all the shapers of society, the priest-king was the most powerful. It is no accident that the pharaohs of Egypt, who were both secular and spiritual leaders, were powerful enough to mobilize the vast resources necessary to build enormous personal monuments and to convince their people that such memorials should be built. Other people later in history tapped the potential for social leadership inherent in a combination of the two functions. The emperors of Rome often strove to establish their status as gods; the pagan kings of Europe frequently took pains to insert religious figures into their ancestry and to emphasize in other ways their special relationships with pagan gods, or, after their conversion, with the Christian God; Christian bishops sometimes acted as political and military leaders and assumed control of secular principalities that resembled city-states.

In those parts of the eastern Mediterranean and the Near East where early cities developed, many varieties of social organization appeared. Some of the social structures proved sturdy, others not. Notable among the failures were female-dominated societies that had evolved from the authority generated by the old female mysteries of fertility and birth. These were probably unsuccessful because the development of heavier farming implements and the growing importance of warfare placed a premium on strength in farming and on militarism in social leadership.

Despite the tales of the Amazons, few women were effective in these areas. Within the societies that did prove viable, at least for a time, a great deal of experimentation went on. For example, people tried various ways of raising revenue, as well as different methods of obtaining labor and materials for public projects, punishing transgressors of community laws and regulations, and maintaining community discipline. In addition to the refinement of the technical advances that allowed city growth, there was the refinement of the idea that at least some people thrived in large, densely populated urban areas and that living in cities set people apart from the rest of humanity that did not do so. There also emerged the enduring idea that city people were the innovators in all fields of technology and culture.

The technical discoveries made in the river valleys enabled people to live together on a scale and in a density previously unknown. The greater degree of security from hunger, the less physically exhausting life, the expanded leisure time, and the additional pleasures available, at least for some, drew increasing numbers of people to these communities. The development of the first cities and the growing concentration of people in them heralded the opening of a new phase of human history, one so significant that it has been called "the urban revolution."

The City-State

Without a reliable food supply capable of sustaining the population over some decades, no large community can develop, and even small ones cannot long thrive. Early cities thus needed to secure the areas on which they depended for their supplies of food and to expand those areas if city population grew. They generally attempted to assert socioeconomic control not only over their own citizens, but also over people in the surrounding food-producing areas and in any smaller communities within them. The early cities of the eastern Mediterranean region were the most wealthy, technically advanced, and highly organized units of their day. Little could stand in the way of their drives to dominate their food-producing hinterlands except another city. When a city had stamped its influence over the surrounding area and gained effective control there, that city became, in effect, the nucleus of a larger geographical, political, and economic unit: a "state." Ancient societies in which the city dominated the state and in which city and state government were

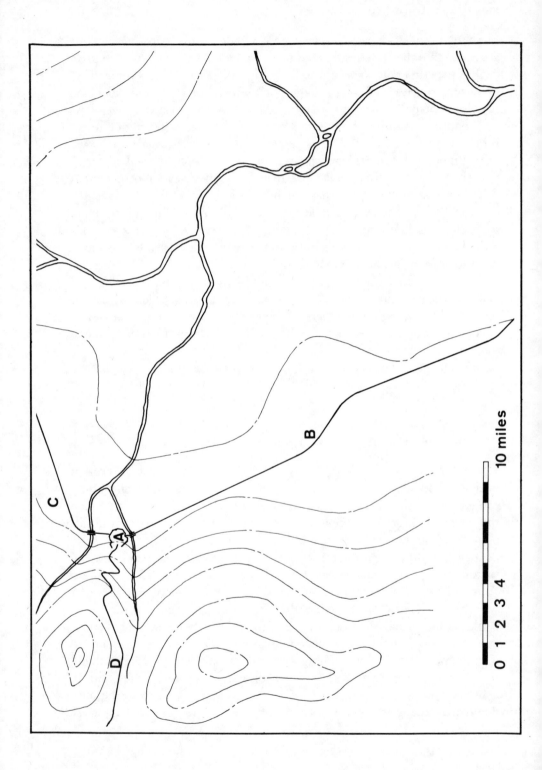

0 1 2 3 4   10 miles

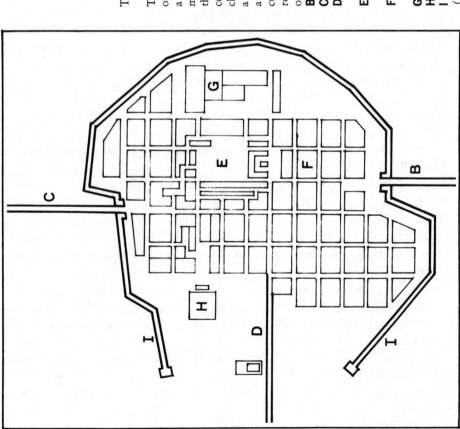

THE CLASSICAL CITY c. 100 A.D.

The site (**A**) was chosen because rivers and mountains offered water supply and protection while still allowing a commanding view of the valley. The road from the mother city into the interior was constructed to pass through this settlement, which also acted as an important communications center where travelers could, for example, change horses, find food, shelter, and protection. Originally a military base for the river valley, it continued to act as a military center while it served as a collection agent and cultural center for the area. The food, taxes, and military recruits gathered in this region were sent to the mother city on the coast.

B Road to mother city on coast.

C Road to frontier post in interior.

D Road to limestone quarry which provided building materials; continued to outpost city in next valley.

E Open plaza; trading center surrounded by public and religious buildings.

F Military section; grid plan derived from original military encampment.

G Stadium and public baths.

H Theater.

I Defensive wall.

(MAPS DRAWN BY SATHIT CHAIYASIN)

identical were numerous: Tyre, Sidon, Argos, Thebes, and many more. The best-known of them, however, is Athens, a city-state that reached the peak of its influence in the fifth century B.C. In the twentieth century A.D. few such states exist, but variations on this early form of urban political unit survive in "city-states" such as Andorra, San Marino, Monaco, and Liechtenstein.

In the centuries preceding the birth of Christ, however, the city-state was the characteristic stage of Western urban development. As was the case with the earliest cities, various forms of social organization developed, and all city-states differed to some extent in specific aspects of their social makeup. Even states that grew up within the same area often had very different forms of social organization. For example, Athens prided herself on the practice of the peaceful virtues of intellectual activity and the development of the arts by her citizens; in contrast, the nearby city of Sparta emphasized martial traditions and virtues.

Despite the many differences in details between the social forms of the city-states, they shared some basic social forms in common. Following the precedent set in earlier cities, an elite composed of a small percentage of the total population typically ruled the city-states. In Sparta, for example, the military leaders governed, while free residents who could vote on community decisions ran Athens in its "golden age." In most cities, dictators or "tyrants" took control at least occasionally. All city-states retained some kind of strong religious cult or cults near the core of both the social organization and the urban fabric. City residents made their livings by manufacturing desirable craft goods and by trading valuable and scarce commodities. Fairly limited transport technology restricted all to a population that could be fed mainly by crops from the neighboring agrarian areas. Some cities imported food items, especially those that could make extensive use of ships, which could carry bulkier and heavier items than land transport vehicles. Even port cities, however, received their main food supply from the farmers of the immediately surrounding areas. Although cities with more fertile hinterlands could naturally achieve a greater size, the limitations of transport generally acted as an automatic population control. Since the passion for making censuses and surveys is a recent development, the size and composition of the population of ancient cities is a matter of much speculation and controversy. Estimates vary, but it seems probable that the population of the majority of the city-states was about ten thousand, with a few of the larger ones, such as Athens in the fifth century B.C., reaching several times that number at the peak of their growth.*

Despite the need of farmers for peace to produce food, and of buyers, sellers, and manufacturers for peace to conduct their trading and manufacturing activities, the city-state was not generally a peaceful place. Despite the many experiments, one line of development that most of the cities of the eastern Mediterranean tended to follow was in the direction of military conquest. Protection and expansion of the food-growing area usually necessitated some military organization, as did the maintenance of security for traders. Military personnel and institutions inevitably proliferated as the need for territory and the possibility of conflict with other cities grew. Equally inevitably, the presence of a large number of soldiers within the cities had an impact on their functions, customs, and activities. Once war was established as a fairly common means of settling disputes between city-states, the city, the nucleus of the state, also became a military center. As such, it required even larger and more complex fortifications against enemy attack. These massive, expensive defenses often effectively closed its boundaries. The encircling defense works could be removed and rebuilt at a greater distance to allow for expansion of the city center, but the more complicated and expensive fortifications became, the less likely were the citizens to knock them down and rebuild farther out. The most massive ones, therefore, tended to remain in place for some time, cramping the physical growth of the city. Some cities thus restricted before reaching their maximum population level often became overcrowded. In many cases military emergencies plus the need to control the overcrowded and occasionally unruly citizenry produced problems that only an overall planner and controller could solve—an individual who could direct military forces against external enemies and who could crush violent expressions of social unrest within the city itself.

Despite the experiments with oligarchies and limited democracies, some form of monarchy or dictatorship seems to have best served the needs of the city-states. Autocrats commanded the military forces, which they used for domestic peace-keeping as well as warfare. In addition, many held high office in or were in other ways supported by the religious structure. Perhaps most importantly, their authority derived in part from the fact that they offered an end to the confusion and dissension inherent in systems in which authority was divided among several people or

* The population of Athens at its peak in the fifth century B.C. is estimated to have been about two hundred seventy thousand, including freemen, slaves, and foreigners, in both the city itself and its nearby port of Piraeus.

groups, systems that were slow to produce action in cases of emergency. Although the legendary Athenian experiment in democracy was an apparent exception, it was limited in time, scope, and the definition of "citizen." After the tyrant Hippias was expelled from the city in 510 B.C., a citizen democracy governed Athens for a century or so. Only free adult males born in Athens of Athenian parents qualified as citizens, and only they could participate in the processes of debate and decision; citizens made up only a small proportion, probably less than one-third, of the total population of the city. This city-state experiment was therefore by no means an exercise in mass participatory democracy. It was certainly government by a privileged minority, and it might indeed be characterized as government by an expanded oligarchy.

Technical advances, the growth of urban industry, and the expansion of trade led to an increasing specialization of occupations among the inhabitants of cities. As the urban economy became more sophisticated and the range of specialties more complex, people identified themselves more and more in terms of their occupations. Craftsmen in special trades such as boot making, metalworking, carpentry, stonemasonry, pottery, and boat building came to feel a sense of community with others who worked in the same trade. Merchants and sailors involved in similar commercial processes felt an analogous affinity. As a result, a new type of social system began to develop within the cities, one based on specialization. In addition, the preoccupation of the city with commerce and profit gave rise to the beginnings of a system of social stratification based on wealth. Just as the extent of a farmer's holdings and the yield of his land indicated his degree of success, so the volume of business and profits evidenced the worth of a city man. Although the development of an urban social structure in which wealth would almost exclusively determine class stratifications was far in the future, the seedlings of such a social form were growing in some of the city-states.

While within their own city walls people were developing new social definitions, the most significant social distinction city people made was between themselves and noncity people. Despite differences in religion, architecture, and government, the many cities that sprang up in the Mediterranean region had major elements in common that united their inhabitants while setting them apart from rural people. Intercity commerce linked urban trade and production centers, transcending the minor regionalisms and uniting cities in an effective, if often quarrelsome, commercial community of interest. Even when cities were at war, they were nevertheless united in their involvement in commercial pursuits and in their common subscription to the whole ethos of commercial and manufacturing activity. The inhabitants were aware that they had common interests with other city people and they came to think of themselves as a separate group, more at home in foreign cities than they were in the farming communities in the immediate vicinity of their own city. Despite cultural differences, their personal economies and life-styles brought them together while setting them apart from farmers, hunters, and nomads. The increasingly obvious and increasingly stressed differences between townsmen and farmers eventually obscured their interdependent relationship as the gap between the rural and urban experiences began to widen. The processes of trade also tended to produce a racially, culturally, and linguistically mixed population in cities. This differentiated city people even further from rural people, who normally saw few strangers and were rarely exposed to people who did not look, dress, speak, and behave like others in their home district.

Two significant differences in the urban and rural ways of life were the larger amounts of leisure available to city people and the greater variety of stimuli they experienced. At any time, rural people normally work more hours each day, more days each week, and more weeks each year than do urban people, and this was very much the case when there were few mechanical aids to help the farmer. He had to tend his crops, care for his animals, and do the milking according to the needs of the crops and the animals, not according to his own convenience. External forces, not his own fancy or the whim of any human agent, determined his day, week, and year. The townsman, on the other hand, normally made his living at some occupation that, apart from other people, involved only inanimate objects whose productive capacity normally remained unharmed if they were untended for a while. He could therefore determine for himself the hours and days on which he worked, unless an employer or master who could impose his wishes on both tools and workers dictated them. Thus the townsman could take time off whenever he wished, when he had produced enough for a comfortable income, or when his employer allowed him to do so. Urban man could, in short, survive very well by playing his role in the complex economic structure of the city for a relatively short span of time. The shoemaker or potter knew how many shoes or pots he had to make each day, week, and year to secure the income he considered necessary. Once they were made, he was free to use the remaining time as he pleased. Similarly, the merchant or sailor involved in some trading venture had to work many hours each day for many weeks and months, but he expected that this extended working time would produce a return large enough to sustain him through the next venture and also through an extended rest and relaxation period. The time over and above what he spent earning the basic necessities of life might be spent doing extra work to obtain luxuries, living idly, or enjoying some pleasurable pastime. Since the range of goods available was relatively limited then and since amassing a fortune required the expenditure of much energy and time, most city people chose to spend their leisure in pleasant pursuits rather than in doing extra work.

City dwellers had a wider range of leisure-time diversions than did countrymen. In his comparatively limited free time the countryman could choose to pursue some marginally useful occupation, such as fishing or hunting, or some domestic handicraft, such as making or mending tools and household equipment; he could walk around his village or converse with other farmers. Whatever he did was limited by the narrow society of his small settlement, and the opportunities provided by the immediate environment predetermined even solitary occupations. By contrast, the townsman had a wide range of alternatives available. He could choose his companions from people of a variety of occupations and places of origin; the fluctuating population of traders, travelers, soldiers, and sailors in the city further enlarged his choice. In large communities in which many people had a great deal of leisure time, providing amusement became a social necessity and a profitable business. For example, most cities had drinking houses of some kind, as well as brothels and places offering singing and dancing. As types of amusement multiplied, townsmen could generally find some interesting debate, group meeting, game, theatrical performance, religious spectacle, sports event, or public lecture to fill the time. Craftsmen's shops, docks, trading centers, and busy streets generally provided variety, activity, and interesting sights which even slaves and the urban poor could enjoy.

The large number of people with leisure time living within the small area of a city contributed to the remarkable cultural fertility exhibited by many city-states. For example, in its "golden age" Athens produced remarkable public buildings like the Parthenon, artists such as the sculptor Phidias and numerous anonymous but highly skilled potters and metal-workers, playwrights such as Aeschylus and Euripides, the philosophers Socrates and Plato, and the unknown and unnumbered people who elevated debate to a fine and noble art, logic and reason to praised skills, and the perfection of the human body and mind to the level of the highest ideals of civilization. Of some importance in this cultural blossoming was the fact that in many places the emphasis on material wealth had not

Sketch of a reconstruction of the Ziggurat at Ur Such impressive temple structures illustrate that early city dwellers possessed surplus labor and materials. They also suggest the complex nature and high degree of organization of the society that built them. From *Ur Excavations* by Sir Leonard Woolley, a publication of the Joint Expedition of the British Museum and the University Museum, The University of Pennsylvania, to Mesopotamia

The Acropolis, Athens These ancient temples atop the Acropolis occupy a site both easily seen and easily defended. The advantages of such a building site often outweighed the additional difficulties it posed in construction.

Greek National Tourist Office

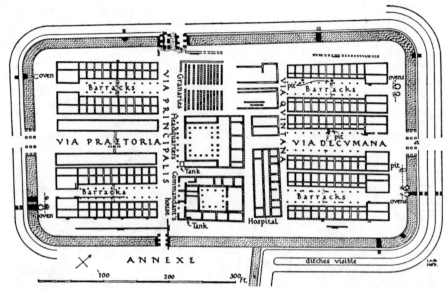

Plan of the Roman fort at Fendoch Military outposts such as this one generally established the basic pattern for cities that were built later on the same sites.

By permission of the Society of Antiquaries of Scotland

View of the excavations at Pompeii This city, buried under volcanic ash in 79 A.D., is exceptionally well preserved. The typical gridiron street plan is evident in this area around the forum. The square was suitable for military displays as well as large public gatherings and was surrounded by temples, law courts, and markets.

Italian Government Travel Office

Model of Rome at the time of Constantine Rome was less precisely planned than most imperial cities, but the Roman passion for order can be seen in many parts of the city. The size and splendor of the public buildings reflect a vital interest in civic life.   Alinari—Art Reference Bureau

developed to a very high level; that is, the inhabitants of many cities had
enough to secure a satisfactory standard of life for themselves but had not
yet developed the compulsion to work all possible hours to acquire as
much wealth as possible. As a consequence, they had time to seek to
improve the quality of life rather than only to count the number and value
of things in it. Many spent considerable time engaged in purely
recreational activities. Others turned to the intellectual and artistic
pursuits that produced the artistic, literary, dramatic, scientific, and
philosophical accomplishments for which the classical period is best
remembered.

The Great Urban Empire

The first phase of city development reached its apogee with the
foundation of the greatest urban empire, that of Rome. The early stages of
the development of this city closely resemble in broad outline those of the
other city-states of the Mediterranean. Probably about 1000 B.C., people
from southern Italy moved north and founded a settled community in the
valley of the river Tiber. By the time Greece was in its golden age, Rome
was already a considerable power on the Italian peninsula. The city
evolved as a jumble of workshops, houses, meeting halls, marketplaces,
and public buildings. Rulers occasionally cleared sections of the city and
initiated great public works projects that produced sections of order amid
the chaos of streets and buildings, but the haphazard nature of the original
development pattern and the constant pressure of population in the city
ensured that Rome never became an entirely orderly, well-planned city.
In this and many other respects it was not a typical "Roman" city, for it
did not exhibit, in their purest form, the characteristics of planning and
development shown by the cities Rome scattered throughout Europe. The
importance of Rome lies in the fact that it became the center of a vast
urban-oriented empire in a predominantly agrarian age. The citizens of
Rome spread their own ideas of urbanism, their particular ideas of city
forms and functions, throughout the empire, and along the way they
found some of the solutions to the problems inherent in large-scale urban
living, solutions that would eventually be forgotten until their rediscovery
many centuries later.

The Roman Empire was not urban in the sense that a majority of its
people lived in cities, for townspeople remained a minority of the total
population throughout the centuries of its existence. It was urban in the

sense that the whole empire was established by and revolved around *the* great urban center from which it took its name, and in the sense that the whole imperial organization and its social and economic structures were urban oriented. The Romans could not conceive of an acceptable level of human life without the special amenities and functions of cities. They considered no region civilized until it had within it a thriving, well-planned, and well-equipped city to which people could repair at intervals to refresh their bodies, minds, and souls. When establishing its empire, Rome used the city as a civilizing instrument, introducing it to or imposing it on conquered people. As a result, the expansion of the empire spread the idea and practice of city dwelling to people who before Roman troops arrived were still a long way from establishing cities on their own. As a consequence of empire building, the city-centered way of life and thinking that had originated in the Mediterranean area spread, at least for a time, throughout most of the known world.

Although there were minor differences in form, the "typical" Roman imperial city as most of the inhabitants of the empire knew it was an almost prefabricated settlement built to house the imperial administration, to garrison the army, and to conform to Roman ideas of what a city should be and do. Their sites were chosen according to the purposes the Romans expected their cities to serve. Generally, they were located at a route center of some kind, on a defensible site where the ground was suitable for building, and in an area fertile enough to produce the agricultural surplus necessary to sustain the population for which the cities were designed. They were focal points in the transportation network, centers on which the roads built by Rome to facilitate troop movements converged. On the frontiers of the empire, the first Roman settlement to appear was the military camp with its neat, orderly, regular gridiron pattern of streets and its symmetrical, defended perimeter. The same military engineers who had planned the original camps often designed the cities founded after a frontier region had been pacified; they followed the same basic ground plan. The gridiron was easy to follow, logical, and orderly; its wide, straight streets readily accommodated either marching soldiers or farm carts. Usually it was modified only for compelling reasons, such as the avoidance of a river or an undrainable marsh on the site.

Even after permanent cities were established, Roman settlements remained military centers. In more peaceful regions the cities served as staging posts and administrative centers of military governors, while in marginally pacified areas they were military garrisons from which troops could be dispatched to quell native insurrections. They were also imperial administrative centers for their hinterlands and contained all the buildings and facilities necessary for them to act as Rome's organizing and collecting agencies. In short, Roman cities were practical settlements built on suitable sites to perform certain specific functions within their areas and within the framework of the imperial military and administrative machinery.

The cities built by Rome had purposes over and above the mundane ones of military and imperial administration, however. Just as the inhabitants of the earlier city-states came to feel that the city was their natural home, so, too, by the time the Romans began building an empire, they regarded the city as the embodiment of all that was valuable in civilization. In areas in which city-states were conquered, existing cities were retained, strengthened, and sometimes expanded. In more primitive areas, people were encouraged to move into and support the new cities built for them and to participate in all the functions that the Romans considered a necessary part of civilized existence. The new cities had to be made attractive to newly conquered, backward people, and also had to contain all the facilities expected by those accustomed to the Roman style of life. They contained theaters, temples, baths, and other sports, recreational, and debating facilities. They had paved streets, markets, meeting places, and often complex water and sewer systems, which the Romans had discovered were essential to the health of large city populations. In short, they incorporated all the equipment that the Mediterranean experiments in city dwelling had shown was desirable for a decently civilized life. Much of this civic equipment, notably the water and sewer systems, represented the Roman synthesis of the results of experiments in solving the problems inherent in high-density urban life. Each was an important element in sustaining the harmony of man and city that the Romans enjoyed, a balance that has rarely been achieved since their time.

As the empire grew, more people were attracted to the great city at its heart, increasing Rome's need for food and supplies and aggravating its already serious overcrowding. In time, the possibility that the hungry crowds within it might one day rise and sweep away the government became a matter of concern to its rulers. When this threat became serious, the rulers devised a policy of "bread and circuses" to divert the people of Rome. Stories of free entertainment and free food, made more glowing by the imagination of each person involved in their telling, percolated throughout the empire; ultimately the "solution" compounded the original problem, stimulating immigration and increasing Rome's voracious appetite for supplies of all kinds. The empire had to satisfy the hunger of the great city that had spawned it, and as that hunger grew, so of necessity did the empire.

Throughout the Roman era (about the first century B.C. to the fifth century A.D.), agriculture remained the basis of the economy and the occupation of the vast majority of people living within the imperial boundaries. The food requirements of Rome, the cities, and the military forces gave farmers every incentive to increase both their efficiency and their surpluses. Through their imperial expansion the Romans introduced primitive farmers to such current agricultural techniques as the use of manure to improve soil fertility and the more careful breeding of cattle to produce better livestock. In many parts of the empire the nature of the Roman social structure and increased farm profits promoted the development of large agricultural estates. Many wealthy citizens established large farms, worked either by slaves or by nonlandholding free laborers, which produced surpluses so large that their owners could afford sophisticated domestic equipment like baths and under-floor heating systems.

Imperial cities had a two-part economic function: they were expected to support themselves and also to act as collection centers through which an appropriate portion of the wealth and supplies of the surrounding countryside could be funneled to Rome. Rome's inability to sustain itself and its large military and administrative structures on the surplus produced by the regions immediately surrounding it provided the initial and continuing impetus for imperial expansion and also stimulated trade and the movement of people, things, and ideas throughout the imperial area. In their local functions, cities acted much like independent city-states, drawing sustenance from and imposing demands on surrounding agrarian areas. In their imperial functions they acted on behalf of Rome as collection agents and the executors of Roman demands on their areas. Experiments with governmental forms were discouraged, for variety gave rise to lack of uniformity, which was incompatible with the smooth running of a vast empire. City government existed to serve the city and the empire; it was expected to be orderly in and of itself as well as to create a climate in which orderliness could flourish. The composition of city governments reflected that of Rome itself; groups of wealthy, upper-class citizens dominated local government. Civic officials were responsible for the planning, financing, and building of public works such as administrative buildings, roads, bridges, and water supply systems. The provision of educational and leisure facilities also fell within their authority, as did the payment of teachers and priests. They were also expected to build baths and theaters and arrange festivals to entertain the population while reminding them of the might and power of imperial government. In addition, government agencies participated in imperial administrative activities such as the collection of taxes and the recruitment of troops. In order to maintain an empire of this size, certain uniform Roman standards had to be imposed through city administrations; local civic authorities were to ensure that weights and measures used in their area conformed to official requirements, and they supervised prices and some productive processes in the interests of empire-wide uniformity.

The cities remained industrial and trade centers, and the needs of the empire for food and supplies of all kinds generated a great volume of commerce; but the Romans made few major technical advances during these centuries. They developed metalworking and other skills vitally important to the maintenance of the military machine to a high degree, but introduced little that was actually innovative. Although the civic buildings of the Romans, as well as their roads and aqueducts, were admirable for their size and magnificence, they embodied no new discoveries of a magnitude comparable to that of the column or the arch, which earlier civilizations had developed. The Romans succeeded in their conquest of the known world not because they invented or discovered important new techniques of manufacturing, processing, building, or transportation, but because they raised existing techniques to a high point of efficiency and applied them on a vast scale. They had a passion for order and organization, and a genius for administrative efficiency. Even in their cultural products there was little that was entirely new, but the fine detail and high polish of their visual and literary arts and the precision and orderliness of Roman law offer further illustrations of their capacity as organizers and improvers of the products and ideas of other people.

Rome imposed a kind of peace over the known world, which lasted several centuries and brought cities and city-oriented ideals of civilization to many backward groups of people who were far from developing cities and enduring civilizations of their own. It consolidated the achievements of earlier civilizations and spread them over a wide area, and, by the very existence of the empire, promoted the development of ideas about unity and cooperation on a scale that embraced not just individuals and communities, but many cities, regions, and races. The notion of the universal empire born in the time of Pax Romana would persist in the future and influence many ambitious individuals, from Charlemagne to the twentieth-century dictators. The vision of world peace that Rome had generated would surface from time to time in the form of such dreams as Pax Britannica and Pax Americana.

Of more immediate and more practical significance was the association between the worldwide empire and Christianity. The standardizing influence of the empire was of the greatest importance in aiding the spread of Christianity, for it ensured that once Rome had adopted the religion, so too would the rest of the world. The one universal empire both preceded and made possible the one universal church. After the collapse of the temporal power of Rome, the Christian church saw itself as the heir of the empire, as the sole remaining supranational, unifying institution, and it was determined to exercise again the worldwide dominance it had enjoyed as a result of its association with the empire. In its formative years, the church existed within the imperial framework and shaped its structure and organization to fit that of its parent secular empire; this framework lingered on within the Catholic church long after the empire had faded. Echoes of it can be seen in the continued dominance of the city and bishop of Rome in the Catholic church, the insistence of the central church that all its members observe its rules and traditions regardless of local conditions or customs, and the urban-centered nature of the ecclesiastical hierarchy based on bishops in cathedral towns acting in obedience to the bishop of Rome. The fact that the universal church was the child and heir of the orderly, organizing, standardizing, but not very innovative universal empire may well also help explain why the church became a conservative institution and subsequently had such difficulty adapting to the innovations of the Renaissance and the Reformation.

The Romans solved many of the basic problems of city living. In their civic pride, civic planning, and life-supporting water and sewer systems they left many valuable lessons in urban living for later generations. Although they made advances in many areas of urban life, however, they were unable to change the fundamentally parasitic nature of their cities and of the military and administrative organizations necessary to sustain them. The failure to cope with this urban problem partially explains the eventual collapse of the great imperial structure. The process of conquest and expansion had begun, essentially, because the city of Rome could not continue to expand while it depended solely on the surplus of its immediate hinterlands for supplies. The need for a larger supply area had led to conquest, the establishment of the empire, and the buildup of the military forces necessary to ensure imperial peace and continued growth. The ever-expanding demands of Rome, the imperial forces, and the cities it conquered and founded ensured that the need for ever-wider supply areas would continue. Implicit in meeting these needs was the simultaneous expansion of the military structure, which pushed back the boundaries of the empire, and of the administrative organization necessary for the management of resources and the coherence of the whole complex.

Even the best transportation, communications, and administrative systems available at the time had limited capacities and ranges. Eventually the empire exceeded those capabilities, and its structure simply became too unwieldy to hold together with the equipment and techniques available at the time. Any small additional strain, external or internal, would inevitably cause fracture and ultimate collapse. Whatever the immediate causes of the dissolution of the Roman Empire, the fundamental one was its inability to sustain one vast and many smaller cities in an agrarian age with relatively limited technological capacity and a relatively simple economy. The cities that generated and spread the Roman way of life were, on the one hand, civilizing instruments and the means by which the most advanced current technical developments spread throughout the Western world; but on the other hand they functioned to a large extent as economic parasites on the body of a predominantly agrarian world. The Romans lacked the means to change this element. With the collapse of the empire, the cities that had been its greatest achievements shrank, and many died; all that the imperial structure had implied and carried with it faded rapidly, leaving only a few important by-products to remind Western man that such a great urban empire had ever existed.

THE
MEDIEVAL 2
CITY

Although urban life went on much as usual in Constantinople and in the communities within its economic orbit, in the West the disintegration of urban centers accompanied the collapse of the great urban empire. The few forces that favored the continuance of urban life were not very powerful. Many of the "barbarian" groups that moved within the old imperial boundaries were acquainted with some aspects of Roman civilization and tried to preserve at least a little of what they had admired. Some native peoples in areas once ruled by Rome had become so thoroughly converted to the Roman way of life that they could not accept the passing of the empire and clung for some time to the cities and towns and to such Roman ways as they could preserve. Bishops and other church functionaries with established bases in cities continued to maintain them as ecclesiastical administrative centers and as points of pilgrimage. Such forces sustained some of the old urban centers long after the empire had vanished, but their life was now tenuous, only a flickering shadow of what it had been at the height of the Roman centuries. Some cities, especially those on the outermost fringes of the old empire, were soon completely abandoned and remained only as dead monuments to a vanished civilization. The Roman way of urban life had depended on the empire for its existence; when the empire broke up, it foundered.

Although it is true that many barbarian groups, such as the Angles and the Saxons, shunned the alien environment of the decaying towns in favor of their own smaller, less sophisticated, largely agrarian communities, cities did not die because the barbarians murdered their inhabitants and destroyed the cities themselves. The real cause was the collapse of the imperial economic structure whose establishment and expansion had given them birth and life. Widespread trade had sustained the lesser urban centers of the empire and had been vital to the life of the larger cities, including Rome; when that trade ended, the urban centers faded because they lacked a function.

The Breakdown of Urban Life

By the fourth century the empire was overextended, and active "new" people pushing in from the north and from the south challenged its control. Beginning in the late fourth and fifth centuries, Germanic tribes, many of whose members had been trained as soldiers in Roman imperial armies, moved over the northern and eastern boundaries of the empire, settled, and made great sections of what had been the northern imperial possessions of Rome their own. This incursion and settlement severely disrupted trading and administrative activities in the northern parts of the old empire, dealing the cities of the area a severe blow. In the seventh and eighth centuries new threats emerged, as the Saracens began to dominate what had been the southern and Mediterranean parts of the empire and the Vikings started to terrorize the shore lines and river valleys of the north and west.

In the eighth century, the old Mediterranean trading structure collapsed as the forces of Islam wrenched the southern shore from Christian control and pressed Constantinople and Spain. The Mediterranean, the core of imperial economic activities, was no longer a safe area for commerce; mobility and trading volume were thus reduced throughout the Western world. With the dislocation of the economic system, towns and cities that had depended on commerce languished. A short time after the Moslems began laying waste to the Mediterranean, the Vikings swept in from the north. They were excellent sailors but far from peace loving, and when they sailed from their cold, rocky, often barren lands, it was in search of plunder from lands better favored. They ranged the northern seas, the Atlantic, and the Mediterranean, some journeying even as far as North America; they were certainly known in places as distant from their homes as Constantinople and southern Russia. No trader was safe from the attentions of these predators who brought seaborne trade, the main bulk-carrying trade of the Western world, almost to a halt. They also disrupted the life of farming settlements near coasts and major rivers. Whenever the weather was good enough for sailing, the raiders came without warning, landed, took horses from coastal and riverside communities, converted themselves into cavalry and foot soldiers, and plundered the countryside. Farming settlements, in which most people still lived, were particularly vulnerable to these raiders because they came without warning in good weather when people were dispersed in the fields tending crops and found it most difficult to defend themselves. The threat of attack led many communities to turn to a military leader who could offer them some protection. In return, the leader was often granted ownership or control of some part of the land or its produce as well as military and civil power over the members of the community. Land and military service thus became bound together in the relationship that later formed the sociopolitical basis of feudalism. Churches and monasteries, with their accumulated treasures, were particularly attractive to the Northmen because they contained much treasure in one location. As a result, the coastal and riverside religious institutions of Europe were emptied of many of their literary and cultural as well as material assets, for the Vikings destroyed whatever did not interest them as plunder.

Despite these tribulations, the church clung to many of the ideas and ideals of the age in which it had been born. It remained in urban administrative centers wherever they survived the heathen invasions, and as it reached out to convert the heathen in what had once been the imperial area, it established new centers. By its insistence upon having urban centers in which to station major regional officers, the church helped preserve some semblance of city life throughout this uncertain time. Abbeys and monasteries were often almost urban settlements in their own right, at least in their concentration of relatively large numbers of people, their specialization of function, and their provision of the facilities necessary for the preservation of community life. This survival of the city in the form of cathedral cities, monasteries, and abbeys, however, was merely a holding action that kept alive the barest essentials of urban life but hardly promised regeneration. These church-centered urban settlements were sustained not by any vital activities and functions of their own, but by the income the church derived from its landholdings. Because of its emphasis on spiritual rather than temporal matters and its inclination to shun the worldly, the church could hardly promote the active trade and industry from which dynamic new urban centers would spring.

Urban life reached its lowest ebb about the ninth century when the flow of its lifeblood of trade and industry slowed to a trickle. Even Rome, an imposing settlement that had held about a million people under the empire, crumbled into ruin and saw its population reduced to a few thousand. From the tenth century on, life gradually began to return to cities. Historians have advanced a variety of explanations for the resumption of urban life in the Middle Ages. Henri Pirenne suggested that the revival of long-distance trade restored the cities to life; although later scholars have disputed various points in his argument, and although all of them do not apply in the cases of some specific urban settlements, the main hypothesis stands. Certainly no one has yet advanced a more plausible argument than this; however, to rely on one explanation for the growth of medieval cities is obviously to oversimplify. Many forces were involved: the formation of nations, the restoration of relative peace and order, the church, the increasing sophistication of legal structures, even the improvement of agricultural techniques. Although particular details varied under different circumstances and in different regions, all these developments and others combined with expanding trade to produce the dynamic medieval city.

As their exercise of power became habitual and their ambitions greater, the most powerful men in society tried to eliminate private feuds in their territories and to extend their control over ever-wider areas. Counts in France, princelings and prelates in Germany, lords and kings in England wanted to establish law, peace, and order in the areas they controlled, for all this fostered prosperity and enhanced their power over the rest of the people. The rate at which peace and stability were restored varied in both pace and depth from area to area, but with every degree of improvement, Europe came closer to reaching the conditions under which long-distance trade could again flourish. There were also signs that population was beginning to increase again; the draining of marshy areas in Flanders and similar projects designed to increase the extent of agricultural land certainly indicated a renewal of vigor.

As the church overcame the setbacks of the barbarian invasions, it began to realize that although a single secular empire no longer protected it, the regulations and geographical extent of a powerful political state also no longer restricted it. As it gained confidence in its ability to function without the empire and began to add more secular concerns to its religious ones, the church began to take a greater interest in what was happening in the temporal world. It undertook vigorous missionary activity and turned its attention to ideological rivals, especially to its greatest, the religion of Islam. In its campaign to remove the Moslem infidel from the land of Christ, the church enlisted the aid of its fellow landowning powers: kings, princes, and other nobles. The Crusades, which were undertaken from time to time from the late eleventh to the thirteenth centuries, complemented the spirit of militarism that permeated the upper levels of society. To the joys of battle and the happy prospects of plunder for the raiding parties they added the sanctions of divine purpose and high morality, and all Europe stirred for the effort.

The Crusades did not succeed in dislodging the Moslems from the Holy Land, but they did revive communications and help stimulate activity in Europe and throughout the Mediterranean area. People began to travel again and to learn about new wonders and desirable commodities from the East. The Crusades reestablished contact between north and south, east and west, and thus played a part in the regeneration of the European economic system that had disintegrated with the collapse of the Roman economy.

The primary general stimulus for the resumption of dynamic urban life was the reappearance of long-distance trade. Trade had continued even through the most disrupted period, although it had been more or less local in character and limited in volume. International trade, mainly in small quantities of luxury goods such as fine textiles and wines, had not been of sufficient scope or volume to sustain much vigorous urban economic life. The resumption of long-distance trade between all parts of the Western world in the Middle Ages gradually created a new wide-ranging economic structure that infused a new life into old cities and generated new ones. Medieval cities were dynamic, though very different in character from the Roman variety; they opened up a new phase of Western urban development.

The Resumption of Urban Life

In the fifth and sixth centuries, people fleeing from the barbaric Huns, Goths, and Lombards found refuge in the inhospitable salt marshes off the northeast coast of Italy. Although this unpromising site offered protection, the refugees found that a comfortable existence required more than the salt and fish available in the marsh. Consequently, early Venetians soon became adept at trading their salt and fish for other foodstuffs with nearby peoples. The marsh dwellers eventually developed a talent for the trading into which they had originally been forced by circumstances, and they refined it into a polished and profitable art. At the

time the community of Venice was founded, northeastern Italy was still
within the orbit of Constantinople, the center of the Eastern empire.
Situated between land and sea, hidden in the salt marshes, Venice was
hard for enemies to find and even harder to attack. It survived the
centuries of disruption and remained Eastern in orientation despite all the
disturbances that might have turned a less well-insulated community
toward the West. When the worst of the barbarian turbulence had
passed, the Venetian traders stood astride two worlds: they were Eastern
in attitude, but Western in geography. They were uniquely situated to
benefit from the earliest stirrings of trade between the two worlds, and
they became the preeminent carriers and suppliers of the Mediterranean,
serving East and West, Constantinople and Rome, Moslems and
Christians. No particular master, region, or ideology bound them; their
first and greatest commitment, which had led them to the islands in the
marshes in the first place, was to their own survival and to the community
that gave them shelter and the means of making a living. As time passed,
the Venetians adjusted their sights, though not their basic principles,
changed their allegiance from mere survival to prosperity, and continued
to serve and trade with any and all customers as well as to manufacture
profitable items such as ships and Murano glassware and mirrors.

When Mediterranean commerce resumed, Venice was its focal
point. The activities of the Venetians began to revitalize commercial
centers all around the Mediterranean because they needed other ports as
transshipment points and other communities as supply and market
centers. Communities in nearby parts of Italy, such as Verona and
Bergamo, began to grow into important centers, and because most major
trade was still waterborne, port settlements, such as Marseilles and
Naples, began to flourish. The greatest impact of the initial revitalization
of trade based on Venice was inevitably felt in the area nearby that
supplied it with food and many trade goods. All over Italy vital new urban
life developed in the shape of independent, prosperous trading communities whose trademarks were dedication to business and freedom from
outside interference. In time, Italian merchants widened their range of
activities to look for greater profits, new markets for established trade
commodities, and new commodities for established markets. In the course
of this expansion, they traveled farther and farther into northern Europe.
Italian merchants were in Paris by 1074 and in fairly large numbers at the
fairs in Flanders by the beginning of the twelfth century.

Flanders, the natural trading center for northwestern Europe,
became the second great European trading nucleus. The mouths of two

great rivers, the Meuse and the Schelde, opened in Flanders as did the mouth of the Rhine, which offered easy water access to much of central Europe. Moreover, for contemporary trading and shipping purposes the Thames, which gave access to England, could also be considered a Flemish river. Flanders had more than geographical advantages, however. The Vikings had been attracted to this northern water route center and had made it a target of their plundering operations. When the edge wore off their violence, many of them settled in Flanders and in the region to the west of it along the Norman coast. By the time the Venetians made contact, the people of the area had become relatively peaceful; with stimulus from the south, the traders of Flanders, whose Viking forefathers had ravaged the region, began to use their ancestral seafaring skills to extend trade to Iceland, Ireland, and around the shores of the Baltic. As it established trade over most of the northwest accessible by water, Flanders became the northern counterpart of Venice.

Exchange between the northern and southern trading centers flourished, for within the economic orbit of each were goods the other wanted. The northern area produced fine woolen textiles while the south produced wine and oil. The stimulus provided by the two great trading centers revived towns and cities throughout Europe, especially on the seashores and on the banks of the great rivers. Roman centers that had barely managed to survive found renewed vigor; new settlements were established on abandoned sites or arose on new sites. Active communities developed at trading and route centers where merchants and craftsmen found it most convenient to meet. The time commercial operations got under way in surrounding areas determined when any given community began to grow.

Many medieval urban centers, especially the towns, which soon reached their optimum size and had stable population levels, served more or less local economic functions. Larger, more active settlements that became the cities of the Middle Ages, such as Genoa, Florence, Bruges, Ghent, Paris, Cologne, and London, owed their success and their growth to their involvement in international commerce. Each depended to some extent on the inhabitants of distant lands or other cities; consequently the people of the cities were often much more aware of a close economic link with foreigners than with the rural people in their own surrounding districts. For example, the woolen textile-manufacturing cities of Flanders depended on raw wool shipped to them from England through London. The fact that English kings were occasionally able to use the threat of cutting off raw wool supplies, crucial to the Flemish economy, to bring

Flanders into line with English political ambitions clearly illustrates the importance of trade in the Middle Ages.

Although large cities formed economic and cultural affinities that transcended national boundaries, they remained dependent on their immediate surroundings for basic supplies. In many places some towns-men grew at least part of their own food either in gardens within the walls or in fields immediately outside them, but as had been the case in premedieval cities, long-term survival depended on the ability of agricultural hinterlands to produce food surpluses, especially in smaller towns. The main function of many of the latter was to supply craft and industrial goods to the surrounding countryside and to provide market services for the rural people in the nearby districts. Even the larger cities that participated in international trade acted as suppliers and market centers for their immediate hinterlands, which in return supplied food. To this extent, all medieval towns and cities were locally self-supporting.

One of the most important developments of the Middle Ages was the growth of healthy, dynamic, urban life in northern Europe, an area that had made little or no original contribution to urbanism in pre-Roman or Roman times. The new dynamism of the north was partly attributable to the three-field system of crop rotation. This important advance in agriculture appeared in the eighth and ninth centuries and became fairly common by the tenth century. Mediterranean people had practiced a two-field rotation: half the cultivated land planted in winter grains and the other half left fallow. The three-field system, in which one-third of the land was planted with winter grains, one-third with crops such as oats, barley, and peas, and the third part left fallow, proved more efficient, especially with the heavy, fertile soils of the damp northern lands. With the area under cultivation at any one time increased by just under 20 percent, the three-field system could produce more food than the two-field rotation. The extra feed grains this system produced made it feasible to keep more horses, which in turn could replace oxen and make many farming processes faster and more efficient. The additional human food produced by the new system fostered the growth of a larger population in the north and also added to the food surpluses necessary to support a larger urban population.

Surrounding defensive walls were a characteristic of most medieval cities. Indeed, the character of medieval urban settlements was partly a result of the fact that they began to grow up in an age when disruption and violence were still more common than not. People still found it necessary to form cooperative and protective groups to secure a reasonable amount of stability and tolerable working conditions. Rural and urban people alike needed the protection of a local lord for their property and persons. Some communities relied heavily on natural defensive systems, as did the Venetians on their islands and lagoons, but many had no natural defenses and had to build artificial ones. Few of the town walls built at this time could withstand prolonged, concentrated military assault, but at least they discouraged enemies. They also provided the enclosed communities with protection from casual bands of marauding and roving lawbreakers and other miscreants outside the mainstream of society. The walls, pierced only by a few narrow gateways, allowed the city to close itself up at night as well as in times of disruption and danger. In addition to providing protection, they marked a clear physical distinction between the urban community and the outside world and further contributed to the essential character of the medieval city by giving the citizens within a sense of community. These distinctions were echoed in differences of occupation and way of life between urban and rural residents, between those within the walls and those outside.

Society in the Medieval City

Few medieval urban centers were cities at all by twentieth-century standards of assessment that are largely based on population. The vast majority had under ten thousand people, and very many had five thousand or fewer, but the most dynamic cities engaging in long-distance trade were larger. In the fourteenth century Florence probably had about one hundred thousand people; London, thirty-five thousand; and Lübeck, about twenty-five thousand. The population of most towns and cities, like that of Europe in general, declined in the fourteenth and fifteenth centuries as waves of plague, including the "Black Death" of the fourteenth century, swept through them. There are no precise statistics about the number of plague deaths, and estimates vary from region to region, but most parts of Europe have been estimated to have lost one-third to one-half of their people. Cities and towns probably suffered to an equal or greater extent than rural areas. As a result of these great epidemics, the overall size of the urban population generally increased very little between about 1300 and 1500. Epidemic disease hit urban communities particularly hard because people were densely packed inside the walls, and disease was readily transmitted from person to person. Whenever the plague struck a city, many people ran away to seek shelter

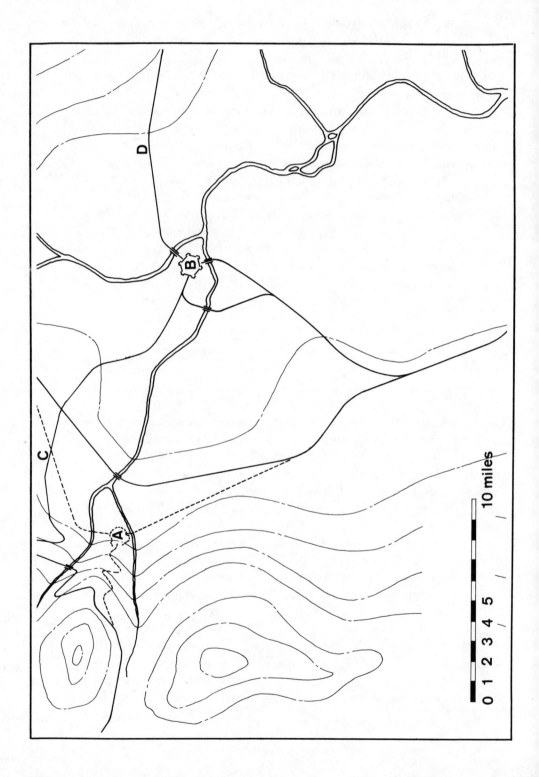

THE MEDIEVAL CITY c. 1350

The classical city (**A**) fell into ruin after the collapse of the military-commercial system that had sustained it. Medieval city (**B**) developed on a new site in response to the needs and patterns of the new trading system. The site was chosen at the intersection of rivers and roads, a natural route center that offered plentiful water, natural defenses, and an ample food supply from the surrounding agrarian area of the valley. The city was a trading and commercial center; craft industries produced goods for trade and for exchange with farmers of the surrounding area who supplied food, as well as many of the items involved in long-distance trade. Many old roads were still used; the old road to the limestone quarries (**C**) was maintained for transport of building materials. A new road (**D**) was developed in response to new trading patterns; it also provided access to timber stands, which provided raw materials for building and for craft industries.

E Cathedral.

F Market plaza.

G Guildhalls, craft and trade centers.

H Fortress of local lord.

I Movement within the city was mainly pedestrian so narrow streets with many angles were not constricting. Some wider, more open streets allowed passage of horse traffic involved in long-distance trade.

J Defensive walls with turrets at intervals.

K Moat outside defensive walls.

(MAPS DRAWN BY SATHIT CHAIYASIN)

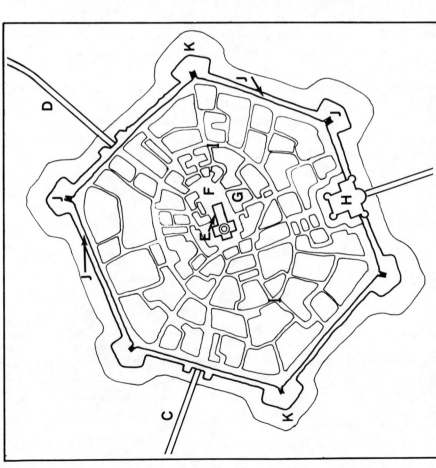

in the next town or village, often carrying the disease with them and infecting the new community. Even if quarantine arrangements could have been made and successfully imposed on the population, epidemics would have remained a problem because their main vectors were rats and fleas, which thrived in dirty and crowded urban areas.

Although medieval cities were not particularly healthy places, especially in times of epidemic, their inhabitants generally made some collective effort to maintain elementary health and sanitary facilities. The vitally important role of a reliable supply of potable water was generally recognized and the water supply was often under municipal control. Most communities with adequate water took pride in scattering fountains throughout the city to provide easy access to this valuable commodity for both resident and visitor. Cities with inadequate supplies went to great lengths to get water. Venice, for example, which had little natural fresh water, constructed elaborate systems for catching and storing rainwater and maintained a regular barge service to carry in water from the river Brenta. Given the limited area within the walls and the care taken to provide as many public fountains as possible, few people lived more than a few minutes away from a water source, despite the general scarcity of indoor water systems.

Waste disposal systems, however, seem to have inspired comparatively little municipal pride and less effort. The example the Romans had set in constructing sewer works was not followed, and although some individuals or groups were responsible for cleaning parts of the city from time to time, virtually all urban centers relied mainly upon streets and rivers for refuse disposal. Human and animal wastes and garbage of all kinds were allowed to collect in the streets on the assumption that the next good rain would clean the streets and wash the refuse down to the river. In the intervals between rains, human and animal scavengers helped keep the garbage down. The poor scrounged what they could from the refuse of the prosperous, while dogs and pigs, mankind's oldest and most reliable garbage collectors, consumed what they could of the rest. Apart from the districts that some individual or civic authority occasionally cleaned, streets and alleys were rarely places in which the fastidious could walk with comfort.

Medieval cities were healthier than they might have been because the countryside literally came right up to their walls, giving townspeople ready access to fresh air and open country. Many of the wealthiest citizens owned land and estates in the country, and poorer people often supplemented their diets with a few fish or some small game. Townspeople usually left the shelter of their walls at harvest time to help local farmers bring in the crops. Although townsmen were careful to make distinctions between themselves and countryfolk, they were also aware, with a sense of immediacy that modern man has lost, that the harvest was vital to their own survival, as well as to that of the farmers. Some urban centers were widely known for their food products in addition to their industrial and commercial activities. Augsburg, for example, was noted for its trout, and up to the mid-seventeenth century the salaries of many civic officials were assessed, and paid, in numbers of trout.

Health problems became serious only when cities achieved a considerable size and a relatively dense population. In the later Middle Ages, although many urban communities expanded, few of them made many advances in community health and life support systems. As a result, high death rates began to be a matter of some concern, even for the more prosperous people who were important, well-educated, and rich enough to leave written records. Infant death rates were especially high, and it became quite common for even the most prosperous people, who could afford to provide the best possible care for their children, to outlive many of them. In the fifteenth century, one Nuremberg merchant had twenty-one children, only nine of whom survived, and this was by no means an exceptional case. During the fifteenth and sixteenth centuries, many notable urban families seemed worried by the poor prospects their names had of surviving through the third and fourth generations. In case after case and city after city, the grandchildren and great-grandchildren of active and intelligent people exhibited physical or mental weaknesses, and after running through the family fortunes, they died without heirs. The reason for this apparent degeneration is unclear, although intermarriage between a limited number of elite families and generations of unhealthy urban living must have been partly to blame. Whatever the causes, the phenomenon was common and especially distressing in an age when people seriously considered the future of their grandchildren and the fortunes of their family in later generations. In the mid-sixteenth century, a German minister writing to his patron commented, "Among all the families of Lübeck there are not three or four in which there is a living member of the fourth generation. . . . May the Lord promise and give to you the fourth successor to your house. . . ." The dying-off of previously successful families and their replacement by others who had been lower on the social ladder undoubtedly created a sense of potential upward mobility in urban society and strengthened the notion that towns were places of opportunity where anyone who was lucky and worked hard could make a better place in life for himself and his descendants.

Despite the very high mortality rate of women in childbirth, there were usually more women than men living in medieval cities. Male infants have always been more frail than females, and fewer of them survived infancy; adult men, as always, had a shorter life expectancy than women, and probably a larger proportion of them died in epidemics. The church encouraged men to become priests, and although the rule of celibacy was by no means always observed, priesthood removed many men from the officially marriageable, breeding, secular population. In addition, a large segment of the male population of towns and cities was mobile and impermanent. Merchants, sailors, and others involved in commercial ventures went away for long periods of time leaving women in effective charge of their households and home affairs. Travel was often dangerous, even in the later Middle Ages, and some traders never returned to resume the responsibilities temporarily delegated to women. As a result of these special conditions within cities, women enjoyed a higher social status and more privileges than they did in rural areas. Although in many places, such as Venice, upper-class women led very sheltered lives, lower-class working women were usually unequally treated in matters such as wages, and rarely did a woman occupy a high official position, some women were nevertheless influential, prosperous, and privileged. After the death of male members, guilds often allowed their widows and unmarried daughters to join and trained them to run the family business. As a consequence of the short life expectancy of males, active, relatively young females held a remarkable amount of urban property. Many journeymen* found that the shortest road to success was by marrying not the boss's daughter, but the widow or unmarried female orphan who was herself the boss.

Unmarried women with no prospect of inheriting property or with prosperous but healthy fathers often found it difficult to find husbands. In some places they voiced loud complaints about the wealthy, oft-married widows who used up the community's supply of eligible males. Women who inherited property from rich fathers or husbands tended to marry and be widowed several times, obtaining, if they were fortunate or wise in their choices, an increase in prosperity and influence each time. The shrill, autocratic, nagging shrew, a female character common in late

---

* Trained craftsmen working for a master or employer who paid wages by the day.

medieval and early modern literature and art, may well be a caricature of the independent, self-sufficient, prosperous townswoman of this period as seen by the distorted vision of economically inferior males and socially envious females.

Urban social structure varied slightly from region to region and city to city, but as a general rule it could be divided into two classes, upper and lower. An important exception was that in some regions, especially in Italy, the most prosperous people rose above the upper class to form a distinct, almost princely class of their own. The urban upper classes were made up of wealthy merchants, manufacturers, and high public officials, while the lower classes consisted of craftsmen, shopkeepers, and workers. Some urban upper-class families were accepted socially by landed aristocrats, monarchs, and princes of the church, while the lower classes mixed socially only with the lower ranks of agrarian workers. Despite distances between the social groups, people within the city existed in a state of relative equality compared with the social conditions prevailing across society as a whole at this time. The crowding of people into relatively confined urban centers made it difficult for distinct, separated rich and poor sections to develop. Although in some places the rich congregated in one area, as the rich people of Venice clustered along the Grand Canal, the generally crowded quarters in medieval cities inevitably forced mixing of prosperous and poor housing. In streets and marketplaces all kinds of people mingled; merchants and money lenders, soldiers and students rubbed shoulders with craftsmen and clerics, apprentices and artisans. Townsmen also derived a sense of unity from their interrelated activities. Merchants depended on craftsmen to produce the goods they traded; craftsmen relied on merchants to sell their products; both relied on the corporate entity of the city to provide them with the physical services and legal protection they needed.

The corporate nature of medieval economic and social organization was both a product of and a strong support for the sense of community. The post-Roman turmoil in Europe had made group action necessary for survival. The groups that emerged in response to danger in due course became institutionalized within the social and legal structures of the Middle Ages and thus remained powerful long after the initial pressing needs for them had passed. The most characteristic and typically urban organization to emerge was the guild.

A variety of earlier organizations, ranging from the trade guilds or colleges of Rome to the guildlike religious and social fraternities of Anglo-Saxon England may be pointed to as the forerunners of the guilds, but no one of them can be said with any degree of certainty to be their direct ancestor. It is also impossible to fix a precise date for the appearance of guilds because a variety of guildlike organizations emerged at different times in different cities. Differences of detail aside, medieval guilds can be divided into three main types: the merchant, the craft, and the municipal guilds. It can tentatively be concluded that merchant guilds were of primary importance in the early stages of development of most towns and cities, and that craft guilds were not very important in most places until the thirteenth century.

Merchant guilds were associations of the major merchants organized either to regulate trade in one particular city or region, or in a commodity in demand in long-distance trade. Guilds of this kind generally protected their members from the competition of other guilds in what they considered to be their trading area, regulated the conditions under which "foreigners" might trade within that area, set up regulations for fairs and markets in which their members did business, and kept an eye on weights, measures, and conditions of trade in general.

Craft guilds were vertical organizations with a place in their structure for everyone engaged in a specific craft, from the poorest apprentice to the wealthiest master. Goldsmiths, brewers, hatters, fishmongers, carpenters—all kinds of trades and occupations had such organizations. These guilds regulated the quality of raw materials used in their trade, set standards for the weight or size and quality of the finished product, determined what kinds of tools and manufacturing processes to use, established the terms of apprenticeship and the procedures for the advancement of a member from apprentice to journeyman to master, and generally supervised and regulated everything concerned with the product of the particular guild.

Municipal guilds varied in composition from community to community. In some cities they were composed of representatives of the leading families, in others, the heads of all the other guilds in the city. In many places the members of a small, elite "electorate" whose qualifications were strictly regulated chose guild representatives. In time, membership in the municipal guild of some cities became merely a decorative office, a status symbol or a reward for distinguished service, but initially the duties of municipal guild members were weighty ones. Their functions roughly paralleled those of later city councils and commissions in that they were responsible for running the basic services in their communities. Guild members ensured that the city could raise a suitable militia in times of war or send the required number of recruits to serve in royal armies. They were charged with the duties of "watch and ward," peacetime protection and peace-keeping services, and with providing and synchronizing timekeeping facilities such as bell towers or town criers. They had to ensure that public works were maintained and attend to any matters of city-wide importance that affected the well-being of the inhabitants. In some cities the duties were so onerous that qualified people often tried to avoid serving in the higher ranks of civic government. There were many cases in medieval Venice of individuals inventing disqualifications for themselves, pleading that the demands of business would prevent them from serving and asking acquaintances among the electors not to vote for them.

Although there were rivalries between guilds and many street fights between gangs of apprentices belonging to different trade guilds, they were, on the whole, a cohesive rather than a divisive force in the social structure of medieval towns and cities. Virtually all townspeople were in some way associated with a guild, either belonging to one or being affiliated through a husband or father. Members of the upper classes were often members of all three types. A wealthy merchant from a prominent family who dealt in woolen textiles might be a member of the weavers' guild, the merchants' guild, and the municipal guild, with all of the concomitant privileges and duties of each. Most people had friends, neighbors, and relatives who belonged to guilds other than their own, and in any event, in most cities the guilds had to cooperate to ensure the smooth running of business affairs. While municipal guilds might make general regulations for the conduct of industry and commerce, the operations and precise definition of the regulations would be entrusted to merchant and trade guilds.

Corporate controls served a variety of purposes in commercial and manufacturing processes, and their enforcement both depended upon and reinforced the sense of community. Most communities, for example, tried to impose controls that would secure a monopoly of the commercial processes for their own residents. Outside merchants, however, played a necessary role, especially in long-distance trade, and some allowance was generally made for "foreign" merchants in the shape of regulations that, while ensuring every possible advantage for natives, allowed foreigners to operate at a profit. Controls to regulate the conditions and hours of trade at fairs and markets protected merchants from loss of profits resulting from inefficient operation. Since goods were identified with their city of origin, one or two unscrupulous merchants introducing shoddy goods, short weights, and overpricing into the market could give an entire city a bad reputation and discourage buyers; regulation of these matters was strictly enforced, too.

In general, the corporate structures within a community worked together to enforce regulations in the interests of community prosperity. The strong sense of community welfare and the corporate nature of regulating agencies both indicate that the medieval townsman's need for protection and cooperation was greater than his need for individual freedom of action. Medieval townspeople had no room within their framework of assumptions for notions of free trade and open competition except on an elementary level within the community itself. Thus townspeople strove to obtain monopolies of all kinds, not only to secure the position of the "native" against the outsider, but also to prevent journeymen from moving to nearby communities and perhaps establishing rival production centers that would draw business away from the city. Monopolies also ensured that rivalries between individual merchants did not cause serious disruption that might be detrimental to the community as a whole. Corporate, restrictive, monopolistic economic organizations became deeply entrenched in medieval urban society. Innovations were few and only slowly accepted, and for a long time there appeared no compelling need to change the institutions that had worked well in the past and to which people had grown accustomed.

In addition to their economic functions, most guilds provided a variety of important social and recreational services. They cared for the widows and orphans of members and provided assistance for members who were the victims of accident or circumstance. They supervised the training of apprentices and provided them, and often the children of members, with a rudimentary general education. Major social affairs and many civic ceremonies took place in the largest and most important guildhall; many guilds had smaller halls that were used to put on special shows and banquets and for the celebration of the feast day of the trade's patron saint. Craft, municipal, and merchant guilds cooperated in staging major community entertainments such as sports events in addition to presenting the mystery plays that were performed during religious festivals.

Medieval urban life was often harsh and brutal, but because the cities were relatively small and the social structure orderly though comparatively rigid, life was generally stable and harmonious. The nature of urban existence and the social structure that stressed the corporate nature of society promoted in most townspeople a degree of civic pride, a sense of civic awareness, and a feeling of community responsibility that have not been paralleled since.

The Urban Church in the Middle Ages

To be fully functioning members of urban society, townspeople had to belong to some corporate structure; in order to be fully functioning human beings both urban and rural medieval people had to be members of the Roman Catholic church. Religious minorities, notably Jews, were recognized as being mostly outside the mainstream of society. In many urban centers Jews were required to live in special areas and were subject to special laws and requirements that applied only to them. Practically the only institution that outlasted the Roman Empire, the Catholic church was the one, largely unchallenged church. To be cast out from it was the ultimate rejection by society, for without its acceptance an individual was a spiritual leper whose situation was in some ways worse even than that of a physical leper, who was at least allowed to receive charity and the superficial ministrations of the church and the community. The church forbade any member to give aid or comfort to an excommunicant, and anyone who broke this law was himself also liable to excommunication. Excommunicants were deprived of many of their legal rights, too, such as the right to inherit property, and few people would live or work near them. An individual could seldom escape the consequences of excommunication by moving to another community, for this was still an age when strangers were suspect and a stranger without an unassailable reason for leaving his previous home was not likely to be readily accepted. Being cast out of the church was tantamount to being rejected by the human race.

Although membership in the church was an essential condition of life, the majority of medieval people, both urban and rural, understood the forms of religion only imperfectly. They were illiterate, but even literacy in the vernacular was no aid to reading church books written in Latin. Most people could not study church documents and dogma firsthand; indeed, the possession of any kind of theological knowledge on the part of anyone but a clergyman or well-educated nobleman was suspect. Church ceremonies and masses were also in Latin, and the congregation had minimal active involvement in them; services thus held little immediate interest. Because church rituals were not translated or presented in the vernacular and few people understood them, the intellectual and emotional appeal they held was essentially mystical or magical. The church offered little moral preaching, leaving this mainly to a few eccentric itinerant monks, and it reserved its educational offerings mainly for the few people who would themselves become clerics. Thus, although the church occupied a central place in their lives, the religion of the mass of the people was generally a vague set of rather simplistic notions bound together by faith. Most people understood that some actions were "good," some "evil"; they were afraid of being consigned to hell and aspired to go to heaven. The religion of the church of Rome was also often still confused with the remnants of "the old religion"; the ancient magical practices and the nature and spirit worship that existed in pagan Europe were never entirely supplanted by the Christianizing efforts of the church.

The essential, practical social services the church performed considerably strengthened its position at the center of society. The church, like the guilds, provided for the care of the young, sick, old, and incapable. It was for a long time the main dispenser of charity and solver of social problems, both of which, coupled with its great social influence, often led to its being co-opted to act as an extension of government for dealing with social matters. The church was the chief, almost the only, educational institution of the age. In an era characterized by rigid social distinctions, it provided one of the few avenues of upward social mobility. Many energetic and ambitious young men of low birth, such as Thomas à Becket, were able to rise to prominence within it. In addition to their spiritual, charitable, and educational functions, church institutions provided refuge for many people who could not cope with life in the lay world. Men who sought refuge from the often harsh realities of secular life frequently joined monastic orders, either as monks or as lay brothers. Convents, in addition to their spiritual functions, held out the hope of a similar refuge for women who could not find husbands or who refused to marry the husband found for them. The numerous, widely scattered establishments of the universal church were often used as resting places by travelers on both commercial and religious business. Church institutions helped oil the wheels of overland travel and commerce by providing safety, a bed, and a meal for travelers and merchants.

In rural settlements the church had little competition as the social center, but even in urban communities where guilds and their halls provided some alternatives, the church organized many social activities and provided a great deal of recreation and entertainment. The time that hard-working people were expected to spend in church on Sundays and feast days was an important period of relaxation and recreation for them, especially since in comparison to their ill-lit and generally cramped homes, the major urban churches were colorful places in which to spend a few hours. The sheer size and spaciousness of the interiors must have been awesome to people accustomed to living in the confined spaces of medieval houses and workshops. Church builders provided carvings, statuary, stained glass, and other decorations to glorify God, please the clerics, and divert, if not stimulate, the people who lost interest in rituals they did not understand.

In addition to its regular services, the church presented morality or mystery plays based on biblical and other religious sources that were performed in the church on special days, providing entertainment and possibly acting as teaching aids. In some cities there evolved the custom of consigning each play to a single craft guild; for example, the carpenters usually presented the play about Noah and the ark. The preparation and presentation of these brief plays soon led to friendly rivalry between the guilds and came to be regarded as an opportunity to enhance guild status. Guild members strove to design ever more splendid costumes and sets for their plays, the dialogue and action of which also became more entertaining and less spiritual as time passed. Eventually the plays were moved into the marketplace and streets where, removed from the atmosphere of the church, their sets could become more impressive and their dialogue more earthy. The traditions and forms of the troubadours and other wandering tellers of tales and singers of songs influenced mystery and morality plays once outdoors. By the end of the sixteenth century this combination was so refined that playwrights like Shakespeare could create highly structured, secular plays of great complexity and present them in recognizable, fixed theaters.

The physical relationship of the main church to the town or city symbolized the importance of the church and its central role in society. Churches were normally situated close to the active heart of the city, at the hub of the network of main roads, as were St. Mark's in Venice and Notre Dame in Paris, for example. Medieval churches, often situated on the highest site in the city, towered over all other buildings, even surpassing the walls in massiveness and grandeur. They undoubtedly acted as signposts to travelers many miles away, announcing the distance to and position of the city in an imprecise but extremely effective manner. The great cathedrals were by far the largest and most impressive structures of their age, and their builders lavished a remarkable amount of care, money, and time on them. Medieval townsmen, whose daily lives were filled with production, transport, trade, and profit, nevertheless built no such stone songs of glory to commerce. Equipment was elementary: hammers, chisels, wooden scaffolding, carts, pulleys, and ropes. They had for the most part only an elementary knowledge of architectural and engineering principles; many projects came to grief, and church building was a hazardous as well as a time-consuming occupation. A few cathedrals were begun and finished within a lifetime, but most, such as the magnificent one at Chartres, which has a twelfth-century portal, thirteenth-century doors and porches, fourteenth-century chapels, and a sixteenth-century spire built on its ninth-century foundations, took many generations to complete. The finished structures were often a mixture of several architectural styles and a combination of various degrees of technical expertise. The superhuman efforts needed to haul large quantities of quarried stone long distances and then to shape and fit it into spires, towers, arches, and buttresses can only be imagined. The misaligned windows, irregularly spaced arches, and other errors that came from building over generations, usually without the benefit of any master plan, only serve to underline the enormity of the effort.

The innate majesty of medieval churches and cathedrals is only one of their wonders; another is the motive that inspired people to build them. Why, with limited technical capacity and restricted bulk transport facilities, did these people spend such time and effort on the construction of buildings that were of no commercial or economic value? Many of those involved in cathedral building simply wanted to create something to glorify God and were convinced that God's house should be larger, more impressive, more richly decorated, and more durable than anything built for the use of humanity. Others were doubtless influenced by the vague but apparently eternal desire to create something grander than had ever been built before. Civic pride may have moved others to participate, the cathedral being a symbol of the wealth, power, and prestige of their community. Whatever the motive or mixture of motives for building cathedrals, the finished products certainly provide eloquent testimony to the importance of the church in the medieval urban community.

Cities in the Medieval World

The livelihood of the overwhelming majority of medieval people was agriculture; the economic and social functions of narrowly defined local areas circumscribed their lives. The urban minority lived by trade, which required that they be free to operate without the limitations and the parochialism that permeated the lives of the rural majority. The restraints, payments, and obligations that feudal lords customarily imposed on people living on their domains were not easily applied to people who manufactured and traded things rather than grew them. Furthermore, the members of urban communities perceived that the restraints and requirements applied to agrarian people restricted the mobility necessary to trade and eroded the profits of commerce. In general, the leading merchants spearheaded the drive to obtain community rights and freedoms in return for community payments to the feudal hierarchy. In addition to developing long-distance trade, the small towns that grew into dynamic cities also had to win the battle for independence from feudal restraints. They used any means to win, including playing off one lord against another, pitting king against church, negotiating compacts with other parties with similar interests, extending loans to key aristocrats at favorable interest rates, and a variety of tactics such as bribery, armed rebellion, and land purchase.

The usual signal that an urban community had won the first round of the struggle for freedom from feudal restraints was the granting of a charter. Charters varied in detail and were renewed, amended, and changed in various ways from time to time, but most of the major cities in those parts of Europe where feudalism existed had one kind or another by the thirteenth century. In the most general terms, a city or town charter granted the community concerned exemption from some or all feudal and agrarian regulations, which not only gave them the freedom necessary for their economic survival, but also placed them outside the sociopolitical framework of feudalism. The practical necessities of urban life led to townspeople enjoying "civil liberties" that people of a similar rank in rural society did not have. For example, most charters granted citizens the right to buy, sell, and bequeath their property as they pleased, limited only by the most nominal restrictions; they were allowed to hold fairs and markets at appointed times and to impose their own regulations on commercial activities; they had the freedom to travel about both inside and outside their home districts.

The privilege of greater freedom, an important by-product of the advent of city charters, heightened the townsman's sense of being "different" from his rural contemporaries; phrases such as "the air of the towns breeds freedom" were often used to express this special status. In many regions, by legal provision or by general custom, an escaped serf who lived in a town or city for a year and a day became a free man and

View of Venice, by Zoan Andrea Vavassore (c. 1517) Islands and lagoons made
Venice an ideal defense and trading center. This busy manufacturing and
commercial city set the pace for the revival of trade in the Middle Ages. The
relationships of water, prosperity, and civic affairs to one another can be seen in

the palaces of the rich merchants along the Grand Canal and in the proximity of
the main square and church to the waterfront.

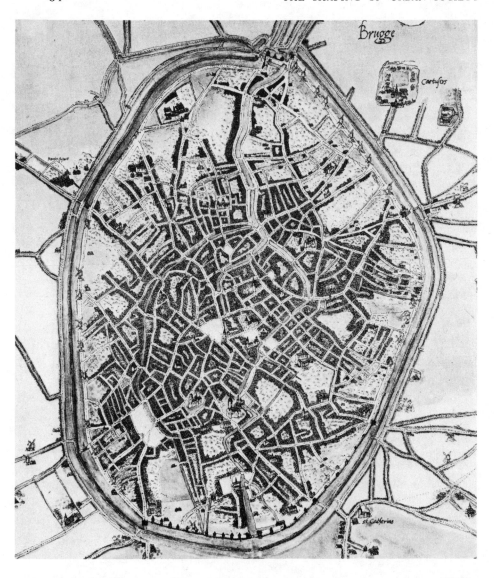

Bruges in the sixteenth century The defensive moat and wall, typical of medieval cities, can be seen. Note the waterway that runs through the city and the apparently unplanned street pattern. The many open areas within the walls indicate that this city was not choked by its own defenses. [NOTE: Although these drawings of Venice and Bruges are from the sixteenth century, they represent the earlier city well. Many medieval cities stagnated after the fourteenth century as new centers assumed leadership in urban development. They changed little after that time and their sixteenth-century appearance accurately reflects that at their apogee.]   Map Division, The New York Public Library; Astor, Lenox, and Tilden Foundations

Berne, Switzerland High ground surrounded on three sides by a steeply banked river loop provided an excellent defensive site for this city. The cathedral, marketplace, and main street of the old city can still be seen on the highest part of the protected site.   Swiss National Tourist Office

MAKING AND SELLING SHOES
Goods in the Middle Ages were typically made by hand in an establishment that was the center of both manufacturing and sale. The customer dealt directly with the manufacturer and could often see the goods being made, as is the case here.

From Hans Sachs, *Book of Trades* (1568), illustrated by Jost Amman

Fountain of Justice, Berne
Many cities in the Middle Ages took pride in providing water for all comers, animal as well as human. Splendidly decorated fountains such as this manifested both civic pride and concern for water supply.
Swiss National Tourist Office

Chartres Much of the medieval character of this city still survives in the twentieth century. The massive and beautiful cathedral, with its great interior spaces, color, and decoration, soars over the cramped, rather drab secular buildings of the old city.
Photograph by the author

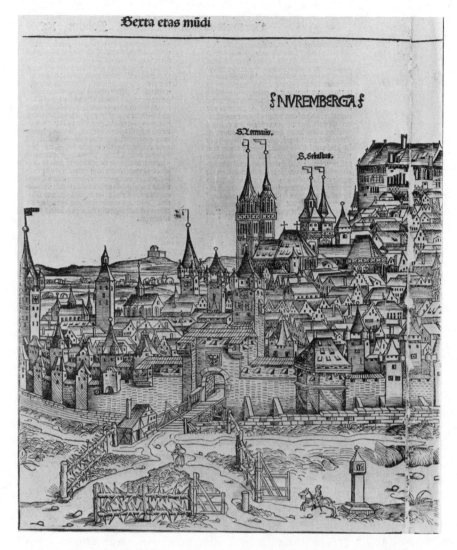

Berta etas mūdi

§ NVREMBERGA §

S. Lorenus.

S. Sebaldus.

VIEW OF NUREMBERG FROM THE SOUTHEAST (*1493*) The medieval city was densely packed with houses; its defensive wall marked a clear dividing line between it and the surrounding countryside. The wall was pierced by only a few narrow gates, and special provisions were made to protect these weak points.

The Metropolitan Museum of Art, Rogers Fund, 1920

was allowed the same privileges as all townspeople. The charter of Bologna, for example, stated that the people of the city had a right to be free, and the city also offered compensation to the owners of runaway serfs whom it placed on its own tax rolls as free individuals. This custom attracted some rural people to urban communities. It offered cities a means of expanding their labor resources, and it also meant that they generally attracted the better people in rural society—those with the wit and enterprise to escape and the adaptability to change their way of life. The successful runaway in effect had to work to support himself for a year in the urban community; this period of transition gave townspeople time to judge his worth. If he proved a useful and active addition, he would be accepted; if he proved to be idle or incompetent, he could be left to the mercy of pursuers, sent back home, or simply abandoned outside the walls and denied readmission. That mere acceptance into an urban community could transform a serf into a free man gave towns and cities a special place in the minds of contemporaries, both urban and rural.

In some areas, a medieval variant on the city-state form of urban development appeared. These city-states resembled tiny, urban-centered kingdoms in many ways; for example, they exhibited strong local loyalties and tended toward rule by princes.* This urban form generally appeared in the areas most affected by the earliest resumption of commerce in the early Middle Ages. It was common in Italy, where strong rivalries between cities were frequent, and in the Rhine basin, the main avenue of trade in central Europe and an area in which the pattern of political fragmentation was often shaped by the existence of urban centers. Where the formation of city-related units of political geography was widespread, the formation of nation-states tended to be delayed.

On the fringes of the main patterns of early medieval trade, urban communities developed more slowly, and their desire for freedom of action often coincided roughly in time with the determination of the greatest feudal lord to be a national monarch. In the more slowly developing areas, such as France and England, cities often allied with the new monarchs because they shared a common interest in ending restrictive localisms and control by local lords—the cities for economic and trading reasons, and the monarchs for reasons of nation building and centralized power. The

---

* Here "prince" is used not as a title but as a description of function. Under this heading fall such rulers as merchant princely families, like the Medicis of Florence; elected heads of state, like the doges of Venice; the many bishops of "Germany" who acted as the heads of their own little states revolving around the clerical administrative center of the bishopric; members of families who made up fixed urban oligarchies; and lords, princes, and electors of all kinds and titles.

fact that the activities and goals of the cities and national monarchs were usually mutually supportive strengthened this alliance. Both sought to establish a national, uniform legal system, the kings to strengthen their position as rulers and the cities to stabilize trading conditions; kings wanted to forge nations out of a collection of regions to give themselves wider political effectiveness and to form a broader power base for foreign adventures, and the cities wanted wider market areas with uniform trading conditions. Kings needed expanding incomes to finance domestic and foreign undertakings, and taxes and other levies on trade provided an elastic revenue source that could increase if trade were stimulated, while townspeople were always ready to cooperate with anyone or anything that promised growing trade and greater profits.

The demands imposed on the wider economic and social structures by medieval urban centers must be counted among the forces that helped change the medieval world, especially in Atlantic Europe, the region that would exhibit the most dynamism in the early modern phase of urban development. One product of urban expansion, which was well under way in Atlantic Europe by the thirteenth century, was a growing need for food surpluses to feed the swelling urban population. Agricultural surpluses had always been a major precondition for urban growth, and even greater surpluses were inevitably a prerequisite for the growth of more and larger towns and cities in the Middle Ages. The fact that rural people had to produce the excess to sustain the urban population meant that the pressures of urban growth also affected rural economic and social structures. Increasing demand for food meant that the production of food surpluses* became an increasingly profitable proposition for landowners and landholders. As the demand for food expanded, more farmers, especially in the areas surrounding urban centers, tried to enlarge the surplus they had for sale. Few advances had been made that increased yield per acre, and increasing surpluses generally meant augmenting the acreage of land under cultivation.

Increased production of trade goods was also implicit in city growth, which depended upon expansion of urban economic activities. As trade swelled, a greater demand for raw materials and trade goods was made on the rural economy. Farmers and landowners consequently found it increasingly profitable to produce cash crops, such as wine, oil, and wool, for sale to merchants. In order to take advantage of this opportunity,

---

* Mainly grain surpluses; the diet of most people at this time consisted of bread, beer or wine, a little meat and cheese, and a few vegetables.

however, it was necessary to expand the cultivated or grazing acreage; this placed great strains on the essentially static, land-based order of established economic and social arrangements.

In some areas new land was cleared for use, in others, marshes were drained and made productive. In many areas the most obvious way to increase acreage was to clear the common, land belonging to no one owner but to the rural community in general. Although common land was not farmed land in the general sense of the term, it was not unused, for much of it had traditionally been the means of survival of many poor rural people. Peasants grazed their animals on it, trapped small game, collected acorns for their pigs, found firewood for domestic fuel, and gathered some food items, such as mushrooms, to supplement their generally meager diet. Many rural people lived constantly on a narrow margin of survival that shrank to a knife-edge when bad luck or a poor harvest beset them. In order to survive at all, the poorest rural people did a variety of things: farmed a little, worked for pay on occasion, made a few things to sell or exchange, and made some use of the resources of the common. The sum of all these activities was little more than survival; because the margin was so narrow, the failure of any one element could mean hardship or even starvation. Clearing of common land by landowners trying to increase their surplus yield chipped away at the semiwild fringes of common land around many villages. Eventually in these villages too little was left to allow freedom of grazing and the number of cattle on the common had to be restricted. As people tried to pursue their traditional activities on a shrinking area, each found less game, less firewood, and fewer acorns.

The poorest people were the first to find it harder to survive when their share of the products of the common dwindled. Faced with starvation, many of them had to find some way of replacing the living they had gleaned from the common land. Meanwhile, landowners who had expanded their acres of cultivated land needed more labor to work the new fields. They now found it unprofitable to give each laborer the use of a patch of land in exchange for his labor and more economical to devote all of their holdings to cash crops; many began to pay workers in allotments of food or small amounts of cash. Thus, the same processes that forced the small landholding peasant off his holding also produced an alternative occupation for him: that of landless agricultural laborer, hired and paid for his services by his master.

Such changes took place slowly and the pace of change varied from region to region, affecting different people at different times even within the same village. The diminution of common land quickly forced the poorest, those who depended most heavily on the common for survival, off their small official holdings. People who depended relatively little on the common and had relatively large official holdings might not feel the effects of its shrinkage for several generations until some disaster, such as a run of bad harvests or a series of untimely deaths, beset their families and exhausted their other resources.

Some peasants forced off their traditional holdings moved to the towns and cities and increased the urban population yet further, but most had no marketable urban skills and lacked the daring to move away from familiar surroundings. Although the majority remained to work the land, they operated in a very different social and economic context from that which had existed before the reduction of the common and the cultivation of cash crops. They no longer had rights to their own piece of ground in return for which they rendered services to their lord; they were landless workers, hired hands of an employer who paid them food doles and money wages. With this change, the land-for-service contract that had been the foundation of the whole manorial structure faded from significance, and the socioeconomic edifice that had been erected upon it began to crumble into disuse.

Gradually, farming communities in more and more areas of Atlantic Europe moved away from the small-surplus, essentially local subsistence farming that had been characteristic of the medieval economic system toward the growth of cash crops of food or raw materials for sale to some merchant. As cash profit became an increasingly important element in farming operations, rural areas began to adopt many "urban" notions, such as the specialization of function and the production of items for sale in distant communities. For example, many farmers in suitable districts concentrated on the production of wool that ultimately found its way into the thriving textile trade; others, such as some English monasteries, devoted all their suitable land to the cultivation of grains which they sold in bulk for cash. Such cash-crop producers often bought food for their own needs from smaller local producers. In short, the specialization, complexity, and cash-based economy that had been characteristic of urban settlements began to invade the countryside.

The development of a rural cash economy, beginning in some places as early as the later Middle Ages, widened the gap between poor and prosperous, and by the seventeenth and early eighteenth centuries a new rural social order was in operation. The poor laborer had only his labor and occasionally some surplus food, both of which he used to pay his rent.

He could not accumulate surpluses of either of these resources and therefore could not increase his landholdings. When common lands began to disappear, he became dependent on a landowner for employment, no longer having the right to the fruits of his own labor since he no longer had a right to the land. Thus, poor people embarked on a downward spiral that ended with their descendants accepting a new social role as landless workers surviving on payments from an employer.

On the other hand, some moderately prosperous people were able to get on an upward spiral that eventually improved the economic and social standing of their descendants. Their prosperity was generally the result of owning or holding relatively productive land and of having light obligations to the lord. They had more time, more and better land, and were able to produce surpluses. Less of their excess was committed in advance as rent or other payment; consequently they were less dependent on the common and so less affected by its shrinkage. A few such people, especially those fortunate enough to have large, healthy families to supply labor, could sometimes produce a surplus large enough to be worth taking to a local market. If they were lucky and worked hard, such people could, over the years, transform their surpluses into that infinitely conservable and convertible medium of exchange, money. When the opportunity arose, they could use their savings, often accumulated over several generations, to buy or lease more land from which they could expect even larger surpluses, which in time would produce the cash to buy yet more land, which might be cultivated by hired laborers. With continued good fortune and hard work across the generations, a few families eventually gained economic prosperity and social respectability.

By the seventeenth and eighteenth centuries, the rural medieval social distinctions in much of western Europe had broken down and a new social system based on employer-employee relationships and on money transactions had come into operation. The complexity of this process defies brief description for its manifestations varied with time and place. Even in those areas where changes took place relatively quickly, several generations passed before they were complete. In this process, the economic and social influence of cities played a large part. Cities had never fitted smoothly into the economic, social, or political structures of the dominantly agrarian medieval world, and their inhabitants consciously struggled to free themselves from agrarian restraints. At the same time, the continued growth of cities and of their demands undermined the whole agrarian framework and helped transform a subsistence agricultural economy into a more specialized, productive, cash-based operation compatible with urban needs and practices.

In time, of course, the typical medieval community also began to break up. New challenges, such as those implicit in the great explorations and the discovery of new lands, the technical innovations such as water-powered machines that could be used to make some productive processes more efficient, and the depletion of some raw material resources for which substitutes had to be found, brought a need for new attitudes and methods of working. The corporate substructures of the medieval cities were, like most organizations, innovative and useful in the early stages of their development. They filled current community needs as urban settlements matured, but in time they became entrenched and rigid. When new forces emerged, they lacked the flexibility to deal with them effectively. The guild hierarchies, originally essential to the organization of urban enterprises and later a stabilizing influence in the maturing cities, ossified. Custom took control, and guild composition and practices came to be based almost entirely on precedent rather than on immediate practical needs. For example, it became customary for the number of masters to be fixed, thus preventing many qualified journeymen from becoming masters. Journeymen and apprentices with no prospects of advancement came to resent the restrictions imposed by outdated customs, and when they saw opportunities to move outside urban centers, many were more than ready to seize the opportunity to leave the communities whose social and economic organizations they felt had served them badly. With changes such as these, urban monopolies began to break down, regulations were bypassed, and community loyalties began to fade.

New industries grew up outside established guild structures, and some old, established industries began to change and take on new forms that made their growth incompatible with guild regulation and urban monopoly, including even the long-established textile industry. Raw and partly treated wool and finished textiles had played a central role in the trading activities of northwestern Europe since commercial activities resumed in the early Middle Ages. As was the case with other medieval industries, guilds usually controlled the processes of production and sale. During the late fifteenth and early sixteenth centuries, however, guild monopolies began to break up as textile manufacturing spilled out of urban centers, beyond the reach of their outdated and rigid controls. Fulling, the process of matting or felting the surface of woolen cloth to make it smoother and more resistant to wear, had traditionally been done by using human labor to pound the cloth in baths of water and fuller's earth. This process could, however, be done more efficiently in a water-powered fulling mill. The earliest reference to such mills is in eleventh-century Normandy, but by the sixteenth century they were common all over the textile areas of northern Europe. Other processes, such as dyeing, could also be carried out with the aid of water-powered mechanical devices. These mills were set up outside established urban centers where they could take advantage of cheap rural labor, swiftly flowing streams, and clean water while avoiding guild regulation. In spite of the complaints of the officials of affected guilds, other cloth-making processes, including spinning and weaving, also gradually moved out to the countryside.

In the textile industry, and in newer industries such as coal mining, the general trend was a breakdown of effective urban community controls and monopolies and a growing importance of capital, individual organization, efficiency, and expanded production in the manufacture of major middle- and long-distance trade goods. The effects of these changes varied in place and time, but the net result was the obsolescence of the craft guild system. The guilds did not vanish entirely; indeed, many of them fought hard for survival, trying, for example, to persuade monarchs to give guild regulations the authority of law. Their attempts to resist innovation and turn the clock back by legal and other means failed in the long run, however, and industry gradually came to depend more and more on capital and individual enterprise. Although a few guilds survived as social clubs and some as anachronistic elements in urban government, they eventually faded away. Established urban industrial centers continued to produce and to be important manufacturing centers, but they were less subject to guild regulation. Their monopoly of industry was broken, and they faced a growing challenge from the new production centers that began to grow from villages into new little towns.

The development of nation-states played a role in breaking up the medieval city form. As monarchs turned their attentions to the conquest of new territories and to contests of strength or of national interest with other monarchs, they needed more money. In trade and industry they saw lucrative fields for taxation, and they attempted to nourish commerce, as well as to offer concessions to wealthy merchants who were willing to advance loans. When monarchs became more successful in their attempts to impose law, order, and peace on their territories, the need of townspeople for community protection became less pressing. Some merchants, aware of this, severed their "home town" connections and prospered as a result of their high degree of mobility and lack of obligations to anyone but themselves. As technical innovations began to change productive processes and as national and personal considerations began to carry a greater weight in economic operations than did community interests, the communal urban entity, the dynamic medieval city, began to fade in many parts of Europe.

THE
EARLY 3 The City
MODERN
CITY of
Princes
and
Merchants

Between the fifteenth and the eighteenth centuries, a spate of new ideas, inventions, and discoveries changed the Western world and opened up a new phase of urban development. Many of the initial innovations came from the long-established center of the urban world, the Mediterranean area, where people explored new frontiers in art, science, literature, and philosophy. The people of Atlantic Europe, however, did much of the practical application of the innovations and most of the exploration of new geographical frontiers. The dynamism in city development gradually passed from the Mediterranean to the nations on the Atlantic seaboard. The western lands that began to set the new patterns had, of course, had towns and cities in the Middle Ages when the Mediterranean had dominated urban-related activities, but they had mostly been secondary communities on the fringes of the main flow of trade. Gradually their role changed in this period, and they came to set, rather than to follow, the dynamic patterns of urban growth and change.

The Forces of Change

The application of technical innovations and the development of many new processes led industries to depend more heavily on equipment and capital investment than had been the case in the past, and some industries tended to move toward a primitive capitalistic mode of operation. As they began to outgrow the old supporting and controlling structures that had evolved on the basis of more primitive industrial techniques, many industries moved away from both guild controls and established urban manufacturing centers.

Coal mining provides a good example of a rapidly expanding industry that was not readily controlled by guilds and whose development required increasing amounts of capital. In the sixteenth and seventeenth centuries coal, used locally on a small scale in some districts for centuries, became an important fuel item in commerce. A thriving coal trade grew up near the rivers Rhone and Loire in France, for example. Mining activities began to increase all over Atlantic Europe, the largest producer and consumer being England.* The greatest demand for coal came from those districts in which wood was becoming scarce. Wood was a raw material with many uses like building houses and ships and making tools and furniture. In relatively densely populated areas, such as around London, the supply was rapidly diminishing; where wood became too precious to burn, the importance of coal grew. London and southeastern England provided a lucrative market for the coal produced on the Pennine, south Wales, and especially the northeastern coal fields. From Liverpool, Sunderland, and especially from Newcastle, coal was shipped by sea and up the Thames for sale and use in London. By the reign of Elizabeth I, the use of coal as a fuel was so widespread in London that the city had a smog problem; even French visitors, no strangers to the use of coal, wondered how Londoners survived in the thick, noxious fumes.

As markets expanded, coal sources suitable for mining by primitive outcrop methods were soon exhausted, and new methods had to be developed to work deeper seams; shafts were sunk, and elementary drainage systems and lifting equipment were introduced. The new mining techniques required the investment of relatively large amounts of capital. The coal mine, which had previously been a hole scraped in an outcropping coal seam worked by a few people with little skill and a few cheap tools, was transformed into a considerable enterprise employing dozens of people and using mechanical aids bought with the capital contributed in fairly large amounts by one or more individuals. Few established urban centers were located on coal fields, and except for the growth of the ports involved in the coal trade, the expansion of the coal

* England produced more coal than all other European producers combined. The growth of the English coal industry was remarkable in the sixteenth and early seventeenth centuries: annual output increased from about two hundred thousand tons in the 1530s to 1.5 million tons a century later. John U. Nef, *Conquest of the Material World* (Chicago: University of Chicago Press, 1964), p. 169.

industry made little direct contribution to the growth of existing cities. In the long run, its major impact on urban development would be in the development of "new" coal towns.

As national monarchs established peace and order more firmly, the protection of the city walls was no longer as necessary as before. Enterprising merchants saw the advantages of employing cheap rural labor, avoiding town taxes, and escaping from the ancient regulations that hampered the introduction of new manufacturing techniques in the established urban centers. Although textile production continued to be an important industry in established centers, by the early sixteenth century it was certainly not an urban monopoly. A variety of forces combined to generate the drift of the textile industry to the countryside in regions such as Flanders, Brabant, Liège, and the west of England. Country people were accustomed to making rough cloth for their own use and could easily be trained to produce the finer cloths needed by international traders. Rural workers were closer than their urban counterparts to the sources of raw materials and food, and thus entrepreneurs could reduce transport costs and wages, avoid urban taxes and regulations, and experiment with production methods without the interference of the guilds. Given that rural textile production had all these advantages, it is not surprising that the increase in cloth production in the early modern period came from rural rather than from urban sources.

As rural textile production expanded, new techniques of organization evolved. Merchants bought raw wool and had it cleaned, spun, and woven by suitably skilled groups of rural workers. Final finishing processes, such as dyeing, were often completed in urban centers. This organization of the processes of production clearly lent itself to individual, direct control and so was more likely to lead to flexibility and experiment than were the old guild methods. It did, however, require that the organizer invest relatively large amounts of capital to buy the raw wool, to finance the various processes of manufacture, and to pay the various groups of workers involved in producing the finished product.

Increasing population made an important contribution to changes in the urban pattern. Lack of censuses makes precise statistical measurement impossible, but it is certain that population expanded, although its growth was often erratic. By the seventeenth century, population levels almost everywhere were much higher than they had been in the fifteenth century. The causes of this growth are matters for speculation, but they undoubtedly included such forces as the waning of the medieval plagues and continued land clearing which made more food available. While

Mediterranean centers expanded relatively slowly, the great trading cities of Atlantic Europe experienced rapid growth. By the early seventeenth century Lisbon, Seville, Amsterdam, and Antwerp all held over one hundred thousand people; Paris had one hundred eighty thousand; and London, two hundred fifty thousand. By the end of the eighteenth century Paris had six hundred seventy thousand people and London, eight hundred thousand, both cities more than trebling their population in two hundred years. The establishment and growth of urban centers, such as Boston, New Orleans, and New York on the western shores of the ocean further enhanced the status of the Atlantic region as the pacesetter in urban development. In the same period, previously small or nonexistent centers in the northern fringes of Europe, such as Berlin, Copenhagen, Moscow, and St. Petersburg, attained considerable size.

The most important force operating to shift the focus of dynamic urban development from the Mediterranean to the Atlantic was a change in the pattern of long-distance trade in the early modern period. Although the Low Countries, an important part of Atlantic Europe, had been an important medieval trading center, the Mediterranean had dominated trade in the Middle Ages. With the exception of the lucrative overland spice trade with Asia, medieval trade had been predominantly intra-European. In the early modern period, the trade pattern continued to be largely intra-European, but trade across the oceans of the world played an increasingly important role. The medieval Mediterranean commercial centers might have played a vigorous part in the new trade, but they were not favorably located to take advantage of a boom in oceangoing as opposed to seagoing trade. The inertia that the continued profitability of their traditional trading patterns generated also held them back. On the other hand, the vigorous, young nations of Atlantic Europe were ideally situated to participate in oceangoing trade, and their people were eager for profit and were unrestrained by strong precedent.

The new trade pattern was based on the discoveries made in the great era of exploration in the fifteenth and sixteenth centuries, during which the main outlines of the major land masses were sketched in on maps of the world. These explorations were much wider ranging than earlier ventures, which tended to stay within sight of the coast, and they involved the crossing of large oceans. Very little land exploration was done and the voyagers found, mapped, and began to trade with new lands from oceangoing vessels. Technological developments in shipbuilding and more refined navigational techniques made all this possible. By the fifteenth century the rigging of ships was more sophisticated and allowed the more flexible manipulation of sails. Other advances permitted the construction of longer, larger ships able to carry the stores and crew necessary for a long ocean voyage. The mariner's compass was put into wider use and the notion that the world was round and not flat was becoming sufficiently widespread to offer temptation to adventurous souls. Curiosity about all natural phenomena increased during the Renaissance and promoted the development of more sophisticated observing and measuring instruments, which were also extremely useful to navigators, especially to those sailing the Atlantic.

A good deal of the outburst of exploration and trading was politically motivated. The ambitious rulers of the rising western and northern states wanted to increase their incomes by expanding the trade from which they derived much of their revenue; they also wanted the international influence and prestige that tended to accompany vigorous commercial activity. Because traditional trade routes to the East through the Mediterranean were blocked by Turkey and effectively controlled by the Italians, new trade routes had to be sought elsewhere. The ocean powers with great lengths of Atlantic coastline and with sailors and ships accustomed to the ocean naturally looked to the Atlantic for these new routes. The desire for increased power and wealth encouraged many monarchs to invest small sums in voyages by adventurous and curious sailors in the hope that a successful journey by even one of them would prove profitable. Much of the royal sponsorship and initial exploring impetus came, appropriately enough, from the Iberian Peninsula, a block of territory that was half Mediterranean and half Atlantic in geography and outlook. In the first half of the fifteenth century Prince Henry ("the Navigator") of Portugal sponsored explorations down the African coast by ships equipped with all the most sophisticated devices then available. Portuguese explorers had crossed the equator before Henry died, and the initiative was sustained with Dias's rounding of the Cape of Good Hope and the eventual establishment of oceangoing contact with India by the sixteenth century. Columbus's attempt to reach Asia by sailing west in accordance with round-earth theories in the late fifteenth century was the prelude to the establishment of the great Spanish and Portuguese empires in a "new" continent.

Silver from the Americas more than returned the initial investment of the Spanish crown, and the hope of finding similar treasure of their own encouraged other monarchs to sponsor explorers. Lured by the promise of enormous profits, merchants followed on the heels of the adventurers, establishing tentative trade routes with the Americas and

India and opening up ocean trade with Asia and Africa. This ocean trade was on a very modest scale by later standards, but was enormously profitable by the standards of the day. For example, the spice merchants who brought in their merchandise through the new ocean routes were able to make a great profit and still undersell spices brought in through the traditional east Mediterranean route. The profits of ocean trade influenced national and international policies of European rulers, stimulated the growth of the great Atlantic port cities, and established two important lines of development that would affect the world for centuries: major ecological changes and European empire building.

As explorers and traders began to roam in ever-greater numbers and ever more widely over the face of the earth, they altered the distribution of a variety of living things—vegetable, animal, and human. Many regions provided ideal conditions for some useful plant or animal native to another area; if profits or convenience warranted it, traders transplanted appropriate species, many of which thrived far from their native lands. Load-bearing animals, especially horses and donkeys, became common wherever Europeans had been, as did chickens, sheep, and other useful livestock. Wheat and other grains were transplanted to the Americas; the potato moved from there to become an important crop in many parts of Europe. Useful plants and animals were, in short, no longer confined to their specific areas of origin but were more widely distributed across the earth. By the eighteenth century human population patterns had altered as well: European peoples had settled in communities all over the world and African peoples had been transplanted to the West Indies and the Americas.

Overseas trading was still a high-risk proposition for the merchant. It held the promise of great profit, but it also offered the possibilities of shipwreck, piracy, and ruin. To offset these high risks, merchants generally tried to secure an official monopoly of trade within specific areas. At the same time, monarchs were discovering that a more complex, far-reaching government was more costly to run and that advances in military technology were making human slaughter more expensive, an important consideration when war was a major instrument of foreign policy. By taxing trade profits and selling trade concessions, monarchs hoped to keep their coffers full. Consequently they were willing to provide merchants with the military support and the monopolies requested in the interests of increasing profits and were willing to conquer new areas, especially when political conditions in Europe made overseas conquest a convenient political maneuver.

Contemporary economic theories intensified international trading competition. In the seventeenth century it was generally accepted that the amount of wealth in the world was finite and that true wealth existed only in the form of precious metals. Each nation tried to obtain the lion's share of these, not only to increase its income and enable it to maintain a larger army, but also to render all other nations poorer and less powerful. There were only three ways of increasing the national supply of precious metals. The most direct was to own the mines, but Spain and Portugal had secured the most lucrative claims very early. A less dependable method was to steal. Privateer-sponsoring monarchs, such as Elizabeth I of England, employed this method although it was an unsound foundation for long-term national economic policies. The third means was to produce a trading surplus to sell to other nations in exchange for gold and silver. Most monarchs found the third alternative the most reliable and profitable, and many of them tried to develop elementary national economic policies, with varying degrees of success.

In general, the policy of the mercantilists was to encourage high-value exports and penalize imports in order to produce a favorable balance of trade. Such regulations tended to hobble merchants, but they had little choice in the matter and needed the protection and support of their monarchs for overseas ventures. In addition, monarchs attempted to obtain overseas trading areas producing commodities that appealed to the prosperous people of Europe, who could pay for them in gold and silver. Accordingly, the most desirable areas were those that produced luxury goods, such as sugar, spices, tea, furs, and exotic baubles. The conquest and protection of valuable trading areas provided the military basis for European imperialism at this time, bringing nations into conflict abroad, such as France and Britain in North America and India in the eighteenth century.

Changes in intellectual concepts about the world and mankind accompanied the changing material and geographical view of the world that resulted from the explorations and the expansion of trading activity. In the fifteenth century Italians had begun to study anew the works of the ancient writers, and they initiated a rebirth of the arts, letters, and secular intellectual activity. In the later fifteenth and the sixteenth centuries, people of central Europe, notably in Germany and Switzerland, began a reevaluation of spiritual values. Although the people of Atlantic Europe would later build upon the achievements of the Renaissance and the Reformation, they played only a minor role in the initial innovations, which came mainly from long-established communities in Italy and central Europe. The peculiar genius of the Atlantic people lay in adapting discoveries to fit practical ends and in weaving them into the fabric of a dynamic new national and urban life.

It was in Atlantic Europe that the stimulation of intellectual and scientific discovery mingled with the excitement of expanding business opportunities; intellectualism met nationalism, and art mixed with political and social ambition. The people of Atlantic Europe took Renaissance joy in life and bent their energies to practical and material as well as to intellectual and artistic ends. They readily adopted the new spirit of inquiry that demanded full exploration of the world and added their share of experiments and discoveries; but they also applied the methodology of inquiry to practical ends such as the development of better navigational instruments and techniques and of more efficient methods of agricultural production.

The upheaval of the Reformation, which gave birth to new Protestant sects, foreshadowed a new kind of spiritual system that soon became an integral part of the nationalistic, mercantile life-style of many urban Atlantic Europeans. The Netherlands, the British Isles, north Germany, and parts of France and Switzerland readily accepted Protestantism; all these were regions that were about to participate in the dynamic commercial expansion of the early modern period. Some people changed religions as an expression of independence or opposition to larger powers, as did the Dutch against the Spanish and the French; some monarchs, such as those of England and Prussia, made it a useful tool of national policy. Protestantism had a natural appeal for townsmen and for moderately prosperous landowners. Townsmen had always had the feeling of being a special, privileged minority group in society, and they readily accepted the new creeds that asserted the existence of an "elite" or "chosen" group in spiritual society. The elitist Protestant sects gave prosperous townspeople a spiritual class system that ensured their supremacy. Although theory held that only God knew the identity of the chosen ones who were predestined to go to heaven, most practical people felt that God was bound to give some sign to the elect. They felt that the ragged, filthy, half-starved majority of the people living in both rural and urban hovels could not be the chosen ones, for God, presumably at least as sensible as his followers, surely would not treat his chosen ones in this degrading fashion. Equally, they were sure that God would not choose his elect from the idle, drunken, disorderly, and dissipated ranks of the aristocracy. Hence, the process of elimination, if nothing else, indicated that this practical, sensible God would choose the elect from the ranks of the sober, hard-working, devout, prosperous middle ranks of society. Their virtues—originally only the practical rules of life of the striving groups in society—along with material possessions and prosperity, were seized upon as signs of God's blessings. Earthly prosperity thus came to be closely associated with spiritual status; the commercial attitudes necessary for the accumulation of wealth became spiritual virtues. The moral code that resulted owed as much to business as it did to religion, and it was with this character that it began to infiltrate the social value system as the influence of the middle groups in society increased. Idleness and frivolity on the part of aristocrat and pauper alike eventually came to be seen as violations of the moral code, while material prosperity and industriousness became virtues that marked the morally superior.

While these adjustments were taking place in religion and the social structure, other changes were operating to reduce the significance of God in the secular world. A wave of scientific investigation and speculation resulted in the development of new ideas about the universe, man, and God; Newton eventually synthesized these ideas into his concept of a flawlessly working universe that operated without either divine intervention or the need for it. Scientists and philosophers generally agreed that God had begun the operation of the universe, but scientific discoveries suggested that it worked so precisely in obedience to discoverable, definable laws that he had no need to meddle to keep it functioning. God was retained in the scheme of things as the maker of the universe providing science with a useful explanation of the origins of natural laws and forming a useful compromise between religion and science. People accepted that God had created the world, but that he no longer interfered with its vital processes or performed miracles that directly involved him in the minutiae of its daily operations. With the advances of the "scientific revolution," God began to suffer a kind of technological unemployment.

The new ideas greatly affected philosophy and theology, so the relationship between mankind and God had to be reevaluated. Although the turmoil and violence of the great religious wars, both civil and international, accompanied the advent of Protestantism, in the long run religion began to fade in importance and recede from the forefront of everyday life. Scientists who uncovered natural laws began to play a more central role, pushing God to the side. Further, the Protestant emphasis on a personal, noninstitutional relationship with God undermined the foundations on which the medieval church had built its central position in society. Once membership in a single, universal church was no longer common to all people, and as the influence of merchants and of practical business interests increased, the church no longer formed a dominant focus of common interests, its institutions no longer necessarily provided a common center for all social activities, and its buildings no longer necessarily dominated urban communities as they had in the past.

The disintegration of the intimate social groupings of the Middle Ages accompanied the new ideas of the wider universe, the expansion of the known world, and the broadening of intellectual horizons. Secure, personal group orientations melted away as the world became a larger, if a lonelier, place. This change in perspective heralded a change in aesthetic values, a change that would have a great impact on urban forms. As scientists emphasized the beauty, rationality, and orderliness of the universe, the people whom they influenced attempted to discover more order, precision, and regularity in their daily lives. The transition from an intellectual desire for organized space and matter to its practical application in planning was an easy one.

City Functions and Forms

Given the great expansion in both the scope and volume of worldwide, ocean-borne trade that took place in this period, it is not surprising that the dynamic city of the time was the ocean port city. This was true even in areas that were just coming under the influence of European people, for the trading ships of Europe needed ports around the world. Cities such as Charleston, Boston, Bombay, and Cape Town thrived in the "new" areas of the world; because recently migrated Europeans whose main concern was trade had built them, they were patterned on the most advanced designs to be found in the great ocean port cities of Europe. Overseas trade was so important to the income and prestige of European monarchs that those who did not have a good seaport strove to obtain one, as did Peter the Great of Russia. He had a realistic, if sometimes crude, grasp of the forces that were making western European nations strong and prosperous, and he subsequently managed to break Sweden's control of the Baltic and to acquire a trading site that would give Russian ships access to the Atlantic region. On this site he planned and built St. Petersburg, a city laid out according to the most advanced city-planning ideas of the time.

Ocean ports were busier than ever before as ships increased in size and numbers and moved in and out more frequently. Everything associated with shipping thrived: more docks and warehouses were built,

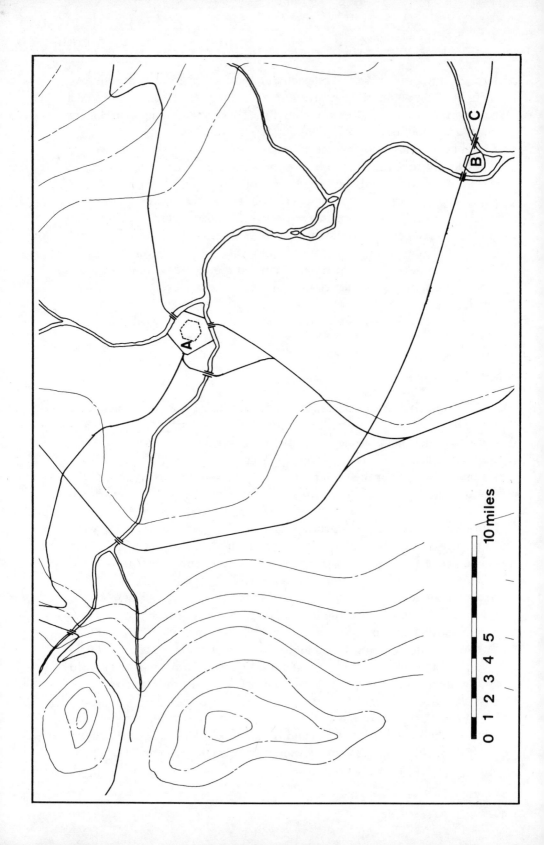

10 miles

0 1 2 3 4 5

THE EARLY MODERN CITY c. 1750

Trade increased in the early modern period and the city grew. The old walls were removed to allow expansion and much of the medieval built-up area was cleared and rebuilt (**A**), although the major features of the old city, such as the cathedral and marketplace, remained. The demand of the increased population for food generated many changes in the surrounding rural area, which also supplied many of the new city residents. Trade and trade-related occupations became the dominant elements in city life and some merchants became almost as wealthy as landed aristocrats. The city became an important financial and administrative center. The prince and many aristocrats built for prestige, creating fashionable, wide, straight streets suitable for their horses and carriages and lined with impressive buildings.

B New settlement. River navigable to this point by oceangoing vessels.

C New road to iron deposits.

D Cathedral and marketplace surrounded by remnants of old city.

E Prince's palace.

F Formal gardens.

G Commercial exchange building.

H Homes of aristocrats and wealthy merchants.

(MAPS DRAWN BY SATHIT CHAIYASIN)

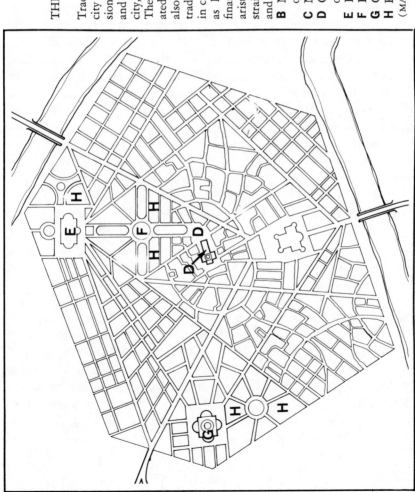

shipbuilding yards were extended, and more rope and sail makers were employed. As activity in the port cities increased, their population grew. There were more merchants, dealers, and traders of all kinds, more sailors and craftsmen who built and serviced ships, more clerks in shipping offices, more shoemakers, porters, barkeepers, milkmaids, butchers, thieves, and prostitutes. The most important port cities became major population centers, often the great cities in their region or nation, while secondary port towns also expanded and attained considerable size. In European settlements in other parts of the world, the port town was generally the first settlement and long remained the largest in any developing region.

As trade increased in volume, range, and complexity, the need for more sophisticated and flexible international financial arrangements and institutions became more urgent. Worldwide trading outgrew the rather elementary commercial mechanisms that had been adequate for the dominantly intra-European, relatively restricted trade of the Middle Ages. As more people from more regions became involved in long-distance trade, fewer could expect to know everyone with whom they did business. There was therefore a need for fixed meeting places where merchants could be sure to find other merchants and local buyers and sellers. In response to this need, the major trading cities established "exchanges" where merchants could be sure of contacting each other and could do business. As trading enterprises became more numerous and wide-ranging, there was a need for internationally acceptable, reliable banks as well as for other institutions that offered both long- and short-term international credit. Merchants also found cash transactions increasingly inconvenient and risky. It was safer and more convenient to deposit their gold and silver money in a safe place and work with slips of paper that gave written authority to call on certain assets from their accounts or from the accounts of others. On this basis paper money, checking, and bank account systems of all kinds began to evolve.

Transoceanic trading, with its attendant dangers from storms, wrecks, thieves, and hostile natives, was a risky proposition, and cautious merchants sought ways of reducing the chances of suffering a devastating loss on a single voyage, appropriately enough, by a sophisticated form of gambling. A merchant or shipowner found someone, or a group of people, prepared to wager that his venture would succeed and willing to forfeit their wagers if something went wrong and the venture came to grief. The merchant, in turn, bet that the venture would fail and that the other gambling party would have to forfeit the prearranged sum for its failure.

The merchant handed over his relatively small stake to the other party, who kept it if the venture were successful and returned the sum many times over if it failed. If all went well, the merchant made a profit on the cargo and forfeited a relatively small sum, but if the ship or cargo were lost, the merchant did not suffer too badly because he could collect the sum of money paid by his "winning bet." If the odds governing the wagers were calculated properly, this system worked to the advantage of both parties, giving the merchant security and the bettors long-term profit for their risk taking. As was the case with the buying and selling of other goods and services, meeting places where such "gambling" could be arranged were essential. At first these were informal, the one that set the pattern being Lloyd's Coffee House in London. As habit persisted and the whole process became formalized, these transactions acquired the name of "insurance" and insurance companies conducted business in offices and exchanges.

The need for meeting places, exchanges, banks, and offices resulted in the addition of new institutions and their buildings to the existing landscape of the major trading cities. As trade and industry became increasingly important in the lives of urban dwellers, these buildings became more and more central to the life and planning of the city. As secular activities became more numerous and complex than religious ones, the church found it increasingly difficult to hold on to its traditional position at the center of community life. A slow shift in the balance of spiritual and secular institutional buildings in the city reflected this change. The church lost its automatic monopoly of the best and most central sites in the city, and in building and rebuilding schemes the impressive and ornate edifices of business and government began to challenge church buildings in site, size, and authority. The bourse or exchange replaced the central cathedral, while banks and government buildings challenged the churches. When Sir Christopher Wren, architect of the current St. Paul's Cathedral in London, drew up a plan for the rebuilding of the city after the fire in the seventeenth century, he retained the old, splendid site for his new cathedral. It was not the plan's sole focal point, however. The Stock Exchange to which Wren's plan allotted the next-best site, challenged its dominance.

Although there was no sudden, sharp break with tradition in this period, urban life and institutions began to refocus as commercial institutions first challenged then replaced religious ones at the major pivotal points of urban centers. Established urban centers that escaped major fires and other disasters retained the great church as the center of their oldest sections, but from that time on, whenever churches were built in cities they no longer dominated the urban scene. The medieval traveler coming upon a city saw the cathedral as the central structure; the traveler nearing a twentieth-century city, by contrast, would find that the great dominant and central structures were governmental, bank, insurance, and commercial office buildings.

The dynamic city of the early modern period was not exclusively the city commercial; it was also the city politic. Contemporary developments within the nation-state greatly influenced the character of the major cities of the time. One development was the growth of the power of national monarchs, which had begun in the Middle Ages and which reached its peak in the seventeenth and eighteenth centuries. Kings were primarily interested in extending and strengthening their personal authority; in order to do so they tried to keep a finger in every pie that might yield revenue, military advantage, or prestige, and to expand their territories wherever possible. The small group of administrators and advisers that had helped monarchs run national affairs in the past was insufficient to cope with expanding government activity, and a large and complex new administrative machine was devised. Specialists took over routine tasks of government, and they needed permanent office buildings in which to work and to store records. The expansion of royal income lay at the root of national, military, and imperial activities, and as ways of raising revenues became more complex, a government's need for a fixed financial center became obvious. Clearly, concentrating all the major governmental offices in one location would be more efficient, and placing the offices of state revenue in a major center of financial and commercial activities would be more convenient than scattering them. Thus the institutions of national and commercial administration tended to gravitate to the same urban center. In the case of some cities, already-existing trends were reinforced: traditional royal centers in major trading cities added commercial institutions and became the undisputed capitals of their nations, as was the case in France and England. In some countries, monarchs attempted to relocate royal administration and court centers in order to make them conform to a convenient pattern. Peter the Great shifted his seat of government from Moscow, the traditional center, to his new port city of St. Petersburg on the shores of the Baltic in an attempt to strengthen the alliance between government and commerce.

As monarchs became more involved in urban activities through the regulation of trade, revenue collection, and the administration of overseas empires, the orientation of national politics, which had been decidedly rural in the Middle Ages, began to take on a more urban orientation. The two revolutions at the end of the eighteenth century confirmed the political importance of the great cities. The political events of the American and French revolutions and the drawing up of their major documents took place not in small villages and obscure fields like Runnymede as had similar events in the past, but in the major urban centers of the areas concerned: Boston, Philadelphia, and Paris. The events of the French Revolution also marked a milestone in the development of urban society with the effective emergence of the mob into the modern political arena.

As moneymaking and politics gravitated towards the cities, active and ambitious people followed. In many parts of the Western world it became the custom for the traditional rural rulers of society to divide their time between country and city in order to look after all aspects of their increasingly complicated affairs. Nobles and prosperous landowners, who dominated politics throughout the Western world and its colonies at this time, did not entirely abandon their country roots in pursuit of their political ambitions, for their landholdings remained their major source of income, their permanent homes, and the effective centers of their existence. However, towns and cities began to enter into the lives of nobles and ambitious country gentlemen who, up to this period, had generally shunned involvement in urban concerns and concentrated their energies on the land. Prosperous landowners with political ambitions found that they were obliged to spend at least some of their time in the royal administrative/political center, and many of them consequently took up temporary residence there. They spent time in the city in the political "season," which was usually arranged to coincide with the time when rural activities were limited by poor weather. During "the season" they also attended to their investments and urban moneymaking activities, enjoyed the pleasures of urban entertainments, gossiped, made acquaintances, and played the upper-class social games of their time and nation.

Some landowners also realized that participating in campaigns for overseas expansion, taking shares in various trading ventures, or investing a little surplus capital in any one of the many profitable activities of the great cities could produce useful additional income. Although the aristocrats of some nations, such as Spain and France, considered commercial moneymaking beneath their dignity, in other nations, notably Britain, the aristocracy felt no such shame attached to commercial enterprise. The brighter, more ambitious aristocrats increased their fortunes by investing some of their land-earned income in trading activities. Wealthy landowners thus spent more time in cities on their own account, on political business, or in their capacity as royal officials than ever before, and their presence added to the adjustments of the functions and the alteration of the appearance of many urban centers.

These new part-time city dwellers, who were becoming quite numerous by the late seventeenth and the eighteenth centuries, needed places to live that not only provided all the comforts of their often palatial rural homes, but also reflected or enhanced their social prestige. They wanted urban houses that echoed the style of the old Italian merchant princes rather than that of middle-class merchants and tradesmen, town houses that by their very design would make a clear distinction between the aristocratic urban dweller and the ordinary merchant. In addition, the houses had to accommodate private parties on an impressive scale. Opulent entertainments, usually given to further social and political connections and to enhance social status, also spawned a new set of urban activities ranging from the design and production of elegant furnishings to the importation and distribution of expensive and exotic foods, frills, and furbelows. The seasonal migration of aristocrats to the cities provoked a boom in expensive housing built in what might be called aristocratic tracts. In the first half of the seventeenth century, Henry IV built the Place Royale (now the Place des Vosges) in Paris to house his courtiers. This square, surrounded by tall, narrow, elegant, and almost identical houses, was widely admired, and it set the pattern for aristocratic housing all over western Europe in the seventeenth and eighteenth centuries. The owners of land on the fringes of the major cities realized that there was money to be made from the building of upper-class tract housing, and they had squares built whose designs echoed that of the Place Royale. In the seventeenth century, for example, the earl of Bedford hired Inigo Jones to design a residential square on his land which was then on the outskirts of London. The result was Covent Garden, a successful development later emulated by the builders of other famous London squares such as Grosvenor and Berkeley squares. In general, the town houses that sprang up in major cities all over the Western world were characterized by impressive, regular facades that reflected the preoccupation of the age with order and regularity.

Getting from place to place on foot did not appeal to prosperous rural people accustomed to riding or being pulled by horses, but the narrow, winding streets typical of medieval cities were unsuitable for horse traffic. The new developments in the aristocratic parts of cities were therefore designed to accommodate horse and carriage traffic. Their streets were wide and laid out in regular patterns. Town houses were generally ranged around parks rimmed by wide roads, fulfilling the needs of the residents for room to turn their carriages as well as the needs of the builders for uniform design and construction. In the less aristocratic twentieth century, many survivors of this type of development would become "embassy rows" and "government squares," their open spaces and wide roads filled with parked cars, their aristocratic pretensions appropriated to enhance the prestige of democratic governments.

In addition to elegant and comfortable homes in which they could entertain and be entertained, the new urban residents also demanded public facilities where they could congregate with people of their own class. To satisfy this demand, theaters and opera houses were built, such as the Opera House in Berlin and La Scala in Milan, both begun in the eighteenth century. Elegant gaming houses, gentlemen's clubs, coffee-houses, and similar meeting places multiplied. Small towns and villages with mineral springs blossomed in both size and wealth as the prosperous came to "take the waters" and engage in the multitude of social activities that made these centers temporary extensions of nearby cities. Because the most popular amusements included gossip and political and business manipulation, meeting areas without much to recommend them except pleasant, undistracting scenery also flourished. These ranged from splendid formal drives, such as Unter den Linden in Berlin, to pleasure gardens, such as Ranelagh and Vauxhall Gardens in seventeenth- and eighteenth-century London. The overall impact of the aristocratic influx into the cities was to open them up, make them more elegant, and confirm them as social and cultural centers.

As shapers of the new city form at this time, however, aristocrats were often outstripped by monarchs whose determination to plan, widen, brighten, and make more impressive was reinforced by the realities of urban dwelling. In addition to the political reasons for stepping up their urban activities, monarchs were intent on gaining international admiration and prestige. Many of them participated in town planning and building of a type that was initially peculiarly their own but that would become the style of government. This style owed much to the enormous expansion of geographical and intellectual horizons that occurred after the beginning of the scientific revolution in the sixteenth century. The results of continued experiment, discovery, and speculation led intellectuals to have great expectations of the capacities of the human mind and great confidence in the future. Admiration for the achievements of the classical era and contempt, overt or implied, of the medieval past and of old,

outdated, and conservative ways of doing things became fashionable. Any
monarch who hoped to gain international renown had to make at least an
outward show of modernity in all things. The current interpretations of
modernity emphasized rationality, order, space, and expansiveness; hence
rulers seeking international prestige and praise felt obliged to construct
new headquarters in impressively large, light, and well-balanced buildings
surrounded by orderly and spacious grounds. In any event, advances in
military technology had made castles obsolete as defensive positions, and
uncomfortable stone towers and cramped, dark little palaces were both
impractical and out of tune with the times.

The paragon of princely building projects was Versailles, constructed in the second half of the seventeenth century. Louis XIV built
this superpalace and its smaller satellite buildings, set in extensive gardens
laid out according to all the best current principles of design, at enormous
expense as a giant playhouse for the French aristocracy. Rebellious nobles
had challenged Louis's power in his youth, and as a mature monarch he
determined to remove all possibility of such a threat reoccurring so that he
could rule France unopposed. To these ends, the aristocrats were
encouraged, and occasionally even obliged, to remain in Versailles for
indefinite periods. Amid these handsome surroundings that glorified
Louis, the Sun King, the convoluted party games of court etiquette and
trivial court intrigues diverted their attentions from serious political
matters. Until its concluding years, military and political success marked
Louis's reign, and the great intellectual and artistic achievements of
France dazzled most Europeans, including other monarchs and princes
who envied the Sun King and sought to emulate him.

The number of rulers who could even aspire to dominate Europe as
Louis had appeared to do was severely limited. Only a few monarchs
could enjoy military success, which depended on many variables
including a thriving economy and sound military leadership. Such chance
matters as favorable shifts in balances of power and well-placed royal
relatives often determined success in international politics. No nation
could produce great artists and intellectuals, much less giants of Western
civilization, upon the whim of its ruler; however, any princeling with
enough money could emulate the great Louis by building a copy of
Versailles, echoing the symmetry and spaciousness of its buildings, walks,
vistas, and gardens. Copies could be as exact or as inventive, as large or as
small, as imagination and financial resources allowed, but all could be
expected to earn praise and glory for their builders if the style were
correct. For example, Karlsruhe in southern Germany was begun in 1715

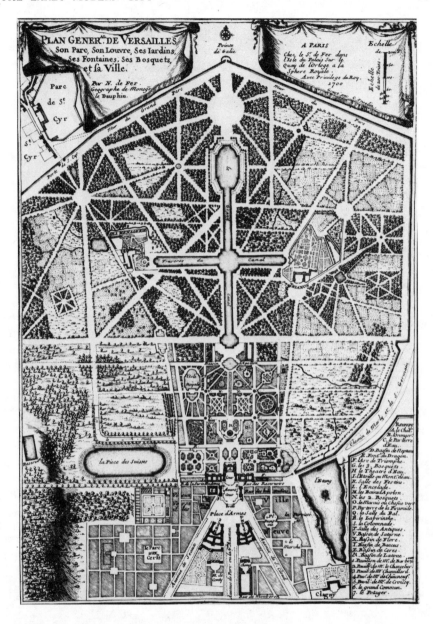

Plan of Versailles The great palace and park of Louis XIV set the basic style for the age of princes and merchants. The regular and often ornate patterns of thoroughfare and open space, palace and formal garden, are typical of the early modern period.

Map Division, The New York Public Library;
Astor, Lenox, and Tilden Foundations

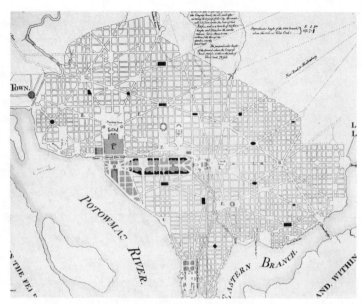

L'Enfant's plan of Washington, D.C. (1792) The style of the early modern princes is clearly evident in this plan for the capital of the new Republic. The civic style of princes became the accepted style of all government centers, and as such, it spread around the Western world in the eighteenth and nineteenth centuries.   Map Division, The New York Public Library; Astor, Lenox, and Tilden Foundations

Karlsruhe, Germany Karl Wilhelm, margrave of Baden, was one of the many eighteenth-century princelings who sought to emulate Louis XIV by building a "little Versailles." His castle was the hub of a series of radiating roads. Those to the south (shown at the top of this picture) formed the framework for the city's pattern of development.
German National Tourist Office

Place des Vosges, Paris Early in the seventeenth century, Henry IV created this elegant living area for the upper ranks of society in what was then a deserted part of the city. The square, surrounded by fine houses with regular facades, with wide roads for horses and carriages, and a central open area for ceremony and display, soon became the meeting place for the aristocracy of Paris and was admired, and copied, throughout the Western world.

French Government Tourist Office

Amsterdam in the seventeenth century, engraving by Pieter Schenk Amsterdam was one of the greatest trading and commercial cities at this time. Its merchants were prosperous, ambitious, and not averse to advertising their riches to the world. While not as elegant as the buildings along the Place des Vosges, these houses are far more grand, regular, and ornate than anything the medieval city offered.

Picture Collection, The New York Public Library

Naarden, the Netherlands Land wars still plagued the Netherlands in this period and cities needed defenses. Where city fortifications were built, they reflected the style of the times as well as the increased sophistication of weaponry. The complex defense works of this city (now converted into parks) can clearly be seen in this photograph.   Netherlands National Tourist Office

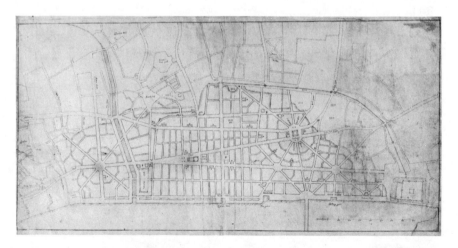

Sir Christopher Wren's plan for London after the fire (1666) The Great Fire of London offered the opportunity to rebuild the city, and Wren planned to do so on the most modern lines. The growing importance of commerce in the early modern city was reflected in the prominence he gave to the Stock Exchange, as the focal point of converging streets (to the right of center).
                                                    The Warden and Fellows of All Souls College, Oxford

GIN LANE, *by William Hogarth* The great early modern cities had a seamier side. In the overcrowded sections of the cities inhabited by the poor, many of the problems of industrial and modern cities were foreshadowed. Poverty, filth, disease, drunkenness, and high mortality rates were endemic.

The Metropolitan Museum of Art, Harris Brisbane Dick Fund, 1932 by Karl Wilhelm, margrave of Baden. As in the case of Versailles, a splendid new palace was the center of the scheme and the hub on which converged a series of radiating roads that served as hunting rides and promenades. Some of these still retain their parklike atmosphere, but those to the south of the palace became the main lines determining the shape of the present city, which is also known as "fan town."

Although the style of Versailles was first copied in palaces and royal parks, it acquired a greater significance when rulers became involved in town planning and renovation projects. Princes, aristocrats, and architects simply used the most prestigious principles they knew and applied the Versailles style to urban development. The governmental formalism that resulted derived a boost from military developments in some areas in this age of aggressive nationalism. Although some urban areas in disputed regions continued to need protection from attack, the simple curtain wall that had surrounded so many medieval towns was no longer an adequate defense. The fortress builders of this later era were forced to use more massive and complex defensive structures; the national government bore at least part of the cost. Because such projects as complicated walls, earthworks, moats, and citadels were expensive, they were often designed with a view to enhanced prestige as well as defense. The military usefulness of straight, wide roads for moving military equipment around within the city and great open squares for marshaling troops reinforced the move toward openness and the deliberate creation of urban vistas.

Because formalism became firmly established and widespread at a time when national monarchies were strong, its patterns became implanted in the official Western mind as appropriate and desirable for government centers. With a few modifications, these also remained the generally accepted patterns for prestigious civic development and redevelopment far into the industrial age. The architecture and design of monarchical national capitals was copied and became the style of governments in general, even of republics. When the United States of America needed a seat of government, her leaders searched Europe for the best official style. They found that formalism was widespread and, associating it with stable and splendid government rather than royalty, adopted it as their own in Washington. Throughout Europe and North America, urban centers with any pretensions to civic pride copied national capitals in one way or another; in this fashion traces of formalism found their way into the provinces and reappeared even in the nineteenth century whenever formal government construction and reconstruction were undertaken. When old rabbit warrens of streets were cleared in

London, the basic lines and principles of formalism produced Piccadilly Circus and thoroughfares such as Regent Street and Shaftesbury Avenue. In redesigning Paris in the second half of the nineteenth century, Louis Napoleon followed the general patterns set by Louis XIV, for by then formalism was the well-entrenched civic ideal; it was also known that wide streets restricted the building of barricades by urban mobs while facilitating troop movements. Furthermore, with their great vistas and impressive focal points such as the Arc de Triomphe, they provided a suitable background for military parades and other displays of power.

What had begun as the style of autocratic monarchies in the age of order and rationality eventually became a civic ideal throughout the Western world, echoed even in cities and nations that had never known a resident monarch. Buildings and avenues that would not have looked out of place in the grounds of Versailles adorned Berlin, London, Washington, and a host of other towns and cities. By the nineteenth century the style was so widespread as to be internationally interchangeable. For example, the Église du Dome in Paris, which was built in the late seventeenth century and which now houses Napoleon's tomb, would not have looked at all incongruous in the middle of nineteenth-century Rome, Washington, or Berlin; at least from the exterior, it could equally well be a Coketown public library or a Podunk town hall of the nineteenth century. The early modern city of merchants and monarchs is therefore important not only because it was a significant evolutionary stage in the development of Western cities, but also because it supplied what long remained the accepted international civic standard of design throughout the Western world.

Cities designed on more spacious and stylized lines replaced the intimate, haphazard, and cluttered medieval urban settlement. Commercial and practical still, the city was now also a place of government, a showcase for military and social displays, and the ordered, formal background for upper-class functions. In most established cities, the reality of the early modern pattern was an armistice between the old and the new rather than a total victory for the new. Most established centers appended new sections with the designs of formalism to their existing medieval cores. The city of Edinburgh illustrates well this kind of development. The medieval pattern is still clearly visible around the castle, while the "new" city, with its broad, regularly planned thoroughfares lined with the impressive facades of houses is across the narrow valley now occupied by the creation of a yet later age, the railway line. In many instances, the compromise between the medieval and the early modern was not so happily accomplished. Great impressive structures clearly designed to be focal points at the end of expansive vistas long existed without such vistas. For example, the Bernini Piazza and Colonnade, added to St. Peter's in Rome in the seventeenth century, clearly cry out for a wide approach avenue from the Tiber that would put them and St. Peter's in proper perspective at the end, but a tangle of streets and houses long stood between them and the river.

Social Changes in the City

In addition to being international trade centers and marketplaces for surrounding regions, cities in the early modern period also became specialized shopping centers as aristocrats and wealthy landowners moved in and generated a change in retailing practices. Just as new town houses and entertainment centers sprang up to satisfy the needs of the new city dwellers, new retail establishments emerged to cater to those people whose social position did not allow them to frequent the rough, busy, noisy marketplace. The aristocrats created a market for fine personal and household goods and for other prestigious commodities whose elegance and expense were in harmony with their social standing. As urban tradesmen began to manufacture and supply these goods, the more farseeing among them recognized that the old workshop-store would have little appeal for fastidious and prosperous customers. Ambitious retailers of goods used by aristocrats began to design their premises specifically to attract rich customers. By the eighteenth century large glass windows that could be used as street display cases had been introduced, as had elegant store interiors in which rich customers buying clothing, wigs, hats, gloves, perfumes, and other personal finery would feel at home. Shopping became a social activity of the prosperous, a pastime in which prestige possessions could be acquired while the purchaser made useful social contacts and kept abreast of the styles of the day. As shopping became firmly established as an upper-class social occasion, store owners increased their efforts to make their shops as attractive as possible to the best-paying customers, and the basic tenets of modern retailing began to take shape. While open markets continued to thrive, they were becoming places that only the lower classes frequented. Aristocratic households relied on markets for food and other ordinary goods, but their servants did the shopping.

The arrival of the aristocracy in the cities placed the traditional urban upper classes—the wealthy merchants, manufacturers, and financiers who had been the urban elite up to this time—in an awkward position; in effect, it added a new top layer to urban society. To make this new social situation even more delicate, wealthy urbanites were becoming even more prosperous and influential at this time. They had acquired awareness of the importance to the national economy and to the revenues and prestige of the government of their efforts in trade and business. As a result, ambitious members of the merchant class had begun to expect a social position commensurate with their achievements. Social friction between the traditional elite and the increasingly powerful merchant class was inevitable.

When land had provided the only kind of income and position that had any social weight, merchants could not compete with the aristocracy for social or political recognition on a national level. By this time, however, wealth was beginning to be recognized as more significant than its source, and in any event, urban activities were assuming a new importance in the eyes of the government and the nation. Merchants could now hope to compete with aristocrats, at least in appearance and within the urban environment, and they were forced into a position of either having to compete or allowing the aristocracy to dominate urban society as they had rural society. Aristocrats, on the other hand, strove to find new ways to enhance the social superiority that distinguished them from the untitled richer merchants. This class competition for power and recognition manifested itself publicly when socially active aristocrats and socially ambitious merchants engaged in conspicuous consumption and the public display of their wealth. Flamboyance in fashion—powdered and ornate wigs, embroidered waistcoats, wide skirts of costly materials and ornate designs—flourished in the seventeenth and eighteenth centuries. Ornate mirrors, ingenious clocks, walls and ceilings decorated with plaster carvings and gilt, and a profusion of baubles and precious art objects became important domestic furnishings. Modern conspicuous consumption and the expenditure of money on nonutilitarian prestige items is traceable to the social contest between aristocrats and upper merchants in many cities in the seventeenth and eighteenth centuries.

This competition also served to widen the social gap between the rich and the poor in urban society as the fashionable and prosperous increasingly disassociated themselves from less wealthy people. The building of tracts of expensive town houses around urban centers led to the separation of the housing of the rich and the poor to an extent that had not often occurred in the past; the rich moved out to more prestigious areas, leaving the poor in the crowded old city. The prosperous were also able to keep the lower classes at a distance through their political and economic power. For example, in 1674, the fruit market in Dijon was moved away from a fashionable part of town because its noise and bustle disturbed the prosperous people who lived there; in Rome the plays, feasts, festivals, and processions customarily sponsored by the rich for the enjoyment of the community in general had been closed to poor people by the beginning of the seventeenth century.

Because social and political competition was at its keenest there, prospective arbiters of fashion, craftsmen, and designers of all kinds flocked to the capitals in order to gain acceptance for their ideas. As a result, the upper classes came to see the capital city as the source of all the most desirable products and designs and all that was fashionable and up-to-date. Because of the mobility of the upper classes, the "capital city" often included select satellite towns, such as Bath where the wealthy English went to take the waters, to cure gout, and to play their part in the social scene. The great arbiter of eighteenth-century male fashion, Beau Nash, held court in Bath and promoted elegance in manners as well as in the tying of a cravat.

As the fashions, goods, and social niceties of the capital rose in the estimation of "the best people," the reputation of local products and provincial styles and designs fell. Even people who seldom left the provinces who wanted to be counted among the best people felt that they had to follow the fashions and acquire the goods currently in vogue in the capital. The ambitious purveyors of prestige items such as clothing, carvings, and household furnishings, and the retailers of imported exotic items such as china, improved their business by moving to the capital from minor port towns, which reinforced the whole trend.

As the capitals set the standards of taste and fashion and became the shopping centers for the upper classes, a new marketing technique, mail order, began to develop. As the demand for goods from the capital increased among provincial people, enterprising businessmen began to set themselves up as agents, some even producing and distributing catalogues listing the goods in which they dealt. This elementary mail-order system helped upper-class social competition extend to the provinces. The socially ambitious wife of an English country gentleman could, by the eighteenth century, place an order with a London agent for items such as a set of Chippendale chairs. Without leaving her home she could acquire fashions from the capital and become the fashion leader within her neighborhood, at least until someone else obtained a more expensive or modish item from her agent. Even in the twentieth century, in spite of the greater appreciation of regional cultures, the products of Rome, New York, and especially Paris have more status value than the products of Milan, Milwaukee, or Marseilles.

Although the social contest with the aristocracy brought some problems and even financial disaster for some members of the merchant classes, on the whole their social position improved. The gravitation of government to the city and the increasing interdependency of national welfare and commercial profits enhanced their social stature and also meant that they became increasingly involved in the formulation of national policy. By the end of the eighteenth century, in fact, this group had become so influential that it could effect decisive changes if it felt forced to do so. The wealthier members of the growing commercial classes in England helped shape imperial policy, while later in the century their American counterparts felt an increasing resentment of the economic regulations imposed by the British government. When attempts were made to tighten those controls, the grumbling discontent erupted into revolt. The merchants and smugglers of Boston, seeing a less profitable future ahead under the new system, moved from economic frustration to impulsive vandalism, put on fancy dress, and flung tea from India, a valuable commodity in trade and smuggling, into the harbor. Similarly, the French bourgeoisie, angered by the actions of an impoverished and economically incompetent government and frustrated by a rigid social system that barred them from the ranks of the privileged aristocracy, overthrew their government and established one more protective of their own prosperity, status, and desires.

The city had traditionally been idealized as the place in which the enslaved and the downtrodden could find freedom and opportunity for advancement. The dynamic commercial/governmental city added to the legend, becoming for many people the dream city that offered instant fame and fortune. Now people lucky enough to participate in one or two profitable trading ventures or to invest in the right thing at the right time could indeed make fortunes. Although this was rare, it was frequent enough to generate legends, especially as tales of sudden fortune were embellished as they passed from person to person. The bustling, prosperous, great cities of this time were so unlike country villages and small towns as to dazzle visitors, who later found it easy to impress rural listeners, and themselves, with tales of glorious adventures, amazing wonders, and great riches. One popular story was that of poor Dick

Whittington, who arrived in London with a few possessions tied in a handkerchief and his cat. He worked for a merchant and became a wealthy and respected citizen in his own right and eventually the lord mayor of the city. Similar fanciful visions made the great city, wherever it was, not only the city of business and prosperity for the merchant, the city of politics for the ambitious, and the city of prestige for social climbers, but also the end of the rainbow, a city of excitement for the bored and of fortune for the poor.

As they began to perform a wider range of functions, the dynamic cities of this period also acquired new inhabitants who, by the eighteenth century, could be considered "typical" big-city dwellers. Aristocrats and politicians became as typical as merchants, bankers, traders, sailors, and ship chandlers. Poor, unskilled, often drunken slum dwellers also became more numerous as dreams of riches that failed to become reality drew the indigent to the city. There had always been poor people in the city as in the country, but in this period they became more noticeable, less assimilated, and less provided for by this new urban society in which most of the communal groups of the Middle Ages had dissolved.

In the dynamic city of the seventeenth and eighteenth centuries, something of the character of "modern" cities and "modern" urban problems began to emerge. The city became more complex and heterogeneous as population grew and city functions became more numerous. The city became a paradox: a source of national pride and the center of crime and vice; a showcase of elegance for the rich and a pit of degradation for the poor; the hub of social and economic life and a sink of disease and high death rates; the center of cultural activities and elegant town houses and of the most brutalizing slums and deprivations; the headquarters of governmental and administrative systems and a blot of corruption and urban maladministration; the site of upper-class planned order and of growing unplanned urban sprawl.

THE
FIRST
INDUSTRIAL 4 Founda-
CITY tions and
Forms

The earliest "modern" industrial towns and cities in the Western world first emerged in Britain in the late eighteenth and early nineteenth centuries and prefigured the course of urban development throughout the West later in the nineteenth century. Although modified somewhat by technological and economic developments, the basic forces that gave rise to the first industrial urban areas are similar to those underlying the growth of cities in the twentieth century. The most important of these forces, therefore, can be considered the major phenomena that distinguish the modern world from all earlier historical periods. They are so vital to its development that a fairly detailed consideration must be undertaken to understand the first industrial city and to explain the evolution of modern, large-scale urbanism.

Population Growth

Cultural, economic, religious, and social factors, both long- and short-term, all affect population size and growth rates, but in essence only two basic, measurable forces operate to change population size: birth rate and death rate. If x people per thousand are born and x people per thousand die in y years in a given area, the population will remain stable because a newborn individual replaces each dying one. Research on animal and fish populations suggests that in the natural course of events population normally maintains stable levels in any given area over an extended period, although short-term, dramatic increases or decreases may occur. Long-term changes seem to happen only if living conditions change—if, for example, feeding areas expand or the number of predators is reduced. The data on human populations are sketchier than those derived from animal observations for a number of reasons: humans live for years instead of for weeks or months, stable and controlled conditions cannot readily be imposed on humans for long periods, and reliable historical evidence covers only the relatively short span of time since the early nineteenth century. From the scant evidence available, however, there seems to be no reason to presume that humans exhibit a much different population pattern from that of animals. Over the whole of human history up to the eighteenth century, human population levels seem to have been reasonably stable. Although the population occasionally declined dramatically in response to such things as disastrous epidemics and crop failures, in general it merely increased very slowly over the centuries. Environmental improvements produced by such things as the development and spread of technological advances that increased crop yields, the clearing and draining of uncultivated land by farmers, and the discovery and development of thinly inhabited regions by advanced peoples probably caused this gradual, long-term increase. The stable situation began to change about the eighteenth century, however, and population grew rapidly.

All statistics are unreliable, even for the West, but indications are that world population increased from about six hundred million in 1700 to nine hundred million in 1800. The rate varied from region to region and nation to nation. Estimates indicate that the population of Europe increased from about one hundred million in 1650 to one hundred forty million in 1750, to one hundred eighty-seven million in 1800.* In England, the population swelled from about six million in 1700 to about nine million in 1800, an increase so alarming as to provoke Malthus to write his famous treatise forecasting that famine, disease, and disaster would strike if some means of limiting population were not found and applied. The population increase was not curbed in the nineteenth century but continued throughout the world; far from slowing down, it accelerated startlingly. By 1850 Italy had about twenty-five million people; England, eighteen million; and Germany and France, about thirty-five million each. The population of the "new" nations in North America and Australasia showed an even greater rate of increase, thanks to

* Eugen Weber, *A Modern History of Europe* (New York: Norton, 1971), p. 428.

migration from Europe. The causes differed somewhat from area to area
and across time, but everywhere the new forces that began to emerge in
the eighteenth century and that multiplied rapidly in the nineteenth and
twentieth centuries acted to upset the long-established rough balance
between birth and death rates. The multiplication of the number of
people changed the face of the earth in about two centuries, even if only
by causing ten or more people to stand where previously only one had
stood. It changed the whole fabric of society, drastically altering
economics, social structures, and even political systems. Perhaps the most
dramatic effects of population growth were on towns and cities and on the
people living in them.

The lack of hard evidence makes it impossible to explain in detail the
causes of population growth in the late eighteenth and nineteenth
centuries in any one region or nation, much less in continents and in the
world as a whole. Historians and demographers have debated the possible
causes. While there are some interesting ideas and even some agreement
about general hypotheses, no precise and specific conclusions can yet be
drawn. Only increasing birth rate, decreasing death rate, or a combination of both could produce the population change; what is obscure is why
the change occurred.

Some historians have suggested that death rates began to fall in the
eighteenth century because people became more resistant to disease and
better able to cope with injury. The great plagues that had periodically
decimated the population, particularly in the Middle Ages, although they
reappeared from time to time in the early modern period, gradually
disappeared, resulting in lower death rates. Jenner's invention of smallpox
vaccination, the improvement of midwifery and of surgical and medical
techniques, and the establishment of teaching hospitals and free dispensa-
ries for the poor in the eighteenth century might also help account for
health improvements, although it is doubtful that any of these affected the
majority of the population very much.

Many specific regional developments may have accounted for
decreases in death rate and increases in birth rate. For example, it has
been suggested that the decline in gin drinking in middle and later
eighteenth-century England might account for some increase in population there. Troops who had fought against Louis XIV returned from
Holland with a taste for gin. Good harvests early in the eighteenth
century made the raw materials cheap and plentiful, and consumption
soared. Cheap gin was less than carefully distilled, and many of the people
who overindulged at this fountain of oblivion died. There were other

casualties too; children who were given gin to stop their crying and to make them sleep occasionally died, and the children of drunken parents were often the victims of criminal neglect. Such is the plight of the unfortunate child shown falling from the arms of its sodden mother in Hogarth's etching *Gin Lane*. When the dangers of badly distilled gin were recognized, respectable distillers worked with the government to regulate production. By the middle of the eighteenth century the official annual average output was falling, presumably reflecting a fall in consumption; this probably reduced the number of alcohol-related deaths in urban areas where gin drinking was most common. Local phenomena such as this undoubtedly had some impact on birth and death rates in the limited areas in which they appeared, but they alone cannot explain the more widespread, long-term population increase.

In the eighteenth century two other important changes took place that also proved to have lasting effects on the Western world: the introduction of sweeping innovations in agriculture and the advent of modern industry. Given their coincidence in time and range, it seems reasonable to suppose that they were linked to population growth. A multitude of agricultural improvements that resulted in higher yields per acre not only made more food available but also possibly improved its quality. Since most people still lived on an inadequate diet on the barest margin of survival, any small increase or improvement in food would clearly have a dramatic effect on health and longevity. Nutrition would also affect birth rates and infant mortality since well-fed, healthy mothers tend to have fewer miscarriages and stillborn children than do mothers suffering from malnutrition. As agricultural advances produced food for more people, industrial expansion increased the demand for labor. While both the number of industries and the volume of production increased, the demand for workers within the nonagricultural job market expanded. "Surplus" people, who formerly would have died because they could not find work on the land or earn money to buy food, now found employment in industry. People whose deaths would have brought the population back to stable levels now earned money in industry, bought their share of increased agricultural production, and lived long enough to produce children. As industrial and agricultural progress continued, later generations lived even longer and produced even more children, continuing the upward surge of population growth.

Later, in the nineteenth century, new forces only tenuously related to agriculture and industry came into play and added to the burgeoning world population. In the second half of the nineteenth century such things as the improvement of urban sanitary conditions and more effective, more generally available medical treatment played major roles in sustaining population increase. The introduction of effective birth control measures at the end of the nineteenth century and their improvement in the twentieth century offered the possibility of restoring the balance between birth and death rates and establishing a stable population again. Although an increasing number of people took advantage of these controls and a fall in birth rates and average family size was visible in some parts of the Western world by the end of the nineteenth century, lengthening life-spans, reduced deaths in childbirth, and the tendency of most families to produce more than two children meant that the population of the world still continued to grow at a rate that was alarming by earlier standards.

In summary, the initial population increase of the eighteenth century involved falling death rates and rising birth rates accompanied by economic expansion in the shape of improved agricultural yields and industrial growth. The answer to the question of why the population increased is therefore not a simple one, for it involved a variety of forces that were so interdependent and mutually supportive that it is difficult to say which caused the increase and which resulted from it. These forces, however, do have a common denominator; the unique mechanism they created and sustained and through which they all acted on society was the first industrial city.

Food Supply

Agricultural techniques that improved yields and quality were introduced only slowly between the time of the initial development of farming and the later seventeenth century. In all these centuries, naturally, some advances were made; new land was cleared for cultivation and new tools were introduced, such as plows with moldboards that cut and turned the soil in one operation. At no time, however, was there such a dramatic and rapid improvement as that which began in the late seventeenth century. Then and in the eighteenth century the heightened interest in worldly problems and the spate of scientific investigations that followed the Renaissance began to have an effect on agriculture. Some farmers began to wonder if the fallow year, during which the land was allowed to recover from crop growing, could be used for the cultivation of a crop that would be useful while helping improve, rather than reduce, the fertility of the soil. Experiments indicated that crops like turnips and clover enhanced fertility while producing useful cattle fodder. The Dutch, always handicapped by low-lying, wet ground, led the way in experiments with better drainage systems, and all over the Western world more and more hitherto useless, boggy ground was converted into arable land. Some experimenters, including the eccentric Englishman Jethro Tull, endeavored to find more productive ways of ploughing and planting. After visiting Holland and the French vineyards where he saw the effectiveness of deep hoeing and frequent ploughing, Tull began to experiment with these techniques on his own estate. He ploughed frequently, hoed regularly with a horse-drawn hoe to eliminate weeds, and developed the seed drill, which sowed seeds at uniform depths in even rows and was more efficient than the old, haphazard hand scattering. His eccentricities amused or appalled his neighbors, but his techniques increased yields and others soon copied them. Experiments in selective breeding produced healthier, more productive cattle. For example, a cow in the Netherlands or Germany yielded about one hundred fifty gallons of milk a year in 1750, but with better breeding and better feed from the new crops, selectively bred cows in the same areas yielded about four hundred gallons of milk a year by 1800.

These and many other similar advances may seem insignificant when considered individually, but together they constituted an impressive array of improvements. Before they could have much impact, however, they had to be widely accepted. Contemporaries often regarded advocates of new techniques with some amusement; for example, an English nobleman who experimented with the growing of turnips and who extolled their virtues to anyone who would listen acquired the somewhat derisive nickname of "Turnip" Townshend. Nevertheless, the new methods were adopted fairly quickly because their increased efficiency was beyond dispute. The expanding demand generated by a growing population promised high profits from increased yields, and landowners were quick to use new techniques that produced larger surpluses for profitable sale. Many less-enlightened farmers were forced to adopt the new techniques through terms regarding such things as four-course rotations and the growing of turnips and clover that more farsighted landowners wrote into leases. Selective animal breeding was also widely adopted; the walls, hedges, and ditches that kept the animals from eating crops were also used to separate them into groups, which, once the principles were understood, made selective breeding much easier and more efficient. The production of a greater quantity of winter feed, such as clover, turnips, and sainfoin, facilitated selective breeding of livestock because more animals could be kept alive through several breeding seasons. The increased volume of winter fodder also meant that stock no longer had to be slaughtered in the fall because of sparse winter grass. Under the earlier system, fresh meat was scarce in winter and salt meat was often putrefied by early spring, and there was a seasonal shortage of milk and butter. The new system allowed more cattle to be kept alive and hence more fresh meat and dairy products were available in winter. The more productive animals produced by better breeding and better fodder effected a considerable improvement in human nutrition.

Although the increased volume of agricultural products was essential to feed the rapidly expanding urban population, in the late eighteenth and early nineteenth centuries the lack of efficient techniques and facilities for preserving and transporting food made the process of getting adequate supplies into the towns and cities very difficult. Vegetables grown on the fringes of urban areas could be taken to market by cart and did not present too much of a problem, nor did grains that could be brought in, stored, and milled as needed. The main difficulties concerned fresh animal products—milk, meat, and eggs—that could not be stored for long periods. Before commercial canning and refrigeration processes were introduced and before carrying cattle by rail became feasible, many cities had to have their meat brought in on the hoof; the cattle had to be slaughtered in fairly central urban locations and the meat distributed from there. The thoroughfares of early industrial cities, unlike the wide, high-curbed streets of the "cow towns" in the western United States, had not been built with cattle drives in mind. As the towns grew, more cattle had to be driven through longer stretches of urban streets. When only a short built-up stretch had to be covered to reach the slaughterhouse, cattle drives were a minor nuisance. As urban areas expanded, however, cattle had to cross longer and longer stretches in which no food or water was available, and the problems became acute. In some towns and cities animals panicked in narrow streets, frightening and injuring people and sometimes damaging property in the crush and confusion. When the animals reached the slaughterhouse, serious problems had only just begun. Facilities were relatively small and primitive but had to accommodate increasing numbers of animals. Slaughterhouses constituted one of the major public nuisances and dangers to health. Blood was often allowed to run down the street; hair, hides, fat, and bones were burned, spreading foul smoke and smells; offal and other untreated or partly burned waste was frequently thrown into the river, which usually supplied water to people living downstream.

Milk cows, egg-laying hens, and pigs produced additional sanitation problems. Although cows and hens kept in commercial establishments to produce fresh milk and eggs for urban customers added to the problems of refuse disposal within the city, they were less of a problem than pigs. In many parts of Europe, countless generations of rural families had kept a pig in the yard as a kind of insurance against starvation. To such people the family pig represented tradition and personal security, and many of them were not willing to abandon old customs, or the pig, when they moved to town. Thus, a great many pigs were kept in early industrial cities; they were fed scraps and refuse and housed in primitive pens in small yards; when no open space was to be had, they were kept in the family living quarters. These primitive, essentially agrarian ways of dealing with animals worked well enough in the countryside, but in an urban setting they produced massive health and refuse disposal problems, adding to the stench, dirt, and dangers of early industrial towns.

As time passed, solutions to some of the problems of urban food supply were found. In the first half of the nineteenth century, the development of railway systems made it easier to bring in fresh meat and produce from surrounding rural areas. The next important innovation came in the latter part of the nineteenth century with the improvement of processing and global bulk transport. Trade in foodstuffs had increased after the great explorations when widely separated people began to exchange commodities such as seed grain, live plants, and salt fish, but it was only in the latter decades of the nineteenth century that global bulk food carrying, which enabled industrial nations to obtain their food from agricultural lands, became a reality.

The example of Britain in the nineteenth century illustrates the growing interdependence of agrarian and industrial regions linked through improved transportation. Although it was the first nation to industrialize and urbanize on a modern scale, Britain lacked large areas of arable land. Consequently, the nation was increasingly unable to produce food surpluses to feed all the people. Agricultural improvements that increased yields had sustained her initial population growth in the eighteenth and early nineteenth centuries, but after these improvements had been adopted, the supply of home-produced food could not expand much further. If population and urban growth were to be sustained after the middle of the century, new sources of food had to be found and the means to transport them long distances developed. The "new" regions of the world, especially the Americas and Australasia, had vast areas of virgin soil on which to grow huge surpluses; the railroad, the steamship, the tin can, and the commercial refrigerator allowed these surpluses to be sold to, and to help keep alive, the urban industrial population of Britain.

Population increase and innovation in transport opened up the underdeveloped areas of the world. Called upon to feed the population of the urban industrial regions, the "new" areas thus established an interdependent relationship with the "old." Changes in one area affected the other, just as medieval towns had generated forces that brought changes to their agricultural hinterlands. The interdependence and interaction of urban and rural functions that had existed for centuries within a local or regional frame of reference began to operate on a worldwide scale in the nineteenth century, a phenomenon that ultimately influenced national and international social and political patterns.

Transportation

The initial improvements in transportation in the eighteenth century were refinements of existing modes; the clipper ships that brought tea and other exotic goods from the East to Europe and North America were merely refined, much faster versions of the ancient sailing ship. In the eighteenth century river transport became more important as people began to build their own waterways instead of relying entirely on the good offices of nature. Canal building was first undertaken on a significant scale in France and Holland, and canals were a major form of transportation for industrial materials in Britain. Barges were slow because horses and humans pulled them and because level changes and locks hampered movements. They were desirable goods carriers, however, because unlike rivers and oceans they were under human control. Furthermore, canal barges were ideal for moving heavy or bulky materials at low cost. Since the cheap transport of coal, iron ore, other basic raw materials, and food was vital to the development of early industry and since speed was relatively unimportant at this stage, canals served their purpose well enough, although they depended on favorable geographic features and water supply.

Under suitable conditions, canals had a revolutionary effect on the transportation of bulky commodities such as coal and wheat, dramatically reducing the costs of transport and thus the market price of the goods carried. The construction of the Erie Canal between Lake Erie and the Hudson River in 1825 provided impressive proof of the benefits of canals; the cost of shipping a bushel of wheat from Buffalo to Albany fell from

$108 to $7. This canal also meant that the grain-growing regions of the American interior were made accessible and were effectively linked to the east coast; from there, products could be exported all over the world.

The French led the way in improving roads by establishing a school for the Road and Bridge Corps of civil engineers in 1747. After the middle of the eighteenth century, stone-surfaced highways began to replace earth tracks in France, Austria, and Germany. Later, the British engineers Telford and McAdam developed better, stronger roadbeds and new surfaces. In the nineteenth century all over the Western world, well-drained, soundly constructed, hard-surfaced roads steadily replaced muddy, dusty, potholed, rutted, and rocky tracks that had long made road transportation difficult, expensive, and unreliable.

The development of land transport accelerated with the advent of the railway, which was to be by far the most important overland carrier of the nineteenth century. To some extent, railways were also a refinement of older forms of transport; the original principles were borrowed from the systems of wooden rails on which horses had pulled strings of carts over short distances from one fixed point, such as a mine entrance, to another. The large quantities of high-quality but cheap iron produced by innovations in the iron industry and by the development of techniques that allowed steam engines to drive wheels made possible the modern railway. A system that ran steam-powered engines on iron rails was constructed in England in the 1820s, and it proved so useful that the development of signaling, braking, and other subsystems was rapid. The spread of this reliable, cheap new form of land transport was also rapid. In 1830, Europe had 316 kilometers of rail, while the United States had only 65; by 1840, Europe had 3,534, the U.S., 4,509 kilometers of railway line.

The pioneering work on railways was done in Britain. The Victorians, heady with the achievements of British industry and enchanted by this invention's power and promise of profit, indulged in an orgy of railway building that covered the British Isles with a closely packed network of lines, integrating all regions and creating a nationwide supply-and-demand area. In central Europe, the expanding railway network helped create the market area that the German state would eventually surround, and it made possible the development of superior techniques of military transportation that contributed to the success of the wars that welded Germany into a nation. Outside Europe the railways also played an important part in bringing young states to effective nationhood. The east-west railway lines played a vital role in welding the vast and very different regions of the United States into a single national entity. Even now Canada bears the obvious stamp of the uniting east-west railway.

Apart from its cultural and political functions, the railway served a very practical purpose as an inexpensive overland carrier of bulk commodities. It made possible the movement of surpluses from the prairies to the cities and ports of North America and facilitated the creation of national and international markets so complete that people of one area no longer starved while those of another produced food surpluses. The railway also strengthened the growing economic interdependence of the world. The Old World supplied the technical knowhow, skills, capital, and often much of the immigrant labor for the building of railways in the New World, which in turn supplied Europe with ever-larger quantities of food and raw materials to sustain its industrial system. French capital helped build railways in Russia; British capital helped build railways in North America and Australasia; Scots engineers were almost anywhere building was being done. Meanwhile, imported wheat was used in an increasing proportion of the loaves of bread eaten by European industrial workers who built rails, rolling stock, and other equipment for export.

Steamships were the railways of the sea, completing the global transport system that revolved around great ports such as New York and London where the railway met the steamship line. Steamships first became important carriers on the great rivers of the Western world, such as the Rhine and the Danube. The Mississippi had two hundred steamboats in 1830 and over one thousand by 1860. Oceangoing ships at first combined steam with sail because they could not carry enough fuel for long journeys, but even these hybrids promised well for the future. The first Atlantic steam-sail shipping lines were established in 1816; the ships of Mr. Cunard then took only seventeen days to cross between Liverpool and Boston. More efficient steam engines, the establishment of a worldwide network of coaling stations, and advances in iron and steelmaking improved steam-powered metal ships, which became more numerous than wooden sailing ships by the end of the nineteenth century.

In spite of inefficient engines that required large quantities of fuel and the limitations of the paddle wheel, the steamship, because it was not subject to the whims of the wind, was more reliable than the sailing ship, and it was soon faster than all but the most speedy sailing vessel. In the 1860s more efficient engines were developed and screws replaced paddles, producing more efficient ships that were far cheaper to run. This resulted in a fall in world shipping rates and an increase in the volume of goods

Water-powered hammers, Abbeydale Industrial Village, Sheffield, England Much
of the equipment of early industrialism was extremely massive and primitive.
Each part of these mammoths had to be fabricated by hand. Because of its
dependence on water, and later on coal, machinery was often located away from
established urban centers.   Photograph by the author

South Street, New York City (c. 1900) The fast sailing ship, and later the
steamship, completed the worldwide transportation system that the railways
began. The greatest cities of the nineteenth century grew up where the major
rail lines met the major ocean lines, as at New York City. Steam and sail existed
side by side in the ports of the world for many decades.

Central Railway Station, Newcastle, from a drawing by John Dobson (1850) The efficiency and cheapness of the railroads promoted increased mobility of people and things and encouraged development of industrialism.
By permission of Newcastle upon Tyne City Libraries; photograph by Kris Walton, R.A.

OVER LONDON BY RAIL, *by Gustave Doré* Railroads increased the misery of the poor, especially those living under the elevated lines. The grime and noise they added to the filth and overcrowding of this part of London is obvious.   Prints Division, The New York Public Library;
Astor, Lenox, and Tilden Foundations

Nineteenth-century workers' housing, Denaby, England These houses have changed little since they were built. Although the road is now paved and water and electricity have been installed, survivals such as these indicate the bleakness, crowding, and monotony of working-class living conditions in mining and factory cities of the nineteenth century.   Photograph by the author

Back alley, Denaby, England Rows and rows of cheap houses surrounded mines and factories. Apart from the streets, the only open spaces were back alleys like this one. The high brick walls enclosed tiny dirt yards, which now form part of the structures of outdoor flush toilets and coal storage places.
          Photograph by the author

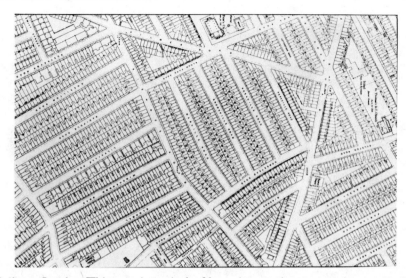

Fulham, London This area is typical of late nineteenth-century cheap suburban housing. By this time elementary building codes were operative, yet development was still dense, even in the suburbs. In the area shown, the average acre contains twenty houses plus space for roads, churches, schools, works, and playgrounds.

Reproduced from the Ordnance Survey Map of 1909

New Lanark, England (1825) Some early industrialists attempted to solve the new problems of urban society. Robert Owen, who designed this early nineteenth-century model factory, was one such innovator. His experimental communities failed, but his ideas were incorporated into the cooperative movement. Bridon Fibres & Plastics Limited

LUDGATE HILL, *by Gustave Doré* The crush and confusion of the great industrial cities can be seen in this engraving of London. In the major thoroughfare, crossed by the railway, were crowded together humans and animals, adults and children, buyers and beggars, public and private transport, fruit and funerals, while above it all early forms of advertising transmitted simple messages to any who could read.   Local History and Genealogy Division, The New York Public Library; Astor, Lenox, and Tilden Foundations carried in the late 1860s and early 1870s. Refrigeration added an important new dimension to ocean transport. Originally ice was used in attempts to preserve food on long journeys, and supplying it became a thriving small industry in America. Ice cut from rivers and lakes in winter was stored in icehouses and exported in special containers, but its bulk and perishability limited its usefulness. The great advance came with the installation of refrigeration machinery in steamships in the later 1870s. Beef, mutton, and other perishables could be carried long distances across the equator in refrigerated holds to people in urban industrial areas who were hungry for fresh meat. The steamship contributed to the emergence of many other phenomena in addition to improved food transport and continued urban expansion. For example, it was a powerful incentive for the building of the great international canals through Suez and Panama, which clipped hundreds of miles and many days from voyages; its fuel needs led the maritime nations to search for secure "coaling stations" around the world where their ships could be refueled in safety. The growth of imperialism in the later nineteenth century and its economic and political ramifications resulted in part from the development of the steamship.

These improvements in transportation were vital to continued urbanization because they made possible the long-distance movement of cheap food necessary to feed the industrial urban masses that swelled the towns and cities of the nineteenth century. They also aided the transportation of industrial raw materials and the marketing of industrial products. In addition, transportation had profound direct effects on the development and shaping of cities. The canal, the steamship, and the railway were the veins and arteries of industrialism, and at the same time were themselves rapacious consumers of the iron, steel, coal, and equipment turned out by the industrial system. Later in the nineteenth century, railways and new transport forms such as trams combined to expand and develop the areas surrounding established urban centers, further modifying city forms.

Industrialization

Even from this simplified account of population increase and improvements in food supply and transportation, it should be evident that the new forces that emerged to shape the first industrial city were very closely interlinked and mutually supportive. None of them would have much effect without the others, and as each developed, it stimulated the rest into further growth which in turn promoted the continued expansion of all. One more piece has yet to be supplied for this complex puzzle, the piece around which all the rest fit and which translated their force into urban terms: industrialization.

The first problem that emerges when dealing with industrialization in historical terms is that of definition. If the word means the production of goods for people other than those who made them, there was nothing new about industry in the eighteenth century, for man had done this to some extent ever since he had become civilized. The specialized production of commodities by certain groups, that is, specialization of function, also will not suffice as a definition of eighteenth-century changes in industry, for that had been evident in medieval and even earlier cities. Nor will the use of powered machines serve to distinguish this phase of industrialization from all earlier ones, for windmills and water-powered grain and fulling mills had long been in use. All of these elements were present in the developing industrial system of the late eighteenth and early nineteenth centuries, but they cannot be applied solely to this period as its distinguishing characteristics. What makes this period stand out from all earlier times to the extent that it is commonly called the "industrial revolution" was the enormous acceleration in the pace and expansion of the range of industrial development. Industrial production and all that accompanied it changed so rapidly and radically that the word "industry" acquired a new meaning and a whole new set of implications.

Between the mid-eighteenth and the mid-nineteenth centuries the specialized production of goods rose so rapidly that it reached a rate of increase that had never before been equaled or even approximated. Specialization of function and production also took place on an unprecedented scale, and the size of the specialist group, the people concerned with the production and distribution of manufactured goods, expanded enormously and new subspecializations developed. The new machines introduced at this time differed from earlier ones in that they had more components and were far more sophisticated. The mechanical loom was more complicated than the hand loom, and the later steam-powered loom was even more sophisticated. The complexity of machinery and the increased amounts of capital involved in its purchase, housing, and operation combined with increasing specialization of function to involve more people in the process of manufacture and to concentrate those people, to an ever-increasing extent, in the growing urban areas around the factories that housed the machines and the mines that produced their fuel.

Apart from the scope and pace of growth and the magnitude of production, perhaps the most significant new element in this phase of industrial development was the use of machines that consumed the fuel that drove them. Fuel had been used for centuries, and machines powered by wind and water were also of ancient lineage, but until the introduction of the steam engine, fuel raw materials were not consumed and destroyed in the process of making machines move. Steam engines, which consumed coal to produce power and thus depleted that resource, were used in growing numbers for a widening variety of purposes in the later eighteenth century. A visitor to the works of James Watt, inventor of the first efficient steam engine, asked his business partner, Matthew Boulton, what the two were making and what they hoped to gain. Boulton's response captured the essence of this new phase of industrialism: "I sell, sir, what all the world desires; *power!*"

The evolution of fuel-consuming machines, which were more efficient, productive, and reliable than the old wind-, water-, or muscle-powered ones, was crucial to the beginning of the industrial system that generated the great burst of urban expansion in the nineteenth century. One of the earliest of these machines was the coal-consuming steam pump, which used steam to drive a pivoted rocking beam whose vertical motion could be used, appropriately, for draining mines. The usefulness of the pump-action engine was limited, for it could only make things rise and fall while most mechanical processes involved wheels and things that moved horizontally. The next vital step, devised before the last quarter of the eighteenth century, was the refinement of means by which a steam engine could generate rotary and horizontal motion; once power could be applied to wheels and horizontal driving belts, the potential of the steam engine was almost endless.

A strong, plentiful, cheap material was required for building steam engines and stronger power machines; iron filled this need. In the early eighteenth century, Abraham Darby found a way of smelting iron with coal instead of charcoal and thus ended the dependence of the iron industry on scarce wood resources. In 1784 the "puddling process" for making pig iron into malleable iron was developed, allowing more efficient production of a greater quantity of better, more workable iron. Iron and coal were the most basic materials of the nineteenth-century industrial system; iron became cheaper and easier to use. By 1825 English iron making was so efficient that English cast iron cost two and a half times less than the French product. Iron was made into boilers, rails, bridges, machinery, and coffins. It made possible the mechanization of industry, the refinement of steam power, and transport improvement. Buildings were constructed with iron facades. Iron caught the fancy of the age; some people in the early nineteenth century even dreamed of utopian cities made entirely of it.

Steam power could not replace hand, wind, and water power in existing machine operations, for the old machines did not have the strength or durability to withstand its onslaught, nor did they have the capacity to keep up with its speed. New machines had to be designed to operate with steam power. The first industry to use them to any great extent was the English cotton industry, which first used steam-powered machines for weaving. The acceleration of cloth production resulted in a correspondingly larger demand for thread, which gave inventors the incentive to develop steam-powered spinning machines. Their success in the cotton textile industry led to the development of power machines in other industries too.

The manufacture of woolen textiles had for centuries been England's single largest industry, and by the eighteenth century it was firmly established and well protected. The increased demand for cheap clothing that accompanied the growth of English and world population promoted a greater demand for cheap cloth. Cotton textile manufacturers faced the problem of providing a good product at low prices to lure people away from traditional woolen clothes. In order to take advantage of the expanding market and to challenge the position of the established product they had to use whatever innovations promised to give them an advantage over wool in quality, production, or price. Power machinery that could produce a uniform product more quickly and cheaply than hand-operated machines gave cotton manufacturers just such an advantage, and they adopted it relatively quickly. The early powered textile machines did not work as well with woolen threads as with cotton ones; woolen manufacturers adopted powered machines only after these technical problems had been ironed out and when they felt the pressures of competition from the growing cotton industry. The increased productive capacity of the latter industry soon outstripped the ability of the traditional sources of supply, Egypt and India, to produce long-staple cotton. The southern United States produced cotton, but only the short-staple variety, which was expensive because the seeds were difficult to remove and cleaning had to be done by hand. Eli Whitney's cotton gin, which made the rapid, economical, mechanical cleaning of cotton possible, opened up the bottleneck in supply. While the reign of "King Cotton" was to have catastrophic political consequences in the United States, it made industrial urban growth around Manchester and the surrounding cotton towns and cities of England inevitable. In addition to its direct effects on industrial cities, the transatlantic trade in raw cotton stimulated the expansion of seaport cities directly involved in the cotton trade, and also gave a boost to transport and related industries.

Of all the nations in the Western world, including Holland, France, America, and Canada, why did England take the lead in the process of industrialization? The small size of their country and its lack of industrial raw materials hampered the Dutch; the French lacked adequate financial machinery and political stability. The United States and Canada were both new nations with huge resources, but neither had the necessary maturity or population at this time. In England in the second half of the eighteenth century, on the other hand, all the preconditions for modern industrialization developed more or less simultaneously. The population grew, providing a surplus of labor that could be employed in industry; agricultural improvements produced larger food surpluses; inventors produced a variety of new machines; coal was abundant, and people with mining experience were available to exploit the growing demand for it. England had shown initiative in world exploration, conquest, and trade in the early modern period. As a result, she had an excellent military and commercial navy to import raw materials not found at home and to command world markets for her exported products. The participation of many English investors in the ocean-borne trade boom of the early modern period also meant that the country was well endowed with capital and people experienced in sometimes hazardous commercial ventures who could direct expansion in new fields and who were willing to take a few risks in expectation of high profit. The relatively open social structure, much more flexible than that of most European countries in the eighteenth century, allowed Englishmen of promise to advance their social as well as economic status and thus gave an additional incentive to individual effort and risk taking. England had developed a fairly sophisticated banking and commercial system flexible enough to cope with the needs of expanding industry. Besides providing a stable political framework within which economic expansion could occur, the government interfered very little with domestic commercial operations, allowing the new industries the freedom they needed to experiment and develop.

Once industrialization was under way, especially after the Napoleonic Wars, England faced no challengers to her industrial supremacy for over half a century simply because she had been first. Her industrial leadership also meant that she was the first nation to become urbanized on anything like a modern scale, and as a result, the first industrial city, the "nineteenth-century city," wherever it existed, showed a marked resemblance to its British prototypes, the pacesetters of early industrialism.

The Shape of the Industrial City

Before fuel-consuming machines appeared, wind, water, or muscles powered industrial machines. Few provided employment for more than two or three people, and most required only one. Because it was not necessary for people to cooperate to use machines, concentration of a labor force was simply a convenience or an accident. However, one steam power source that could run several machines collected a large number of people around it, creating a concentration of people born of mechanical necessity rather than of human convenience. The power source and the machines it drove were housed under one roof for maximum efficiency, and workers perforce settled around the factory to form the nucleus of the dynamic urban form of the time, the industrial city.

A major consideration involved in the use of steam-powered machines was the availability of coal, a heavy, bulky fuel that was not easy or cheap to carry very far, even after the development of canal systems. Because of the nature of the fuel, it was cheaper and more convenient to move machines and people to it, rather than the reverse. The impetus in urban development in this period was no longer confined to trade centers and capitals, but also came from wherever large coal deposits were found. Coal mining was vital to this whole coal-based phase of industrial expansion, and wherever there were economically exploitable coal deposits, towns and cities sprang up. Often this meant that regions of no great significance in the past rose to national and international prominence and boomed in population. Small villages and little towns blossomed into large towns and cities in a few decades. Mines, factories, and houses appeared on the British coalfields in the Tyne-Tees area, on the flanks of the Pennines, and in south Wales, as they did in the Belgian coal district and in Pennsylvania. Major port cities such as Amsterdam, London, and New York continued to attract population and to grow in size, but only such large route centers could provide any kind of population counterweight to the coalfields once industrialization got under way. For example in Britain, whose center of population gravity had always been the fertile agricultural lowlands of the southeast, the whole balance of population shifted in the nineteenth century as people flocked to the booming industrial cities of the north and the Midlands.

In all the Western nations that industrialized in the eighteenth and nineteenth centuries, not only did population increase at a startlingly rapid rate, but it also shifted to areas that were unprepared for large-scale urban development. This state of industrial regions, however, was not as significant in giving the new cities their character as was the unprepared-ness of the people. The new industrial settlements often had existing small villages as their cores, but they rarely possessed mechanisms for directing their growth; many new urban concentrations grew up on sites where there had been no significant prior settlement. Manufacturers and mine owners chose sites for their industrial utility, generally on a stream or river, near a road crossing, or on or near a coalfield. On such a site the manufacturer built his factory or sank his mine, employing the most up-to-date machines and techniques available, while workers drifted in drawn by rumors that there was work to be had. Most manufacturers and mine owners, apart from a few atypically humanitarian ones, looked on their workers simply as necessary elements in the productive process and were only concerned about them during working hours. Their human needs were inconveniences to be disposed of with as little expense and effort as possible. After all, the founders and owners of the new industries were first and foremost businessmen interested in production and profit; they did not see themselves as the founders and planners of the new towns and cities, whose growth was only incidental to personal business concerns.

Nevertheless, some allowance had to be made for human needs, and housing grew up around the factories and mines. Many industrialists made arrangements with a building contractor for the construction of an appropriate number of houses at as low a cost as possible. In many cases, independent speculative builders constructed houses for rent to workers. These were generally of an even lower quality than those built for factory owners. Few people of influence seemed to care very much about the finished product, and few, if any, restrictive bylaws or building codes existed to protect the tenants. Consequently, builders cut construction costs to the bone in order to swell their profits. The working-class housing in the new towns and in the additions to old towns and cities was built as cheaply as possible with no regard for convenience, community needs, or aesthetic nicety. The cheapest kind of worker housing was a

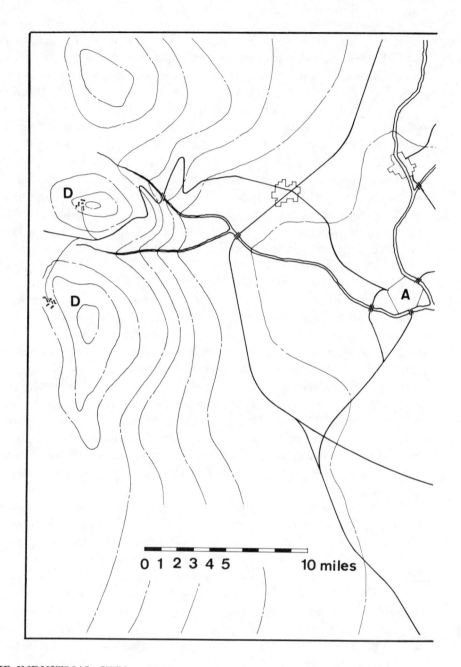

0 1 2 3 4 5   10 miles

THE INDUSTRIAL CITY c. 1850

The ready availability of coal, iron ore, and limestone stimulated development in new
regions. Port facilities and the development of the railroad network encouraged rapid
industrialization.

A Early modern city ceased growing and began to decline as growth impetus moved
downriver to site with port facilities for larger ships.

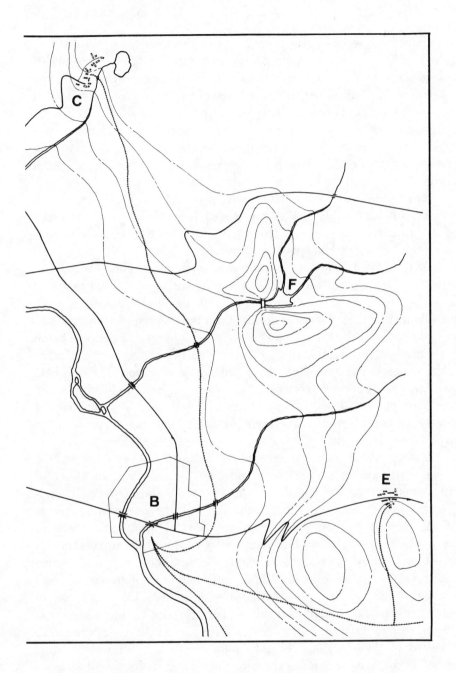

B New industrial city: port and railroad center.
C Coal mines linked to main city by rail.
D Limestone quarries.
E Iron ore deposits, linked to main city by old road and by railroad.
F Reservoir for city water supply.
(MAP DRAWN BY SATHIT CHAIYASIN)

simple brick or wooden box placed in rows to economize on dividing walls. Further savings were possible if two rows of boxes were placed back to back so that they could also share a common rear wall. The earliest worker housing generally consisted of two rooms, one upstairs and one down, with a coal-burning fireplace in the lower room. Except for the ones at the end of a row or terrace, each shared both side walls with neighboring boxes, and in the case of back-to-back terraces, the rear wall. The sets of boxes were themselves arranged in rows or around small central courtyards connected to the street by dark, narrow, alleyways. The net result of this kind of housing development was block upon block of bleak, mean, little houses that provided basic shelter but not much more, and dank, dirty streets that clotted around the mine or factory whose need for labor had spawned them.

Once a viable industry was established in a coalfield location, it tended to attract other industries because its success indicated that coal resources, transport facilities, industrial raw materials, and labor were available in that area. Other factories and mines subsequently joined the original ones, and they, too, spawned worker housing. As the population of a settlement grew, a secondary population of shopkeepers and other service people arrived, swelling the population yet further. The coal field towns and cities grew explosively in the early stages of industrialization, their birth, growth, shape, and character all determined by industrial and commercial considerations, and their problems built into them from the start.

Factory towns, such as the cotton textile towns of Lancashire and the woolen textile towns of Yorkshire, were not the only kind of industrial settlements that boomed at this time. The more industry of all kinds expanded, the greater was the demand for coal; the mines multiplied as did the number of workers drawn to them. Mining cities such as Newcastle, Pittsburgh, and Dortmund soon produced urban centers that were enormous by all previous standards. Because they were inaccessible or lacked flat land, some coalfields did not attract other industries or form great cities but had such good coal that mining alone was profitable. In such places as the valleys of south Wales and Appalachia, towns and villages arose to serve the coal mines and nothing else. In some of the most backward of these regions the inhabitants went straight from simple, almost rudimentary agrarian pursuits, tiny communities, and isolated farms into "modern" industry in a densely populated urban setting. The remoteness of these regions invited employer exploitation of workers. For example, mining companies often established "company stores," "truck" or "tommy" shops where workers bought goods, usually at inflated prices, with company scrip issued in lieu of at least part of their wages.

The expansion of railway networks all over the world and the ever-increasing use of machines in industry generated a great demand for iron. With this, metal-smelting cities, which often became manufacturers of heavy machinery as well because of the availability of raw materials, soon spread across coalfields, and black, noisy, grim industrial centers such as Sheffield and Essen were born.

The ocean port city did not die in this new phase of urban development, but expanded as it assumed new industrial functions. In the nineteenth century more raw materials, manufactured goods, and people moved around within regions and nations and across the world than ever before. As the transport network became more extensive and the volume of goods carried increased, the need for people to handle the traffic at transport interchange points grew. Many new towns and cities appeared in the United States and Canada at points where the food surpluses of the prairies were put on the railway; at major transport nodes, such as Liverpool, New York, and Hamburg, established cities expanded explosively.

The movement of people should be placed alongside the movement of raw materials and manufactured goods as a major force in the generation and spread of urbanization in the West in the nineteenth century. Since urban growth in this period often occurred in places that had previously been only lightly populated, and since the movement of large numbers of people was implicit in the creation of towns and cities in these areas, the time of industry building was also a time of massive migrations. The people who first moved into the growing urban centers represented the "surplus" population that the earlier agrarian economy could not have supported. Some of them moved only a short distance from their rural birthplaces to a nearby growing town; some moved from agrarian districts that were feeling the pressure of overpopulation and surplus labor to industrial regions within their own country; some moved from agrarian countries to industrial ones where, they had heard, there was work to be had and perhaps even a fortune to be made. Within individual nations, the flow of migration was from agricultural areas to the coal fields. In Europe the main trend was from the economically backward east to the more rapidly industrializing west. European industrial expansion did not absorb all of the European population surplus. The most dramatic movement of all was that across the Atlantic; 4.5 million immigrants entered the United States before 1860, and between

1870 and 1900 about twenty million arrived. In addition, many Europeans moved to Canada, Australasia, and, to a lesser extent, to European holdings in Africa and Asia.

People from all parts of Europe swelled the population of the great empty lands of North America. Had this migration not taken place, urbanization in North America, which had land enough to offer many people a living in agriculture, would probably have come very much later in time. Although migrations were important to Western urban growth generally because they distributed the surplus of people more evenly on both sides of the Atlantic, they were important to certain cities in a much more specific fashion. Liverpool, for example, owed part of its growth to the fact that it was the city to which many of the migrating Irish first moved. At the time of the potato famine in the 1840s, three hundred thousand Irish people descended on Liverpool within five months, having a dramatic impact on a city of two hundred fifty thousand people. Some stayed only long enough to board a ship out, others lingered until they decided to which other British city to move, some worked in the city long enough to earn the money to pay for a journey overseas, but many settled permanently. New York experienced a similar growth from immigration, taking in people not only from Ireland but from all over Europe either for short periods of time until they moved west or on a permanent basis.

Many new urban settlements, such as coal or textile centers, developed because their location enabled them to fill one particular industrial function, but the largest cities, like all the enduring settlements in human history, fulfilled a variety of functions and were nourished by a variety of industries and services. Chicago, for example, was a Great Lakes port, a major railway center, a food-processing and marketing center, a major producer of basic metals, an important trade center, and a manufacturing city. Between 1850 and 1853 its population increased from thirty to sixty thousand. By 1870 it had two hundred ninety-nine thousand people, one hundred forty-five thousand of whom were foreign born. The population of New York increased from over one million in 1860 to five million in 1910. In 1837 when Victoria came to the throne in England, six British cities had over one hundred thousand people. By the end of the century twenty-four cities were of this size and 15 percent of the population of England and Wales lived in London alone. Similarly staggering illustrations of the rapidity and the enormous scale of urbanization in the nineteenth century are found all over the Western world.

Modifications of the Form

The lack of planning and foresight in the building of the industrial city combined with its huge area and high population density to make this dynamic city of the nineteenth century also the preeminent city of death. An urban death rate of about twenty per thousand was considered low, and most larger cities in the middle years of the century had a normal death rate of between thirty and thirty-five per thousand, which went higher in times of epidemic.* Infant mortality rates were even higher than those for the general population since the time before a child's fifth birthday was full of hazard and overshadowed by the specter of death. At the Foundling Hospital in Paris in the 1830s, one-quarter of the children died before they reached their first birthday. While foundling hospitals were not the best places to start out in life, this example does reflect the level of infant mortality across the urbanized West. Life expectancy was short for the majority of city dwellers, and death and disease stalked the streets with far more regularity and thoroughness than street cleaners or garbage collectors. The city that offered a livelihood on the one hand, on the other killed its inhabitants and required a continued influx of immigrants from the countryside to sustain it.

The industrial city in its raw and unmodified form was such a death trap that urban growth would probably have stalled in the later nineteenth century without the reforms that modified it a little. If this leveling off had taken place, the high death rates might have counterbalanced the high birth rate and restored the equilibrium between the two. By the middle years of the century, however, some people began to realize that many urban centers were unfit for human habitation and in the latter part of the century gradually introduced improvements to change the situation.

Because the size of nineteenth-century urban concentrations was unprecedented, no one knew how to plan for basic urban services in large areas with high population densities. There were no provisions in the rapidly growing towns and cities of the first part of the century for anything other than traditional methods of disposing of refuse, obtaining water, and other essential tasks. For lack of alternatives, people continued to do as they had always done, but the results were disastrous. People had always disposed of refuse, trash, and human excrement by throwing it

---

* The death rate in most modern urbanized Western nations is now around twelve to fifteen per thousand.

into the river or by leaving it in the streets for scavengers or rain. When urban centers were small and widely scattered and when they produced relatively small quantities of easily degradable refuse, these methods did not overtax the capacity of natural disposal by water. When cities grew and began to produce an enormous volume of waste to which the factories added large quantities, natural means of disposal collapsed under the strain. Scavengers and rain proved unequal to the task of reducing the mounting piles of refuse that packed down and lay, sometimes for years, in backyards and alleyways. In rivers and streams, minute organisms died, plants died, fish died, and for all practical purposes the water "died" and became useless. Many waterways became stinking, open sewers, foul cocktails composed of chemicals, trash, excrement, decomposing organic matter from slaughterhouses, and other rubbish such as rusty buckets and old bed frames. In 1849 a disgusted contemporary described the Thames at London as "a more or less concentrated solution of native guano." In the same year fourteen thousand people in the city died of cholera; the streets and rivers were not only offensive eyesores, but also great breeding grounds for diseases of all kinds. Epidemics of typhoid and cholera struck terror into the hearts of city dwellers much as the plague had terrified their medieval counterparts.

People in many cities had to use water that they or people in an upstream settlement had polluted. Only a few of the largest cities had any provision for the purification of drinking water by the end of the century. Even where such facilities existed, they generally consisted of little more than tanks where solids were allowed to settle before the cleaner water was pumped off the top. When communities were small, few people had lived far from the river or stream from which they drew water, but as settlements became larger and city authorities grew more remiss in providing residents and visitors with water, many people found that they lived relatively long distances from any water source. Even when builders provided standpipes at intervals in the streets of a residential area, these were generally widely spaced and some distance away from many houses. Given the long hours put in by most working people, their miserable housing conditions, and the apparent futility of any battle against soot and dirt, most found walking a few hundred yards for a bucket of water for washing simply too much trouble. The unpleasant taste and smell of the inadequately treated water also discouraged its use. Many people drank only beer, wine, or spirits and used water solely for cooking and occasional washing.

Some were troubled by too much water. The pressure of population in the growing cities meant that land that had not previously been used for building because it was too low-lying, marshy, or subject to floods was used for building. The inhabitants of these areas faced the additional misery of damp cellar floors and frequent floods that left layers of stinking mud and refuse behind. To the filth on the ground and in the water was added dirt in the air. The smoke and soot from factory chimneys and railways and the dust from unpaved streets littered with horse droppings hung like a pall over most industrial cities. Since all but the very prosperous had to wash their clothes in dirty water and dry them in dirty air, most city people were dingy and grubby. The general griminess of the cities as much as the dictates of fashion established the general habit of wearing dark clothing.

In short, the natural life-support systems broke down in industrial urban settlements under the weight of too many people packed carelessly into too small an area. As a result, people died. Because they were ill-fed, their children were stillborn or too feeble to survive the first few years of life in this hostile environment. They died in large numbers as epidemic diseases such as cholera, typhoid, and diphtheria, born in filth and transmitted easily through the packed masses of humanity, swept through cities like brush fires. Survivors of the urban plagues were not unmarked. In the 1840s the French army found that while four out of ten conscripts from rural areas were unfit for military service, the rejection rate for urban conscripts was a staggering nine out of ten. As the evidence piled up from a variety of sources, some medical men, researchers, and humanitarians realized that the high death rates and ill health indicated that all was not well in towns and cities. Even before germs and their role in disease were discovered and understood, some individuals asserted that ordinary occurrences like breathing the foul air from rotting garbage and drinking cloudy and unpleasant-smelling water caused disease. After all, the gases of decomposition from places like the canal basin in Leeds were so strong that they blackened silver watch cases in a few minutes, and it seemed reasonable to some people that such gases were not good for human beings either. Although their analysis of the situation may have had many faults, by the mid-nineteenth century some people were ready to acknowledge that the problems existed and that study, which must always precede solution, had to be attempted. Ideas were only slowly translated into actions, however, because action often threatened vested interests and tradition. Moreover, the people of the nineteenth century were as reluctant as their twentieth-century descendants to undertake to improve the living conditions of the community as a whole if that required inconvenient and expensive programs.

The most urgent needs in the nineteenth century were for new methods of obtaining clean water and removing refuse and for new forms of local government and laws to modify the forces that were "naturally" shaping the cities and making them into charnel houses. Civic authorities had to be created and given the power to provide water and cleaning services for all inhabitants and areas within the urban community. Old water sources had to be abandoned and cleaner ones found and artificial purification systems put into operation. Streets needed to be cleaned "artificially," and household refuse had to be collected regularly and taken away for disposal instead of being left to scavengers. Sewers had, in effect, to be reinvented and connected to all households.

Prosperous people were usually able to improve their own environment to some extent by paying for garbage to be removed, by having cesspools constructed and cleaned regularly, and by having their water brought by cart from some clean source and put into storage tanks in their homes. Lower death rates reflected the cleaner conditions in which the wealthy lived. Death rates in the prosperous quarters of Paris, for example, were two to three times lower than in the slums. The majority of people could not afford to buy special waste disposal or water supply services, and as a result, their commercial development lagged far behind the community needs. If the mass of the people were to receive necessary services, civic authorities would have to be empowered to provide them or to contract for their provision with private companies on behalf of the community. Eventually, the comparatively wealthy people who would have to both advocate and finance such services if they were ever to come into being realized that the situation had become intolerable and had to be improved. Philanthropy and pity for the masses who lived in an incredibly sordid and unhealthy environment motivated some; a sense of *noblesse oblige* or civic pride inspired others. Many were deeply disgusted by the smell and filth of the cities which they also had to endure, at least from time to time. Perhaps the sharpest motivating force was the fact that, once started, an epidemic disease recognized no social or geographical boundaries. Although epidemics generally originated and took their greatest toll in the slums, they often spread rapidly to the pleasant enclaves of the prosperous and killed the rich and their children, too.

In the middle and later nineteenth century, the combination of these motives and the increasing awareness that the deterioration of urban living conditions was reaching a crisis point promoted what might be called a sanitary revolution. An increasing number of effective civic authorities were created and began to finance and construct adequate sewer systems, to provide or regulate water-processing and distribution systems, and to hire street cleaners and garbage collectors. Local authorities in London began to construct a main sewer system in the 1850s; the first state board of public health was established in Massachusetts in 1869; the American Public Health Association, which promoted public health work, was founded in 1872. In addition to providing basic public health requirements, some civic authorities began to take steps to correct other undesirable features promoted by unregulated urban growth. In many towns and cities the civic authorities, sometimes with the aid of national government, began to regulate housing conditions in the hope of reducing disease and ill health. By the end of the century, the formulation of elementary building and housing codes was well under way, and most cities had adequate water and sewer systems. As the various environmental and public health programs became effective, urban death rates began to fall, and by the turn of the century the great epidemic diseases of the first industrial cities were tapering off.

In the later decades of the nineteenth century spreading suburbs and new skyscrapers were beginning to change the form of the first industrial city. Its problems were on their way to solution, and cities were in the process of becoming pleasant places in which to live when the modern city form began to evolve, bringing with it new problems to compound the old.

THE FIRST INDUSTRIAL CITY

5 The Making of Urban Industrial Society

Because the industrial city was such a radical departure from previous urban forms, it generated massive social changes, amplified by the many major innovations that accompanied its development: population increase, expanded food supply, advances in technology and transportation, and industrialization. The social adjustments generated by the industrial city were all the more significant because they affected a higher percentage of the population of Western nations than urban phenomena had ever directly affected in the past. In the nineteenth century, city people had ceased to be a minority of the population; by the early twentieth century, they had become a majority. Even in nations such as the United States that retained their rural majorities into the early twentieth century, thanks largely to the expansion of agrarian frontier regions, the effects of urban industrial expansion directly touched the life of nearly every person. Railway lines cut through farmlands and forests, and trains brought a taste of the smoke and noise of the city to quiet fields and villages. Families were separated and some farming communities atrophied as the siren song of the city began to lure young people away from their homes with promises of prosperity and modernity. Mail-order firms such as Sears used improved transport and communications facilities to peddle urban fashions and household equipment in the most remote corners of the countryside. The growing cities of Europe and North America provided a profitable market for agricultural surpluses and manufactured the equipment with which to cultivate them, thus stimulating the development of the huge agrarian expanses of the prairies.

The Impact of Industrialism on the Social Order

Traditional forms and practices, even those that had evolved within urban society, could not cope with the stresses imposed by the bustling industrial city. Many old social forms broke down under the new pressures, and as a result, instability and confusion prevailed until new social forms developed that were more compatible with the new kind of city.

The new urban forces disrupted society at all levels, affecting even the most basic social unit, the family. In preindustrial times, the individual had rarely operated outside of his family, which traditionally worked as a single economic unit, each member sharing the labor by which the family made its living. Indeed, under certain circumstances, the larger a family, the more prosperous it could hope to become; a large family eased the burden of feudal labor rents and was also better able to work landholdings without hiring outside help. Even when corporate groupings, such as the church and the guilds, began to break down in the late Middle Ages and the early modern period, the family remained an essential, highly functional economic and social unit. Sons had normally entered their fathers' trades when they became adults; the typical commercial unit had been the family firm run by family members as a group concern. The advent of industrialism, however, imposed tremendous strains on the economic and social unity of the family, and many of the bonds that had held it together dissolved or changed.

As factory employment became more common, the economic functions of the family weakened; independent rather than collective efforts were increasingly responsible for income. In some very early factories, including some English cotton mills, families did work as units, but this arrangement became less and less common as industrialization progressed. In most poor families, everyone still had to work to stay alive, but "family income" came to mean the pooled wages of individual family members rather than a total income derived from cooperative effort.

Before modern industrialism, the skills necessary for earning a living changed little from one generation to the next. The strong similarity between the occupations and practices of grandparents and grandchildren made the family a valuable educational unit within which aged family members passed on their skill and experience. Old people who had become too infirm to do much work were teachers for their grandchildren, for they not only had useful knowledge, but they also had time to devote to teaching. Their performance as educators of the young had the added advantage of leaving the active adults free to work without being troubled by child-care problems. When the rate of technical innovation accelerated in the later eighteenth century, however, the family began to lose its usefulness as an educational institution because the continuity of skills was disrupted. Adults outside the family provided training in new techniques, and the practical skills that old people had mastered soon became obsolete and of little value to their descendants. As education gradually became an extrafamily function, another practical bond within the family unit and between its generations weakened.

When family members had worked together to make a living in farming or the family business, their activities had been integrated. They tended to work, eat, sleep, and recreate at the same times, and to be acquainted with the same people; this all strengthened the cohesiveness of the family unit and made it the focus of the social life of its members. With the coming of powered machines, the family social unit persisted, but many of the activities from which it derived its strength disappeared, and convention and convenience increasingly determined its social functions. Members of families in industrial cities worked at different jobs, sometimes in entirely different establishments, and they very often had totally different hours of work and leisure. Consequently, many social contacts were made at work, completely outside the family, while social activities tended to attract individuals with similar backgrounds and hours rather than family groups. The family economic and social unit also began to weaken among the urban middle classes. The basic business unit of early industrialism was the family firm in which fathers and sons, brothers and uncles performed different but closely interrelated functions. As industry and commerce became more sophisticated, however, firms expanded; by the later nineteenth century they began to operate increasingly along "modern" lines, employing more professionals in managerial positions and acquiring more capital from outside stockholders who were more interested in profit from their investment than in who was running the business. Fewer business and professional men were able to work at home or in nearby offices and were thus removed further from social contact with members of their families. Family social activities such as entertaining friends at home and holding traditional family celebrations did continue, and many of the social functions of the family survived, but all the pressures of the urban industrial system tended to weaken rather than reinforce them.

As the nineteenth century progressed, the family tended to dissolve into a group of loosely connected individuals. This social adjustment was in time followed by the making of laws that intervened in family affairs on behalf of individual members. The traditional interrelationships within the family group began to change, and the role of the adult male as its legally unquestioned absolute ruler began to break down. In many industrializing nations in the nineteenth century, women received the legal right to own and manage property independently of their husbands, and in a few places they obtained the right to vote as independent citizens. Children began to be accorded rights as individuals independent of their parents. By the end of the century, in many places children were protected from unduly harsh parental punishment, and excessive beating or mistreatment of a child was no longer a family problem but an offense by one individual against another that was punishable by law. Governments also increasingly treated children as a group of citizens with a special position in society in such matters as the right to education and the legal minimum age of employment.

As the disruptive forces of the industrial urban system gained in strength as time passed, each individual became less an integral part of a family unit and more a single independent entity, a single wage-earning unit whose daily bread did not depend on his working with family members. He was educated with and by strangers outside the home, his social life did not necessarily include family members, and he could live almost as well without a family as with one. The family persisted, but it was an increasingly fragile unit that depended for its survival more on tradition and affection and less on daily necessities.

In addition to disturbing traditional familial patterns, industrialism disrupted life at the individual level. The old regulating agents and rhythms of life were natural and in accord with animal instincts. People got up when it was light and slept when night came; they worked hard in late spring, summer, and early autumn when the weather was best and did very little in winter when the weather was at its most unpleasant. The seasons even regulated manufacturing and trading. In winter, trade slackened because storms at sea were at their height; dirt roads were muddy and impassable, and it was difficult to move raw materials or finished products very far. The streams that powered water-driven machinery were often frozen in winter. Although most people worked long and hard, they did most of their work under the most favorable natural conditions.

In industrial cities people found that natural phenomena no longer directed their lives but rather the demands and capacities of the powered machine. The seasons or light and darkness did not influence them, nor the whole system of production and distribution they supported. To produce optimum profits, machines had to be in operation around the clock all year long. The workers who tended them also had to be available, but no group of workers could work as tirelessly as machines. Thus, shift working was introduced. As this became more common, many workers were required to work at night and sleep during the day, either on a permanent basis or on alternate weeks and months. Those who worked at night were thrown completely out of phase with the rest of humanity which, as usual, was up and about in the daylight hours when night workers were trying to sleep. The mealtimes and leisure hours of night workers did not coincide with others, and they found that in addition to all the other inconveniences of their schedule, they might not even see the day shift working members of their families for days at a time. Nearly everyone worked in winter and so had to become accustomed to the unnatural act of getting up before the late winter sun dawned and leaving warm beds and homes to walk to work through cold, raw, bleak streets before it was light.

At a practical level, industrialism changed time itself. Time had always been a rather vague personal and community matter in the days when most people arranged their lives to correspond with the hours of light and darkness and when all forms of transport were slow and no great degree of group coordination was expected. This casual, "natural" approach to time first became a problem with the development of railway systems. British railway timetables of the 1840s, for example, noted variations of "local time" from "London time" ranging up to almost a quarter of an hour within a relatively short journey. Travelers who owned watches were warned of these local variations, which owed everything to community custom and nothing to longitude, and were expected to adjust to local time when moving from one station to another. Time standardization was clearly a necessity when transport became faster; it first became possible with the installation of telegraph lines that allowed local stations and communities to synchronize with London time, which thus became national time.

These new patterns of life developed in an environment alien to the majority of people. Densely populated large towns and cities with closely packed houses and factories, contaminated water, smoky air, and impersonal crowds were replacing small towns, villages, and sparsely populated rural areas as the living places of most people. An old gentleman testifying before a U.S. Senate Committee on Education and

Labor in 1883 looked back on the New York he had known in the 1820s and 1830s saying that people then "were a great deal happier than people are now. . . . They had plenty of social good feeling, everybody knew everybody." He complained that this cohesive society had broken down as the city grew larger.

For people who had been born and brought up in rural villages of not more than a few hundred people, the number and density alone of people in the cities of the nineteenth century must have been terrifying. For example, in 1837 in Belfast, one of the smaller cities of the nineteenth century, there were nine houses, each with two rooms, in Gutter Alley. The floors of the lower rooms were packed earth and none of the rooms were more than six feet eight inches high. In these eighteen rooms lived 147 people, an average of about 8 to a room. Some newcomers arriving in Paris in the 1830s found themselves living in lodging houses where twelve lodgers shared six beds, while in Manchester in the 1840s, over 7,000 people shared thirty-three privies, an average of 215 men, women, and children to each one. Although the overcrowding reported in these instances may seem exceptionally appalling, such conditions were by no means uncommon, and investigators in virtually all major Western cities in the middle years of the nineteenth century recorded similar examples. It is probable that few people from rural backgrounds coped easily with these new conditions of life within the new urban setting. To the next generation, however, born within the huge, crowded industrial city, streets, factories, and packed humanity seemed normal and the rural life described by their parents largely alien and valueless.

The vast majority of people in the predominantly rural past had never enjoyed an adequate diet, good housing, or ideal sanitary facilities. They had died early and had often been hungry. Even so, life in some squalid rural cottage surrounded by open land was quite a different proposition from life in a squalid urban tenement submerged in a vast sea of brick, stone, and dirt. Escape from small rural settlements and even small towns was easy simply because they were small; for farmers escape into open fields was, in effect, obligatory. As the cities sprawled and the distances from urban centers to rural districts increased, escape, even for a short time, became more difficult. The expansion of the built-up area combined with long working hours, weariness, and poverty to ensure that many urban people saw open country and open sky rarely, if ever. Thus, ever-larger numbers of people were permanently confined to unpleasant homes and dingy workplaces, imprisoned by bricks and mortar, and always obliged to walk on filthy pavements. Apart from the occasional incongruous pig or cow, the only other living things that shared the bleak new cityscape with human beings were scraggy dogs and cats, grimy sparrows, starlings, and pigeons, and pests such as cockroaches, rats, and lice. Given these conditions, it is no surprise that so many urban people lost all awareness of the role of humanity in the scheme of living things, or that anger, despair, and frustration occasionally erupted into drunken brawls, violent crimes, street riots, and senseless acts of destruction.

Violence of some kind had long been an occasional part of urban life. Sporadic fights between rival bands of apprentices, between retainers of rival families, or between townspeople and university students had plagued many medieval cities. With the development of the huge, densely packed industrial city, however, came a new kind of violence, that of the great urban masses, which brought with it the prospect of rule by terror. The frustration, desperation, confusion, and disorientation that produced mob violence were ever-present elements in the daily lives of many poor urban people, especially those with high expectations who had recently arrived from the countryside. Any additional strain such as high unemployment, a temporary food shortage, a labor dispute, or even a political crisis could trigger mob violence in the growing cities. In the eighteenth and nineteenth centuries the middle class rather than the mob engineered political revolutions, but mob action sometimes provided the opportunity for revolutionary leaders to take political control. As urban concentrations multiplied and urban areas became larger, mob action more often accompanied political crisis. For example, fear of the Paris mob came to play such an important part in French politics that Louis Napoleon found it necessary to rebuild large sections of the city, creating the straight, wide boulevards that made the barricading of the streets by the mob more difficult while they facilitated the movement of troops and police. In the twentieth century, working-class spokesmen would emerge and the urban masses would have greater access to nonviolent channels of political and social action, but incoherent, indiscriminate mob violence has yet to be eliminated from urban life. In essence, the diffuse feelings of anger and frustration that fueled the Paris mob during the revolution and the emotions that motivated the urban mobs in the Watts riots in California and in the uprisings in Paris and Belfast in the 1960s are much the same.

In addition to fostering mob violence, industrial cities created masses of people who became basically rootless, without strong family or community ties. The need for work or the hope of a better life wrenched people away from their families and friends, the patterns of life, and the lands they had known and flung them headlong into alien surroundings. Their new contacts were with unknown people who were also struggling to live in a social milieu whose patterns were not yet firm enough to impart a sense of stability. Many families broke up as some men left to seek work in industrial centers, promising to return or to send for the others when they had established themselves but never doing so. Young girls left their families to work as servants in prosperous urban households, and young men left family farms to work in factories. In addition to regional dislocations, the international demand for industrial labor produced segments of the population without firm ties to the nation of their residence. This phenomenon was an important factor in urban instability and unrest in Europe, but was even more visible and more disruptive in the context of the overseas migrations that enlarged as the century progressed.

Initially, at least, displacement of surplus population from rural areas produced the majority of the industrial workers. The old visions of alabaster cities lured some migrants to urban centers, but most people were drawn there because they could not find work or could see no prospect of a decent future on the land. In effect, pressures of population forced them out. The poor majority had little choice because the alternatives were to move to a city and try something new or to stay on the land and starve sooner or later. Ireland illustrates vividly the conditions that produced mass migrations. Discouraged from developing native industry by English regulations and dependent for food on the potato which thrived on her soil, Ireland had become an overpopulated rural slum by the middle of the nineteenth century. The expanding population was sustained by devoting more and more land to potato growing at the expense of other crops. This fed larger numbers of people but also resulted in a heavy reliance on a single crop. The dangers of this were forcefully exposed in the 1840s when the potato crop failed and Ireland found herself with a larger population than food resources would support. Faced with starvation at home, thousands of the more adventurous and desperate people of Ireland took a chance and moved. Few of these emigrants were in a position to make conscious choices between equally desirable alternatives. The majority went wherever they had heard there was work, where they knew someone, or only as far as they could afford to go.

Like the mid-century Irish, the majority of the new urban masses, whatever their origins, came from impoverished rural backgrounds. Almost by definition, most of them had little or no money when they arrived to settle in the city. Many were illiterate, most were woefully undereducated, and all needed to learn new skills in order to function in the urban industrial economy. Although the industrial city was crammed with poor people, it did not make its people poor, for so many brought poverty with them from their original homes like so much excess baggage.

The uprooting of such vast numbers of people from their native surroundings and ways of life and their congregation in urban areas inevitably created friction within the cities and added enormously to the disorienting effects of the new environment and the new patterns of work and timekeeping. The thrusting together of large numbers of people with different languages and social and cultural backgrounds occurred so rapidly and on such a massive scale in the nineteenth century that the new urban dwellers had no chance of acquiring the few generations of familiarization necessary for them to become accustomed to and to accept each other. Indeed, many groups, faced with the problems of adjusting to a new environment and a new way of life, found that their only security lay in building their new lives within a subcommunity of people who came from the same region and spoke the same language, thus compounding the problems of achieving a unified urban social and cultural system.

Increasing mobility and massive migrations did have some beneficial effects, however. Without the developing industrial economy and its growing capacity to absorb labor, the "surplus" people produced by population increase would have starved and died. The international migrations meant that the underpopulated regions of the world acquired the people and the labor force necessary to transform them into food surplus producers able to support urban expansion. Emigration gave a few fairly prosperous people the opportunity of turning their modest assets into huge fortunes. Some people who were discontented but had been unable to better themselves in their original homes emigrated in the hope of better conditions and a more pliable social system. Among the prosperous, vigorous malcontents who moved overseas were many of Europe's more active and disenchanted elements who might have spent their energies organizing riots and revolutions if they had remained at home.

The Masses, Poverty, Slums: Incentives for Urban Reform

The average immigrant left no records and his feelings and experiences can therefore only be imagined, but they must have

WENTWORTH STREET, *by Gustave Doré* Many poor people had no homes and literally lived and died in the streets. Many who were able to rent living spaces were forced by overcrowding to turn to the street for space and recreation. The grim hopelessness of life in the poor sections of industrial cities can be seen on the faces of these people. Local History and Genealogy Division, The New York Public Library; Astor, Lenox, and Tilden Foundations

STREET ARABS IN THE AREA OF MULBERRY STREET, *by Jacob A. Riis* These homeless New York children were comfortable by the standards of the street dwellers. Gratings such as this were much prized in cold weather because they kept out the wind and because the air rising from inside the building provided warmth.   The Jacob A. Riis Collection, Museum of the City of New York

REAR TENEMENT BEDROOM, EAST SIDE NEW YORK, 1910, *by Lewis Hine* These people, more prosperous than the street dwellers, could rent a home; but the squalor, overcrowding, and inadequacy typical of nineteenth-century working-class living conditions are still evident.
Collection of the International Museum of Photography at George Eastman House, Rochester, N.Y.

BELL TIME, *by Winslow Homer* The work force of this nineteenth-century New England factory presents a cross section of the workers of the industrial age: males and females of all ages from children to the very old, from reasonably well dressed to ragged. Among the lower classes it was as common for women to work as it was for men. Reproduced from the collections of the Library of Congress

BREAKER BOYS INSIDE THE BREAKERS, 1911, *by Lewis Hine* Concern for the welfare of children led to government regulation of industry and of working conditions, but even by the turn of the century, regulations concerning children's employment tended to be honored more in the breach than in the observance. Collection of the International Museum of Photography at George Eastman House, Rochester, N.Y.

ITALIAN IMMIGRANTS ON FERRY, 1905, *by Lewis Hine* Unlike this family, most immigrants of the industrial age owned little but the clothes they wore. The very poor were rarely able to afford a transatlantic journey and were forced by population growth and lack of rural employment to move to nearby overcrowded cities. The additional difficulties encountered by immigrants who had to learn new languages and customs were counterbalanced by the increased opportunities for employment in the new lands.
Collection of the International Museum of Photography at George Eastman House, Rochester, N.Y.

Reconstruction of a Victorian parlor Prosperous people in the nineteenth century lived in comfort and clutter. Their enchantment with the ownership of large numbers of objects and the ready availability of cheap domestic labor to dust them is suggested here. The focus of the room is the coal-burning fireplace.   Castle Museum, York, England

resembled the emotional disorientation and physical malaise that the jet age would label "culture shock." If, with all the benefits of education and modern communications, mid-twentieth-century travelers often experience feelings of acute bewilderment, frustration in the face of alien demands, nausea from unfamiliar foods, and numbness from changes in daily routine when confronted with new surroundings, the change of environment must have been much more devastating to the nineteenth-century urban immigrant. The majority of them were uneducated, and if they had any idea of what to expect, it was a foggy one based on rumors and the impressions of other people. Only a few were able to make advance arrangements with someone in the city for lodging, work, and food. Few had anyone to whom they could turn for help in the event of an emergency, and many had never been in any settlement larger than a farming village before they arrived in their new home. Most of them must have experienced problems of communication and understanding; urban residents often ridiculed and took advantage of new arrivals because of their rural accents and their ignorance of city ways, prices, wages, rents, and accommodations. Such problems were, of course, magnified many times over in the case of people who moved to places where they did not speak the language at all.

All this built up to a tremendous burden of disadvantages for the new city worker, the weight of which made it hard for him to capitalize on the opportunities his new surroundings offered. The need to adjust to new routines, to learn new skills, and to become accustomed to city life added even more weight to the burden. The tiny minority who had a little capital to invest, who had some skill they could sell, or who were lucky could prosper or even make the fortunes of which they had dreamed; but the majority, people who had spent all they had on their journey, who had no skills or education, and who were not lucky, became locked into a cycle of poverty that remained unbroken through the generations until a stroke of good fortune or the acquisition of an education or useful skill came along to open an exit.

Many of the immigrants arrived with nothing but the clothes on their backs because they had sold everything else to raise money for the journey, and some were already in debt because they had borrowed the money for clothes, shoes, or fares. Having arrived in a town or city, they had then to find housing; because they were poor, they chose the cheapest accommodation, usually located in the least desirable parts of town. They lived where no one who had enough money to make a choice would live. They settled alongside malodorous rivers and canals, next to stinking open sewers and overcrowded graveyards full of shallow graves, near

smoky, dirty factories and mines, and beside and sometimes even under
the viaducts carrying thundering railway traffic. In the mid-nineteenth
century, thousands of people in the French city of Lille lived in basements
with earthen floors covered with puddles where they slept on beds of
straw or even of potato peelings and ashes. In Manhattan in the 1870s,
almost four hundred seventy thousand people lived in less than fifteen
thousand tenements with little or no ventilation, small rooms, and shared
sanitary and cooking facilities. Such accommodations sapped the health,
determination, and self-respect that were necessary for earning a living
and for self-improvement.

Finding employment also presented problems, although generally
some kind of job presented itself after a few days' search. Skilled workers
fared reasonably well on the job market, but few new immigrants had
marketable industrial skills, and the vast number of unskilled workers
weakened their bargaining position. At the mercy of a seller's market
when looking for a home, the new resident was usually at the mercy of a
buyer's market when looking for a job. Employers paid workers as little as
possible and worked them as many hours as was feasible. Although wages
were low and the hours were long, anything was better than starvation; in
any event, the new worker usually had no choice. By moving to a town or
city, the majority of immigrants could expect to find a job and to banish
the specter of starvation for a little time at least, but beyond this the
prospects were generally bleak. Low wages and high rents and food prices
allowed workers little hope of saving for something better in the future;
long working hours left little time to spare for education or for
organization and agitation for better conditions; unhealthy living conditions weakened workers and reduced their earning capacity. Depressing,
unhealthy, and degrading surroundings both at home and at work drove
many people to seek escape in drunken stupors or in the limbo induced by
patent medicines consisting mainly of opium derivatives. The children of
the new workers, the first town-born generation, were not much better
off than their parents had been, except that they were more accustomed to
cities. Their parents had no money to educate them; low parental wages
made it necessary for children to start work in unskilled jobs at low wages
as soon as they were able. This breakdown of financial and psychological
supports for the individual within the family ensured the perpetuation of
the problems of adjustment and socialization. The early industrial city
offered subsistence survival but not much more, and the poverty that
many of the original immigrants had brought with them was bequeathed
to their children.

Working conditions imposed additional strains on working-class families and individuals. The number of working hours in a day varied in different industries and areas, but in the absence of regulatory legislation, workdays were long everywhere. For example, textile workers generally worked about twelve to thirteen hours a day, and miners, who worked in a physically demanding industry and had to make long underground journeys before they arrived at the coal face, worked about ten hours a day. Sunday was generally a holiday, as were some saints' days in Catholic regions and Saturdays in Jewish enclaves, but employers sometimes required workers to perform maintenance duties on those days. In other words, most workers in the early, unregulated industrial system worked very near the limits of physical endurance. There was little time to spare for preparing meals or performing other domestic chores, and sleeping or dozing on the job must have been a common way of compensating for the rest lost because of tasks that had to be performed at home.

Women and children were much in demand for all but the heaviest industrial labor. They were considered more tractable and dexterous than adult males, but because they were assumed to be secondary wage earners they were paid far less. In the earliest stages of industrialism quite young children were sometimes given jobs that supposedly were suited to a child's capacities. They watched over machines or did other jobs in which small stature was an advantage, such as cleaning machines and the floor under them. In the early nineteenth century it was quite common for the child of a poor urban family to start work in an essentially adult job at about eight or ten years of age. Long working hours meant that few children had the time to acquire an education or an advanced skill that would help them break out of the poverty cycle.

Factory work was often dangerous and industrial accidents were common. Unscreened, unguarded machines, sometimes cleaned while work was in progress, trapped and cut off fingers, limbs, and hair, maiming and sometimes killing workers. Mines were particularly dangerous; miners were killed or injured in numerous accidents involving roof falls, flooding, and explosions that might have been avoided if even elementary safety precautions had been taken. Flying sparks, harmful dust, noxious gases, and poisonous chemicals endangered unprotected workers in almost all industries. Occupational diseases were rampant, especially lung diseases, which were acquired in dusty jobs like mining, stonecutting, and even fur dressing. Because an accident or illness that kept a worker off the job generally resulted in a reduction of the income essential to the survival of his family, many people, especially those with several small children, had to work even when they were ill. Besides contributing to the spread of disease and the resultant high death rates among fellow workers, sick and injured people were themselves prone to further accidents and disease.

In spite of the long hours and high risks, rates of pay were generally low and subject to fluctuations beyond the control of the workers. Wages could be cut off for varying lengths of time for several reasons. Before the middle of the nineteenth century few parts were standardized and easily replaceable, and the early, temperamental machines broke down frequently. Breakdowns could mean hours, perhaps days, of unemployment while workers waited for someone to make a new part or dispatch a new machine. The tendency of the unregulated industrial economy to work in a boom-slump cycle produced periodic underemployment or unemployment. When demand and prices fell, production was cut back and workers lost their jobs or worked fewer hours for less pay. In a deep slump, industries sometimes shut down completely and turned away all employees. This was particularly disastrous in single-industry towns, for when the mine or factory closed, no other employment was available. Service businesses such as grocery stores within the town were also forced to close when the community ran out of money, and a whole town might be out of work for some time.

When there was an interruption in pay, whatever the reason, most people had few options; none of them were pleasant or likely to produce much income. People could sell or pawn possessions of any value, or try to get other work. Children could often find odd jobs or light work of some kind when adults were unemployed. If unemployment seemed likely to be prolonged and farming districts were not far away, people could look for unskilled farm work, especially during the harvest. Some could try hunting or poaching game. Families reduced expenses to the bare minimum necessary for survival, skipping rent and other payments so they could fill their bellies with something cheap but bulky, like potatoes. As a last resort, they might ask charitable institutions, if available, for help. Slumps caused acute misery because many people made barely enough money to feed and house themselves, and few workers had savings to fall back on if they became unemployed or ill. The fact that conditions beyond the control and comprehension of the workers caused many of these periods of unemployment must have generated feelings of insecurity and futility and undermined whatever initiative and self-reliance they possessed.

The life of the "average" urban industrial worker who lived on the margin of survival is difficult to describe for the same reasons that it is hard to characterize the life of the "average" anyone at any time. There were, however, enough strong similarities in the lives of this group throughout the industrializing West to draw a general picture. A family with three children could generally expect to meet basic expenses if the husband, the wife, and at least one of the children worked. They expended about 75 percent of their combined income on food; the rest was for rent, fuel, clothing, transportation, and entertainment. The basic diet consisted mainly of starchy foods, usually bread or potatoes, with inexpensive, highly seasoned items, such as sausages and pickles, to flavor meals. This restricted diet did not promote physical health or mental alertness, but few could afford a more balanced one. Most workers simply filled their bellies as full as possible, as cheaply as possible. Skilled workers had a higher living standard than the unskilled. Their larger incomes enabled them to pay a little more rent and to buy a little meat once or even twice a week, a few vegetables or some fruit or dairy products, and wine, beer, tea, or coffee. The rise in real wages that began to take place in the latter part of the century was generally initially absorbed by a higher consumption of food in general and by the addition of food luxuries like sugar and meat to the diet of the ordinary workers.

Rents in most urban areas averaged about a quarter of a worker's total monthly income. With the exception of the most prosperous, most families expected that their living quarters would consist of little more than one room. Families who could not afford much rent often sublet a corner of their only room to a single person or to a couple, while those who earned more might be able to afford one and a half or two rooms. Only by the end of the nineteenth century were the highest-income working-class families beginning to consider a two-room house as "normal" living quarters. Rooms were small and sparsely furnished. People made the fullest possible use of what they had; for example, a bed occupied at night by a day worker could be used during the day by a night worker. Children had little room to play, and their parents had virtually no privacy. Many people with such mean, cramped little homes preferred to spend their leisure hours in the streets or in the local tavern. Drinking shops of various kinds had long been urban social and recreational centers, but they multiplied rapidly as the urban population expanded and the desire for escape grew stronger.

All urban workers did not, of course, work in factories or mines, but the lives of these workers were very similar to those who did. Industrial establishments set the commonly accepted norms for working hours, and industrial wages largely determined the salaries paid to nonindustrial workers. Thus, salesclerks, whose work was considered to be much easier than that of industrial workers, were expected to work far longer hours for the same or even less pay. Many urban "industries," such as clothes making and cigar manufacturing, operated in a room of an apartment house or in cellars or attics. Such establishments could hardly be considered factories, but because their profit margins were so narrow, their owners were not inclined to pay their workers much more than was necessary for bare survival. Although the details of their working lives differed, the wages, hours, and general conditions of life of other workers such as railwaymen and stevedores were generally measured against those of factory workers.

Some workers did enjoy a higher standard of living than the majority who lived on or close to the margin of survival. Those who had some valuable skill could manage, with a little luck and continued good health, to keep their families in clean, warm, little houses or apartments without their wives being forced to work. A few could even look forward to establishing small businesses or to educating their children in the hope that they would find better jobs. As the century advanced and the industrial system became more sophisticated, the need for skilled workers grew and their incomes rose correspondingly. By the last decades of the century, too, some of the benefits of the industrial system began to filter down to the working classes in the shape of rising real wages, and the group of "prosperous" workers began to increase in size. As all this took place, a gradual rise in the general level of expectations began.

A rise in the level of the generally accepted minimal conditions of living or marginal existence accompanied the change in the level of expectations. In the first part of the nineteenth century, this level had been the clear-cut line between starving and eating, between death and survival. A century later, minimal conditions would be a much less easily defined but no less socially significant line between mere survival and self-respect, between social limbo and social viability. While many people in mid-twentieth-century urban nations are undeniably poor, they are much better off materially than the nineteenth-century poor. The improving standard of living of the majority of urban industrial people had continued to raise the generally accepted level of minimal conditions for over a century. When poverty was synonymous with starvation, the poor starved; when the mass became prosperous, the poor became those with a less than adequate diet, less than average housing, and fewer than normal material possessions.

All these major, rapid shifts in the established order of economy and society brought revision of ideas about governmental institutions and the social order. Institutions that had been designed to deal with the problems of villages and small urban settlements could not begin to cope with the complex problems of the large industrial cities. The private and public charities that had been organized to deal with poverty had worked well enough when communities were small and the poor were relatively few in number and well known to other members of the community. Confronted with the masses of poor people in giant urban centers, however, charities could no longer deal with them on an individual basis; the fact that so many people were strangers to whom the community as a whole felt little charitable obligation compounded their difficulties. All the traditional public offices suffered from similar problems of size and rapid expansion, and long-established agencies for such things as peace-keeping, road making and mending, lighting, and building soon proved miserably inadequate as industrial cities multiplied in number and grew in size.

These inadequacies inevitably attracted the attention of theorists, for the failures of established agencies of social and urban regulation emphasized the need to reassess the basic rules of social organization and government. Old systems and agencies that were, in essence, motley, bastardized versions of those that had operated with considerable vigor in the Middle Ages were seen as completely unworkable without drastic modification to fit them into the new setting. Some people felt that the modifications needed were so drastic that the whole social and governmental system might as well be swept away and replaced with one more suitable for the times.

Of long-range significance was a body of ideas called socialism which began to evolve in the cities and factory towns of the early nineteenth century. Many of the early socialists were French, such as Saint-Simon who fought in the American War of Independence and supported the French Revolution. He and his followers were the first notable exponents of a planned society that recognized urban industrialism. They advocated public ownership of capital and other assets and coordination and regulation of the activities of all segments of industrial society by social "engineers." These engineers would ensure that society operated in ways beneficial to all its members and would also initiate large public works projects such as building canals. Other social theorists later pursued a similar theme. Louis Blanc proposed a system of state-supported "social workshops" where workers could work for themselves without the need for capitalist-supplied equipment. The most famous nineteenth-century theorist who pursued such lines was Karl Marx. His work owed much to the reports of Friedrich Engels, who gathered information on the conditions of people living in English industrial cities in the mid-nineteenth century. Other contemporary investigators, including government committees, agreed with Engels that urban conditions were deplorable. Using these findings as background, Marx developed a social theory in which history consisted of a series of class wars; he predicted that the current industrial system would ultimately collapse as the workers, the real producers, rebelled against their miserable conditions and wrenched control from the middle class.

Other people sought to resolve the material and social problems of the new urban industrial system by creating utopias, communities in which all elements of society would live in comfort, happiness, harmony, and brotherhood. One such utopian was Robert Owen, an English cotton manufacturer. Despite his personal success, Owen felt that industry operated for the benefit of a few people at the expense of the majority, and that as a result, it produced inequity and friction within communities. He tried to establish private cooperative communities in which capitalists and laborers could work together for the benefit of all. When his English experimental community in New Lanark failed, he attempted another, New Harmony, in the land of utopias, the United States, but it failed as well. Nevertheless, trade union and cooperative movements eventually incorporated many of his ideas. Ultimately, if often vaguely, they affected the patterns of English socialism, a far less radical and less doctrinaire version of socialism than that which would develop from the writings of Marx.

While these new theories about social organization would, in the long run, have a considerable and often complex impact on Western nations and on the world, the immediate and obvious responses to the new urban industrial system took the form of practical reactions to the most serious urban problems, the most urgent of which concerned their life support systems. Without adequate sewers, a reliable fresh water supply, decent housing, or public services, the industrial settlements had rapidly developed into death traps. Their builders, without precedents to guide them or much time for thought, had been driven by the speed of industrial expansion and the desire for quick profits and had built badly. By the third and fourth decades of the nineteenth century, evidence from

England, which led the world in industrialization, supported by evidence from urban centers throughout the West, suggested that unless action were taken soon to improve living conditions, the cities and towns would become vast Potter's Fields where only disease thrived and only death prospered.

The essential systems—water supply, waste disposal, and cleaning—would take huge initial capital investments but would yield only small, long-term monetary returns. Building water and sewage pipe systems, reservoirs, and purification and processing plants involved large geographical areas and could not be done without powerful authorities with special legal powers. The need for overall planning, huge investments, and special legal powers ensured that governmental authorities would have to do this work. Many experiments were tried before efficient systems were worked out in the second half of the nineteenth century, of course, but the eventual solutions to industrial urban problems seemed to lie in governmental hands. The vastly swollen urban areas, larger than anything known before, were instrumental in creating vastly swollen government bureaucracies with wider powers than had ever been known before. Big city and big government seemed mutually supportive.

In most cases, change came only too slowly after thousands had needlessly suffered and died, but eventually society again adapted to the new demands imposed by changes in urban functions and forms. Initially, the working classes, the majority of the people, were able to do little to effect change because they were illiterate, disorganized, and poor, all conditions that militate against taking effective action. In many places, outbursts of urban violence were undoubtedly expressions of working-class anger, frustration, misery, and the vague desire to do something about their living conditions, but these were mainly incoherent and undirected and had no permanent effects. The people responsible for the changes that were made in the nineteenth century were not the workers, as Marx had prophesied, but the middle classes. This group had the power necessary to effect governmental changes, and charity, philanthropy, idealism, religious fervor, humanitarianism, and self-interest were all indispensable in getting the process of change under way.

To a great extent, the industrial cities were truly the cities of the middle class, made by them in a short enough span of time that individuals could associate urban growth with their own actions and those of their predecessors. The handful of people whose capital, expertise, and hard work had built the factories that gave life to industrial cities and whose commercial establishments thrived on the products of the factories in time came to feel a pride in achievement and creation that by the later nineteenth century began to color the conditions and fate of the whole urban community. Because they were personally involved in their communities, many industrialists and other businessmen undertook to improve and beautify their cities. Civic improvement produced unattractive statuary by the ton and hundreds of public buildings, like the Town Hall of the English woolen textile city of Leeds, that are so enormously pompous and ugly as to be almost attractive. Despite such frills, the contemporary equation of improvement with efficiency and cleanliness ensured that civic improvement would also include the renovation of government agencies and the installation of sewer and water systems.

A similar group of people with similar motives supported the movements for the reform of working hours and conditions. The humanitarian and religious convictions that had prompted the abolition of slavery and the improvement of cities also sustained the factory reformers. Their initial campaigns and the earliest governmental regulations they produced concerned the exploitation of the weak and helpless, specifically women and child laborers. In the early stages of reform, these regulations were honored more in the breach than in the observance, but by the end of the century they were beginning to have some effects, and in time they helped improve matters for male workers, too. Working conditions gradually became better as hours were reduced and employer demands became more humane, considerably improving conditions of life for the working classes.

As machines and industrial processes became more complex in the latter part of the nineteenth century, industrialists became aware that an educated worker was a greater asset than an uneducated one. Literate workers could read regulations, lists, and instructions, and could more readily understand new machines and processes. Hence, in the establishment of national systems of compulsory education, a strong undercurrent of necessity and self-interest supported middle-class and governmental idealistic egalitarianism.

Once civic and social reforms got under way, the improvements enabled people lower on the social scale to participate in initiating change. The earliest attempts of workers to organize for their own protection and advancement met with little success because few of the original trade union leaders had the experience or the money to gather an effective organization; many were frustrated by the apathy of the very workers they were trying to help. These early failures, nevertheless, gave later unionists a body of precedent and experience on which to build. As time passed and more people overcame their original stupefying bewilderment and adjusted to urban life, an awareness grew among the lower classes that poverty, misery, and early death were not inevitable. Trade unions, which began as small groups meeting informally in beer and wine shops, works, and private houses, gradually acquired legal recognition as organizing and bargaining institutions. Unions first began to become effective in France and Belgium in the 1860s, in Britain and Austria in the 1870s, and in Germany in the 1890s. The first promising American labor unions began to emerge after the Civil War and began to have some effect after the foundation of the American Federation of Labor, led by Samuel Gompers, a London-born cigar maker, in 1886. By the end of the century, union organizations were beginning to operate in virtually every industrialized and urbanizing nation, and union leaders were beginning to bargain, sometimes effectively, for better pay and conditions for their members.

The role of the urban mobs in the revolution of the late eighteenth and the nineteenth centuries clearly illustrates that the urban masses could be dangerous to the established governmental and social systems. The masses could precipitate a crisis that could then be used effectively by the middle-class and intellectual revolutionary leaders. As ever-larger proportions of the population lived in urban areas, the potential damage that mob action could inflict increased, and the destructive power inherent in large masses of people concerned many of those who supported established systems of government. To some extent, the expansion of the franchise can be seen as a practical ploy by established, powerful social and political groups to preserve their positions by giving a little power away. Taking the people into partnership in government seemed to many to be the most likely way to dissipate anger and frustration and to forestall the mob violence that might erupt and rip the established rulers from their positions of power totally and irrevocably.

The expansion of the franchise amplified the political voice of the masses and gave them legal avenues of effecting change. Working people gradually realized that their votes could be used to promote economic and social policies that would benefit them, but not until the twentieth century did mass democracy reach its full potential in shaping living and working conditions and the directions of social change. By the time early industrialism was reaching maturity at the end of the nineteenth century, however, there were some signs, such as the formation of workers' political parties, that the working classes would play a larger role in the processes of change in the future.

The Middle and Upper Classes

The bourgeoisie had always been closely associated with urban settlements, but as industrialism spread, the importance of the middle classes rose so quickly that they almost seemed a new social force. The growing significance of this group was due to the increasing importance of capital and industry in the new economic system. As they became more numerous and their functions more vital to the general economy, the members of the middle class became more important in a social context; they took over many of the traditional functions of the aristocrats and became the founts of generally accepted social codes and philosophies.

The middle class of early industrialism is separable into two main subgroups, the upper and the lower middle classes. The upper middle class possessed large amounts of capital; these were the bankers, the successful merchants, and the owners of large industrial plants. This small group acted as a part of the ruling upper class, and where there were still viable aristocracies, the upper middle class often bought estates and sometimes titles in order to join the traditional elite. The lower middle class was a larger but less prosperous group made up of the owners of modest businesses and industrial concerns, the suppliers of goods and services, retailers, and, at its lower levels, artisans who had recently become owners of small business and manufacturing ventures. As industry prospered and urban areas grew, the increased demand for a wide variety of goods and services greatly enlarged the size of this group. In spite of expansion, people in the lower middle class tended to feel insecure in their positions in the social hierarchy. The upper middle class ignored or patronized them, and as the nineteenth century progressed, they were increasingly under pressure from the ambitious workers below them, especially after real wages began to rise. In the latter part of the nineteenth century, they also had to struggle to preserve their distinct status in the face of the growth of a new middle class made up of managers, administrators, and other white-collar workers. The majority of people in the lower middle class were thus confronted with an increasing number of challenges to their status.

On the basis of its traditional values, the middle class felt some contempt for aristocrats, whom many considered to be sinfully idle and dissipated, and for the working classes, whom they felt to be shiftless and improvident. Its members, however, retained their desire to have their own considerable merits recognized by all other groups in society. Above all, they strove constantly for that elusive social distinction of being thought respectable. Respectability basically involved strict adherence to the Protestant ethic, but it also meant the emulation of the ways of life of envied people in higher social positions and the public display of prosperity and economic success.

The progressive, innovative, dynamic character of the original middle class began to disintegrate as it grew in size and influence and as urban dwellers ceased to be a minority of the population. After the middle class had achieved a powerful position in the economic system and in society as a whole, it was in its interest to consolidate its gains and preserve the new status quo. Thus, ossification tended to set in, and the middle classes became increasingly conservative. Solid prosperity became "respectability" and socioreligious virtues became "morality." Their growing tendency to judge everything from a "moral" standpoint affected many spheres of life from politics to personal relationships and art. Shakespeare was bowdlerized to make his works acceptable to respectable families, and stories and poems with moral messages were much in demand for Sunday reading. Artists painted romantic, "inspiring" scenes of stags at bay in misty mountains and faithful dogs mourning beside the coffins of their masters.

The equation of poverty with lack of moral worth colored attitudes toward the poor, who were primarily the unskilled, the unfortunate, the young, the old, and the sick. To a social group believing that hard work always brought success, that thrift led to wealth, and that virtue made one respectable, poverty was proof of moral as well as economic failure. The poor were subjected to a heterogeneous mixture of the kindly humanitarianism approved by middle-class religion and of the moral reprobation dictated by the middle-class ethic. Because poverty was equated with a lack of personal worth and perhaps even divine displeasure, its preventable causes were long ignored and untreated. As a result, the middle class of early industrial society bequeathed to its modern descendants many problems that have become more difficult to solve as time has passed. One of the greatest of these has been the moral stigma so firmly attached to poverty.

The requirements of the code of respectability were often difficult to reconcile with the practical realities of middle-class life. For example, the pressures of the free economy on industrialists and businessmen forced them into cutthroat competition that was often at odds with behavior required by respectability and humanitarianism. The conflict between social codes and economic realities proved almost impossible to resolve, and a popular way of dealing with it was to pretend, consciously or subconsciously, that the conflict did not exist. The omission of human sexuality from the code of respectability produced another source of irreconcilable conflict. The rampant prudery in Western society resulted in many incredible absurdities. For many decades, people requested the "limbs" of chicken at meals and covered furniture legs with cloth wrappers lest the sight inflame lascivious thoughts in the beholder. Prudery also led to less risible social phenomena. This great age of respectability, when gentlemen did not press their attentions on their wives more often than was necessary to ensure an acceptable number of children, was also a great age of prostitution; since bearing or rearing an illegitimate child was an unpardonable sin, infants abandoned on the doorsteps of charitable institutions were commonplace.

This ethical code also stressed domestic comfort and, hence, material possessions. Initially, the demand for more and better goods and services was a dynamic force and stimulated industrial production, but it later tended to become counter-productive in qualitative terms. Invention and increased production ensured that the number and variety of objects offered to satisfy middle-class acquisitiveness would continue to grow, but neither could guarantee that what was produced was useful or beautiful. A burgeoning uncritical materialism operated in most middle-class homes. Decoration of all kinds flourished for the sake of decoration: wax flowers and fruit in glass domes, stuffed birds, pianos, velvet footstools, and other items that were rarely, if ever, used. Merchant princes in earlier ages had been patrons of the arts, advocates of comfort, and disciples of elegance and good taste; the industrial middle classes became the patrons of machine-made clutter and the advocates of the modern urban industrial philosophy of material acquisition for the sake of social standing.

Adjustments to the Urban Industrial System

The impression that the early industrial city was essentially middle class is to some extent inevitable because it controlled urban institutions, set standards of taste and opinion, put the wheels of change and reform in motion, and generally appeared to dominate. Although the more highly visible, articulate, and influential middle classes were a vital part of urban society and exercised an influence out of proportion to their numbers, their importance should not obscure completely the changes that were taking place at the lower levels of society. Although it is virtually impossible to obtain precise population statistics by class, it is reasonable to assume that by the end of the nineteenth century roughly between 70 and 80 percent of the population of urban areas were working-class people. The rest were middle-class people of various types and a few aristocrats. The values, way of life, and changes that took place among this majority of urban people were not necessarily the same as those among the middle classes, although middle-class trend setting did have a considerable impact upon them.

The lower classes of early industrial society are extremely difficult to describe because they incorporated a wide variety of people, from the prosperous, nearly middle-class artisans at the top to the homeless, the unemployed, the drunks, the thieves, and the derelicts at the bottom. The middle and upper levels included mainly people in specialized occupations created by the increasing complexity of industry and urban services. Unskilled workers and those subsisting on crime or charity comprised the lower levels. One of the most important facts of lower-class life was unfamiliarity with the urban environment. In the 1850s, less than half the people living in London and Paris had been born there, and in American cities the proportion of native-born residents was even smaller. Until the end of the century, the majority of urban workers everywhere were immigrants, people who had to adjust to alien environments and overcome initial feelings of disorientation. To add to these difficulties, lower-class people, although they shared essentially the same economic and social status, differed from each other in accent or language, in traditions and customs, and in values.

Many new urban residents clung to their old ways as long as possible and sought the company of others who did the same. This perhaps gave some of them a sense of stability and identity, but it also helped create ghettos in rapidly developing urban areas. Once established, these tended to be self-perpetuating because new immigrants were attracted to them. Eventually sections of many major cities came to be identified with a particular group: Irish, Jews, Negroes, Poles, Italians, Chinese. This phenomenon was common in the New World, where cities collected a more diverse group of immigrants, on the whole, than did the cities of the Old World. Even in Europe, however, this semivoluntary segregation produced special ethnic sections in most major cities. Many of the old customs preserved in these enclaves, such as regional versions of religious services and farming-village attitudes toward family authority, were irrelevant in an urban context. While their perpetuation was of little practical benefit, the careful preservation of old traditions, even if they were incongruous, seemed to many people to be preferable to the alternative of launching out into a strange, new urban world in which it was easy to lose both community contacts and personal identity.

Other people, of course, turned their backs on everything they had known in the past. They shunned the ghettos and simply joined the formless urban mass. They muddled along on a day-to-day basis as best they could, trying to get along with, or at least achieve a kind of watchful truce with, neighbors whose language or accent sounded strange and whose ways of life were unlike their own. For the most part, these people simply survived and endured, but in spite of the fact that they championed no revolutionary social causes they were instrumental in building a social framework appropriate to the new urban setting. The modern mass urban life-style, which is still in the process of evolution, had its earliest beginnings in those incoherent fumblings toward adjustment to the anonymous urban environment made in the early industrial city. In moving to cities, people lost contact with brothers and sisters, cousins, uncles, and aunts who remained behind or moved to other places. People found that distance, lack of communication, and the lack of common interests diluted their sense of kinship with more remote blood relatives. In an agrarian setting, having an extended family nearby was useful at harvest time, at barn raisings, and on other occasions, but when survival came to depend on individual paychecks rather than on group effort, distant relatives became irrelevant and easily forgotten. Thus, the "family" came to mean simply parents and children; the limitations of urban housing reinforced this new definition. Even grandparents in the immediate vicinity, once they ceased to work, became valueless appendages and were often burdensome family responsibilities.

The church, which had begun to lose its power in the early modern period, now lost even more of its influence over society as hordes of people flooded the cities. Many of the new industrial towns sprang up in places where there had previously been no communities and no churches. In these places the church was usually a late addition to the urban community, not the natural center of a settlement that had grown with it or an institution that had developed a community around itself. Wealthy residents who found churchgoing a pleasant and respectable social occasion financed many new urban churches, but these often proved to be places in which the poor felt uncomfortable or unwelcome and tended to discourage a socially mixed congregation. Many churchmen organized missionary expeditions into the poor districts, and some did manage to build churches there, but few met with much long-term success. Religious groups that did succeed in poor areas, like the Salvation Army, tended to be new organizations whose composition, objectives, and methods took into consideration critical urban problems like poverty, hunger, and drunkenness, and offered some programs for dealing with these conditions. The majority of people experienced practical pressures that discouraged traditional patterns of churchgoing. For most, Sunday was their only day of leisure, and many people found other activities more diverting and pleasant than attending church. The larger the cities became, the more diversions they offered; drinking houses and cheap theaters abounded. Later in the century the modestly prosperous could take cheap railway excursions to the country or picnic in parks. People without the money for commercial amusements or collection boxes simply hung around staring into shop windows or watching activity on docks, building sites, and streets.

The impact of urban expansion on religion is difficult to assess because religious feeling is personal, impossible to define, and hard to measure. It is difficult even to determine its impact on church attendance because people in congregations were rarely counted with any precision over a wide area. Some indication of the effects of urban growth on church attendance can be given for 1851, when England conducted a "religious census." This showed that on a national average about 15 percent of the general population attended church, but while 20 to 25 percent of the people in rural areas attended, only 2 to 10 percent of the population of urban areas did so. In other nations, especially those with large Catholic populations, patterns of churchgoing were different, but the discrepancy between English rural and urban attendance rates suggests that there was a strong negative correlation between urban growth and church attendance.

As traditional social relationships began to dissolve and long-established community institutions lost their influence, tentative new relationships and institutions began to form. Many urban people, having lost all of their village and much of their family systems of identification, began to identify with their neighborhoods and to build their social lives around them simply because these were the areas and the people that they knew best. Initially, few people deliberately chose to live in a particular urban district. They settled near people they knew, in houses close to their work, near people who spoke their language, or in places they could afford. Once settled, however, the immigrants' leisure activities were conducted in the local streets and drinking shops; they made friends among the people who lived nearby; they bought from, and were often in debt to, local merchants. Much as the medieval townsman had identified with his town, the industrial townsman identified with his neighborhood within the much larger urban settlement. Because the rich and the poor tended to live in fairly widely separated parts of the urban area, the rich in the pleasant parts and the poor in the unpleasant, location also eventually became an indication of social and economic status as well as ethnic background. Some neighborhoods became so strongly identified with particular groups of people that by the mid-twentieth century, a reasonable guess about a person's economic standing, skin color, occupation, housing, and political convictions could be made on the basis of knowing where he lived.

Later in the nineteenth century, people also began to identify with fellow workers in similar jobs because they experienced similar working conditions and economic problems. Miners felt they had things in common with other miners, steelworkers with other steelworkers, toolmakers with other toolmakers, and so on. Initially, this kinship was felt among workers in the same establishment, but it later expanded to include all workers in particular occupations within a nation. This was a powerful force in the growth of national trade union organizations. Once these were established, affiliations based on occupation tended to cut across those established on neighborhood lines because people who worked together often lived in different neighborhoods. As urban transportation improved in the late nineteenth and early twentieth centuries, the two systems tended to be divisive rather than complementary. This diffusion of community feelings contributed to the lack of cohesiveness in urban life and to the fading of the sense of community that had been apparent when urban settlements were smaller and fellow workers were also generally neighbors.

THE
MODERN 6 Founda-
CITY tions and
Forms

In the late nineteenth and early twentieth centuries a tremendous explosion of city building took place in all parts of the industrialized Western world as cities became the dwelling places of the majority of the people. The modern city was an outgrowth of the first industrial city, and essentially the same forces that promoted the growth of great industrial urban centers sustained its expansion: technical advance, population growth, transportation improvements, and increased food surpluses. Nevertheless, the new urban complexes differed in many ways from nineteenth-century cities. At the turn of the century, a new industrial and economic system began to evolve, one that was to dominate the twentieth century. Its characteristics were the use of electricity as a domestic, commercial, and industrial power source; the rapid introduction of new powered machines for all kinds of purposes; the development and expanding production of synthetics, including drugs, plastics, insecticides, rubber, and fabrics; the use of petroleum products as fuels, especially in transport; and the enormous increase in general production. Parts of the Western world that had not led in the first stages of industrialization adopted the new industrial system most rapidly. In general, areas that had previously industrialized successfully had much invested in proven methods of production; they resisted change and were reluctant to experiment with new techniques and machines. Industrial leadership, and the urban dynamism that accompanied it, slipped away from Europe to the United States, a large nation with enormous natural resources. The transition took many years to accomplish, and for several decades the old and the new systems operated side by side. By the 1920s, however, the years of British and European leadership were clearly over and the United States led the Western world in industrialization and set the new patterns of urban development.

Since the conditions that had produced the first industrial city had initially developed in Britain, this early stage of industrialism spawned cities around the world that bore a marked resemblance to British towns and cities. In the late nineteenth and early twentieth centuries, especially after the First World War, the United States took over leadership in industry and technology and began to develop the sophisticated form of industrialism that would give rise to the modern city. As American equipment and techniques spread around the Western world, towns and cities everywhere began to exhibit American characteristics, life-styles, social forms, and problems. As far as city form was concerned, the nineteenth century had been the British century; similarly, the twentieth century would be the American century.

New economic and technical developments did not transform established urban centers completely. As in the past, they retained many of their old characteristics and configurations, but added new developments characteristic of the new city form. In addition, the new city-shaping forces modified existing urban patterns in many places; established urban centers added new elements to their already complex patterns that included sections remaining from several earlier types of city development. Paris, London, and Boston added freeways; Berlin, Marseilles, and Manchester added high-rise buildings; Birmingham, Brussels, and New York added great spreading skirts of suburbs around their existing built-up areas. Cities and towns everywhere experienced traffic and parking problems, and many began to wither at the center as contemporary life-sustaining forces dispersed throughout the suburbs.

The new urban patterns were most clearly visible and least influenced by prior developments in the cities of the American West that matured after the new city-shaping forces began to operate. Denver, Phoenix, Albuquerque, and Las Vegas, which became settlements of note only in the twentieth century, provide examples of the modern city in its virtually undiluted form. One of the purest examples of the type, certainly the most widely known, is Los Angeles, where modern industrialism mated with the automobile in virgin territory and spawned the great diffused "car city," the city of the twentieth century.

City-shaping Forces

Technological development and the production of better, more efficient tools are not exclusive to the twentieth century. What distinguishes the present century and has earned it the title of "the age of technology" is the enormous and unprecedentedly rapid increase in the number, kind, range, and effects of technological innovations. The steady pace of one or two changes over several generations had been broken when the inventions of the eighteenth century began to generate new kinds of production and new ways of life, but even the rapid pace of the late eighteenth and nineteenth centuries now seems stately compared with the mad gallop at which innovations have been developed and introduced since the end of the nineteenth century. For example, some people who were young when airplanes were clumsy fantasies in wood, wire, and fabric were still alive to watch supersonic jets and the first moon walks. Within one lifetime, atomic physics was transformed from theory into bombs and power stations; experimental crystal radio receivers blossomed rapidly into cheap, pocket-sized transistor sets. Television went from the laboratory to the living room in a generation. Great strides in the development and application of scientific and technical discoveries of all kinds characterized the twentieth century.

By the mid-nineteenth century people realized that the lack of precise construction in such things as steam engines reduced their efficiency. In addition, the demand for machines and replacement parts provided ample incentive to produce machinery more efficiently, and in the 1850s and 1860s the first machine tools were developed. Standardized measuring gauges that could produce finer tolerances, screw-threading machines, metal-slotting, cutting, and punching machines, and mechanized lathes for turning metal parts were put into operation. These machines that made parts for other machines made possible interchangeable, standardized components and rationalized the whole process of machine making. Standardization also enabled machine owners to order replacement parts from warehouse stockpiles, which reduced the number of production delays and work stoppages. In the twentieth century, machine tools became more sophisticated, and consequently more sophisticated machines could be built to do more with a minimum of supervision or repair.

Many of the technical advances made in the twentieth century were based on the availability of abundant, cheap electrical power, and the electrical generator became a cornerstone of industry and urban life. Electricity, a quasi-scientific plaything in the eighteenth century and a power source for communications in the nineteenth century, became a necessity of life in the twentieth century. It was an indispensable source of power for city lighting and traffic control, for domestic and commercial lighting, heating, and cooling, for running laboratories and hospitals, for public transport services, private cars, and space vehicles. Its ready availability in all urban areas supported the development of vast industries producing all manner of consumer goods from light bulbs to hair dryers and ovens. The modern age of high mobility is also a plug-in age in which many personal activities, from watching entertainment to brushing one's teeth, are restricted by the length of the electrical cord running to an appliance. Massive blackouts like the one in New York in 1965 have clearly demonstrated the almost total dependence of urban society on electricity. Suddenly deprived of electrical power, the city fell dark and silent and people were marooned in high-rise offices and apartment buildings. Others were imprisoned in elevators, and eight hundred thousand were trapped in subways. Millions were lost, frightened, thirsty, and eventually bored. The effects of the loss of electricity did not end when power was restored; they resurfaced nine months later in the form of a marked increase in births.

The machine that became as symbolic of this phase of industrialism as the steam engine had been of the first phase was the internal combustion engine. Work on this device began in the 1860s and 1870s in Austria, Germany, and Italy, and the first major landmark was passed in 1885 when Gottlieb Daimler patented his engine and carburetor. This achievement inspired men like Benz in Germany, Peugeot in France, Rolls and Royce in England, and the Dodge brothers in America to experiment with engines of their own. The invention of the oil-injection engine by Rudolf Diesel in 1893 laid the foundation for the development of twentieth-century heavy road transport. Production followed rapidly on the heels of invention, and by 1914 there were about two million cars, some of which could reach speeds of fifty miles per hour; motor omnibuses first appeared in London in 1904, and by 1916 they had completely supplanted horse-drawn buses. From the second decade of the twentieth century, cars, buses, trucks, and land vehicles of all kinds that used the internal combustion engine multiplied rapidly, boosting the development of a wide range of subsidiary industries. The oil industry, which had supplied paraffin and kerosene for lamps since the 1860s, boomed from a minor industry into a giant. Similar car-related growth took place in industries that produced steel, glass, plastics, electrical equipment, and machine tools. The multiplication of the number of rapidly moving vehicles made it imperative that the problems of mud and dust associated with traditional earth roads be solved, and so all industrial processes associated with the laying of hard-surfaced roads also boomed.

Using the internal combustion engine, Zeppelin built the first controllable airship in 1900. Because it was a vast improvement over balloons, which could not be steered with any accuracy, the dirigible enjoyed some initial success, although the highly flammable contents of the gas bag made it an extremely dangerous and eventually unpopular form of transport. In 1903 the Wright brothers made the first powered, sustained aircraft flight without using lighter-than-air gases, and the airplane was born. The First World War hastened its development, and by the 1920s enough planes were in use that major urban communities were building airports. In the 1940s the Dutch airline, KLM, introduced regular Europe-to-New York flights, and Pan Am began round-the-world flights. Although high fares kept the plane from becoming a common means of public transport until the 1950s, the rate of its development from private experiment to public carrier had been rapid.

Although many inventors were Europeans and some industrial applications of the new machines were devised in Europe, Americans did almost all the important commercial development, taking both domestic and foreign inventions and quickly turning them into profitable commercial and consumer goods. Typewriters became available in the 1870s; cash registers, calculators, and tabulating machines were later introduced. American business became the most highly mechanized in the world, especially after the introduction of the first modern computer by IBM in 1943. The United States was also the first nation to develop and apply new production techniques that stemmed logically from the use of more sophisticated machines. The first time-and-motion studies and the first theoretical works on assembly-line production and modern management began to appear in the U.S. in the last years of the nineteenth century.

In addition to the opportunity to exercise "Yankee ingenuity," the United States had powerful incentives to move rapidly into the new phase of industrialism. Its industrial base was not fully developed in the later nineteenth century as were those of Britain and other European countries, and it was therefore more flexible and receptive to innovation. The nation had vast resources, but compared with Europe only a small population and few skilled workers. Sophisticated machines enabled scarce labor resources to be utilized to their utmost and allowed unskilled and semiskilled laborers to become efficient operatives in a short time. Meanwhile, a variety of efficient, high-capacity machines allowed single farming families to cultivate farmlands that would have kept whole villages occupied in the Old World. The great size of the country gave its people the incentive to develop transport and communications that would effectively reduce distances, and new devices like the telephone and the automobile were vitally important to the formation of a cohesive national unit.

European nations did adopt the new machines and techniques in time, but on the whole they were slow to accept new procedures. There was no general shortage of labor to speed the development of labor-saving techniques, and by the time their development had gained momentum in the early twentieth century many European nations had highly structured industries and well-entrenched unions that made both industries and workers resist change. Manufacturers whose firms had been successful for over half a century were understandably reluctant to alter the machines and procedures that had made fortunes for their fathers and grandfathers. In addition to their conservatism, European nations were constrained by their comparatively small size and limited resources. Furthermore, the two world wars fought on European soil proved to be enormously exhausting and disruptive. Western Europe, which had led the Western world for centuries in creative and innovative activities, lost its economic, political, urban, and to some extent its cultural dominance in the twentieth century as the United States forged ahead. The New World superseded the Old, and the features that would characterize the new industrial system—assembly lines, mass consumption, mass communications, and automobiles—superseded the characteristics of the older system: the ironworks, the steam-powered factory, and the railway engine.

Just as the characteristic features and products of early industrialism had shaped the form of the new city, so those of modern industry molded the modern city. There was no clear-cut point at which early industrialism ceased and modern industry began; indeed, even now there is a great deal of intermingling and overlapping. Nevertheless, modern industry is so different in character and quality from the industry of the nineteenth century that it must be treated as a different developmental stage. The distinctive primary product of early industrialism was the massive machine with relatively few parts that required the accumulation of large quantities of raw materials and fuel by considerable amounts of labor, both skilled and unskilled. Manufacturers expected a high profit return on each item produced. The number of consumers who needed and could afford massive items like railway engines and ships was limited, and hence their market was restricted. A few of the products of this early stage of industrialism, such as cheap cotton cloth, were designed for a mass market, but such products were limited in number and few manufacturers aimed at a modern-scale mass market. Standardization and technological sophistication in modern industry made it possible to produce a wider variety of smaller items. Carpet sweepers, telephones, and washing machines were introduced in the 1870s; vacuum cleaners, phonographs, and electric fans appeared in the 1890s; refrigerators were available for domestic use in the 1900s. These machine-made machines for domestic and personal use opened up a potentially huge new market to replace the relatively restricted old one. The new economy featured the production of small items with many small parts. Each product yielded a relatively small profit but was produced in huge numbers. Cars, radio and TV sets, can openers, telephones, refrigerators, electric razors, and light fixtures were designed and produced not for purchase by a few large firms and wealthy individuals, but by the mass of the people.

Even before the turn of the century, mechanical improvements had increased the productivity of individual workers. In the 1840s a textile worker had been able to turn out nine thousand yards of cotton in a thirteen-hour day, but by the 1880s a worker in a modern mill could turn out three hundred thousand yards in a ten-hour day. At the beginning of the twentieth century Henry Ford vividly demonstrated the productive potential of the new industrial system. In 1907 his moving assembly line for building Model Ts cut assembly time per car from fourteen hours to ninety-three minutes and increased productivity per worker enormously. Similar increases took place in other industries as the twentieth century advanced. The new industrial system increased not only production per worker, but also the number of items produced.

The higher degree of efficiency and greater industrial production eventually resulted in increasing wages, which in general rose about 70 to 90 percent between the 1860s and the 1930s. Higher wages meant that more workers had money left over after paying for adequate food, shelter, and clothing. The rate and time of these wage increases varied from country to country and industry to industry, but by the first decade of the twentieth century they were high enough almost everywhere to allow some workers to become effective consumers. At first, they spent their higher wages on larger amounts of food, especially sugar, and on food luxuries like tea, beer, wine, and canned goods. As more industries turned to assembly-line methods of mass production and joined the new industrial system, productivity per worker increased further, and in the first few decades of the twentieth century real wages increased enough to allow workers to buy small household goods and to save for luxury items like vacuum cleaners and inexpensive cars.

Increased productivity meant that manufacturers faced a new kind of question: how to market the greater volume of goods produced. In order to sell more units, the market had to expand, so production costs and profit margins were reduced to lower the price per unit, and advertising was developed to generate a demand for the products. On the one hand, the new industrial system enabled the workers and producers to become consumers by raising average real wages; on the other hand, the survival of the new industrial system required that they become consumers and absorb the greater number of goods they turned out. Mass production for a mass market, probably more than any other single characteristic, along with high mass living standards distinguishes the modern from the early industrial phase of development in the West.

As time passed and more people satisfied their basic needs, continued economic growth came to be based to an ever-increasing extent on the generation of new consumer demands. People had to begin to "need" goods they had not thought of buying before, and demands had to be generated for products that were not new but merely "different." New cars, for example, generally provided essentially the same transportation as old ones, but redesigned taillights and grills and electrically operated windows and other gadgets satisfied consumer expectation of something new or different. If no new consumer needs appeared, industry would only have supplied replacements and filled the needs generated by population expansion. While this might have produced a reduction in price, the profit per unit made by manufacturers and distributors on mass-produced items was already fairly small and could not have fallen much further without putting manufacturers out of business. A reduction in demand would have meant a cutback in production, falling wages, and unemployment. To prevent economic depression and to allow the new industrial system to grow, production had to continue at high levels. If demand did not meet production of its own volition, it had to be artificially stimulated. Thus advertising, consciously and deliberately persuading people to consume, soon became an essential part of the new economy and a major industry in its own right.

Advertising in the early industrial period was simple, direct, and unsophisticated, simply naming what goods were available and who made them. It was not much different from the advertising of the medieval craftsman who hung a picture of a boot outside his door to show what he made. Later, a list of the virtues of the goods was added to a simple announcement. The technologically advanced phase of industry produced much more sophisticated advertising. New media such as films, radio, and television, themselves products of the new industrial system, were capable of bringing advertising more effectively to more people in more places than newspapers and billboards. In addition, industry produced a wider variety of products to sell and developed more minor variations on basic items. Faced with the necessity of creating a demand for their products, manufacturers began to hire consultants who specialized in persuading people to buy items of peripheral need. Advertisers used all kinds of techniques to inform, amuse, and interest people, but the most effective methods developed were based on the recognition, orchestration, and exploitation of human insecurities and weaknesses. Automobiles became symbols of virility and social status; by implication, anyone who did not own a car with the latest grill or body design and paint colors was an inferior human being of shrinking social status. Similarly, advertisers implied that anyone who did not use their deodorants and mouthwashes would become a social pariah, and that any housewife who did not fling herself into paroxysms of delight about the newest floor wax or dish soap was falling down on her job and likely to become the laughingstock of the neighborhood. Eventually, similar techniques of mass persuasion came to be used in manipulating public opinion in politics and related areas.

The higher living standards, greater mobility, and high consumption of natural resources characteristic of the modern economy were obvious everywhere in the industrialized West by the middle years of the twentieth century. Indeed, by the 1960s the rate at which natural resources were being depleted was giving rise to growing concern. The United States used more fuel and metal between the Second World War and the late 1960s than in the whole of its history before 1941. Virtually every successful daily newspaper in large urban centers consumed about a twenty-thousand-acre forest each year in paper pulp. Before the First World War, water consumption was the equivalent of two and one-half gallons per day for every person on earth; in the late 1960s it had risen to the equivalent of one hundred gallons per person per day. All the features of the new industrialism were crystallized in its city form. In car city,

Valley Stream, Long Island (1933 and 1959) Two of the major characteristics of modern suburban sprawl are the extent and speed of its growth. In the last quarter-century great expanses of productive farmland have been completely swallowed up by tract houses and multilane highways.

Courtesy of the Long Island State Park and Recreation Commission

Freeway interchange, Los Angeles The personal mobility afforded by the mass-produced automobile has been a major force shaping the modern city form. Highways consume great amounts of land on their own account and dominate the urban landscape.

Transportation/Technology Department,
Los Angeles Area Chamber of Commerce

Manhattan skyline The verticality evident in this aerial view of New York City is typical of the modern trend of growth in the centers of old, established cities. The great buildings that dominate the skyline are the creations of the large corporations spawned by the modern industrial economy.

New York State Department of Commerce

Rockefeller Center, New York The skyscrapers that create an impressive skyline completely dwarf human activity within the city. People resemble ants scurrying about at the bottom of enormous steel, concrete, and glass canyons whose tops are entirely beyond the framework of normal human activity.

Courtesy of Rockefeller Center, Inc.

Crawley New Town, England The "new towns" were created to take the pressure of population off London. In some cases, such as Crawley, they have tended to take the form of a cell of typical modern suburban development incongruously transplanted into the countryside.   Commission for the New Towns

Reston, Virginia Reston was built by a subsidiary of a large oil corporation. Clearly, it is not simply a detached cell of suburb but rather an attempt to create a new urban environment. Such experiments are valuable, but they are also expensive, and they generally require special conditions unavailable near ordinary cities.   Courtesy of Gulf Reston, Inc.

Modern shopping center Typical suburban shopping centers are entirely dominated by the car. Note the enormous spaces devoted to parking and to
surrounding roads. Such "holes" are characteristic of the fabric of the modern
city.   Gulfgate Shopping Center, Houston, Texas

Neuhauser Strasse, Bonn, Germany This shopping/pedestrian area attempts to
deny the car completely and to integrate parts of the old city into the modern
one. In order for this type of redevelopment to work, convenient, inexpensive
public transportation must be readily available to large numbers of people.
                                                              German Information Center

consumer city, the minimally consuming, non–car-owning, poor residents would find themselves as cut off from the mainstream of society as lepers had been in the Middle Ages.

Two of the major forces that made possible the development of the early industrial city, agricultural improvement and increasing transport efficiency, continued to be of great importance to the modern city. Although the drift from the land continued in the twentieth century and the rural population shrank, improved agricultural techniques enabled the remaining farmers to produce the expanding surplus of food demanded by the growing cities. Much of the increased food surplus was the result of the application to farming of the products and techniques of the city and its industries. Farmers used larger and more efficient machines, which compensated for the declining agricultural labor force. Chemicals reduced plant and animal diseases and controlled pests, and chemical fertilizers produced higher yields per acre. Advanced scientific techniques led to new and more productive strains of plants and animals. Motor vehicles, planes, and helicopters enabled farmers and ranchers to care for huge areas of land more efficiently with relatively little labor. The techniques of mass production and the assembly line were applied to the harvesting, processing, and packaging of agricultural products, and "battery farming" increased the production of animal products like eggs, milk, veal, and poultry.

The use of chemicals in both animal and vegetable products and the quality and taste of the more efficiently produced food came under scrutiny, and many people began to buy more expensive foods produced without modern industrial and chemical aids. This counter-trend was one of the manifestations of the growing mid-twentieth-century disenchantment with the values of the new industrial urban society, but by this time there was little hope that a movement back to "natural" food production could be successful as long as population remained at current levels and high levels of consumption were sustained.

Although personal transportation received more glamorous treatment, bulk transport was still of vital importance to the industrial system and to the cities, for it carried the food and supplies on which their existence depended. Electric and diesel trains and ships powered by diesel engines improved bulk transport, but the most significant new development was in road transport. Heavy motor vehicles and the large, wide paved highways that could accommodate them were responsible for moving a large proportion of the products of the cities. Trucking was also

instrumental in expanding the consumer market because trucks could take
goods to even the most remote regions.

Major advances in communications systems stimulated city sprawl
by making distances irrelevant in many human and economic functions.
Modern postal services, begun in Britain in the mid-nineteenth century,
were quickly accepted as essential, and the rapid increase in the use of the
mail illustrates the dimensions of the demand for quick, cheap, personal
communications over long distances. The U.S. Post Office sold one and a
half million stamps in 1850, four billion in 1900, and twenty-four billion
in 1960. Improved telephone services and the mass production of
equipment that made telephones cheaper brought them within range of
the mass market. Both business firms and individuals could make
long-distance regional, national, and even international calls quickly and
easily, while local calls in the most affluent parts of the West became as
much a commonplace of life as exchanging greetings with family
members across the breakfast table. By the end of the first decade of the
twentieth century, there were about twelve million telephones; fifty years
later, the number had increased to over one hundred seventy million, over
half of which were in the United States. The tremendous increase in the
number and availability of telephones made expanding urban distances
inconsequential.

From Marconi's transmission of the first radio signal in 1894 and the
first transatlantic message in 1901, the development of radio into a mass
communications medium accelerated tremendously. By the middle of the
twentieth century, few Western urban households were without at least
one receiver. Television developed even more rapidly: the first commercial program was broadcast in the late 1930s, and a little over two decades
later over 80 percent of American and a not much smaller percentage of
all Western households had a TV set. Radio and television services,
which also nullified distances, aided in the diffusion of urban values
throughout nations and across the world. Mass entertainment, their staple
commodity, was an urban phenomenon. Advertisers, who were responsible for much radio and television programming, concentrated on
appealing to areas with a high population density, the urban areas. They
tailored their presentations for the tastes and interests of an urban
audience and broadcast programs on a timetable determined by the
working hours of the average city dweller. People in rural areas also
received radio and television programs but as a result of the nature of mass
entertainment and the influence of advertisers, the messages they received

were urban ones. The mass media transmitted the general idea that cities were the most important and interesting sections of the nation and that big cities were the most important of all. This gave an additional boost to the long-existing drift of people from the country to the cities.

Population increase, which had been closely associated with industrial expansion since the late eighteenth century, continued. Once the problems associated with the breakdown of life support systems in the early industrial cities had been solved, life in the city was no more deadly than life in the country. As advances were made in medicine, cities gradually gained an advantage over the countryside in some respects, since medical care was more readily available. Inoculation and asepsis techniques were introduced, and regulations requiring their practice appeared in many nations, including Britain where the death rate fell from about 22 per thousand in the 1840s to about 15 per thousand by the end of the nineteenth century. Similar improvements in health were visible everywhere in the industrialized West by the turn of the century. The number of deaths from tuberculosis, malaria, pellagra, and similar diseases declined. The introduction of sulfa drugs in 1935 and of antibiotics in the 1940s reduced the dangers of infection drastically, while improved surgical techniques prolonged life and made conditions such as appendicitis, which had generally been fatal in the past, little more than inconveniences. Meanwhile, better cleaning, paving, and waste disposal services in cities combined with the greater availability of running water, baths, and cheap soap to make it easier for ordinary people to keep themselves cleaner and healthier. As a result, the weak and the very young or very old no longer fell prey to the first epidemic that came along and life expectancy increased to sixty or seventy years.

The endemic diseases of the early industrial city—cholera, typhoid, and smallpox—ceased to act as major agents of population control. Modern immunology checked diseases that threatened to replace them in the modern city before they reached their full potential. The number of poliomyelitis cases rose in the 1930s and 1940s and began to pose a serious danger to certain segments of the population. It hit young adults and children hardest and therefore would, in epidemic proportions, have had a great potential as a population regulator. The deaths and disabilities it caused, however, produced widespread alarm and a demand for a cure. The Salk and Sabin vaccines, developed in the 1950s, all but eliminated polio as a threat to life in the West before the disease could achieve epidemic proportions.

Infant and maternal deaths, which were extremely high in the early industrial cities, were important population controls because, like polio, they involved the most fertile and potentially fertile segments of the population. Improvements in pre- and postnatal care, midwifery, and the treatment of childhood diseases such as measles and "toothache," which had been major killers in the nineteenth century, reduced death rates dramatically. Infant mortality, which had been 142 per thousand at the beginning of the twentieth century in Britain, was 31 per thousand only fifty years later, and in some places it was even lower, as in Sweden at 21 per thousand.

Most of the forces that have operated to prolong life in the twentieth century have been most effective in urban areas. While rural people are finding it increasingly difficult to persuade a doctor to live in their communities and to fund hospitals and sophisticated treatment centers, doctors are relatively abundant in large cities where more money is available to finance well-equipped hospitals, emergency services, medical schools, and research centers. Many of the new tools of medicine are expensive, and in order to be efficient they must be available to large numbers of people. A unit equipped to diagnose tuberculosis or to administer polio and other vaccines can process hundreds of people in a short time in a city while the same unit would be idle for long periods in rural areas.

Technological advances and the vast output of the economic system have enabled twentieth-century Western nations to supply nonindustrial nations with the means to increase food supply and the medical equipment and techniques with which to prolong life. DDT helped control pests that damaged crops and spread disease; vaccines introduced preventive medicine on a large scale; supplies of powdered protein, milk, and other foods helped relieve famines. Although Western financial, medical, and agricultural aid was minuscule by affluent Western standards, it had a tremendous impact on large numbers of non-Western people living on the margin of survival to whom a few cents' worth of vaccine or powdered milk made the difference between life and death. With the spread of Western medicine and technology in the twentieth century, the population of the "third world" soared, promising many unpleasant complications for future generations, for while many were given life, few were offered the hope of achieving an equal footing with the affluent West.

Other medical advances held out the possibility of stabilizing the population. The use of birth control by Western people has been most common among the people with the highest living standard, and as the living standards of the masses have gone up, family size has generally gone down. While birth control has had some impact on Western nations, birth rates have not yet reached long-term equilibrium with death rates; in the third world birth control has had little impact. Hence, although the rate of population increase in parts of the Western world has slowed down, population balance such as existed before the first "industrial revolution" is still distant. In most parts of the non-Western world, population increase continually threatens to outstrip the capacity of technological advance to stave off mass starvation.

Longer life expectancy has begun to change the nature of Western society. In preceding centuries when death rates were high, the feeble and old formed only a tiny proportion of the population. Twentieth-century medicine and technology changed this situation, and the feeble and old make up an increasingly large segment of the population, producing new social problems that may become critical if the trend continues. Demands will be made for better provisions for old people, including retirement plans and health schemes to give them an acceptable standard of living. As the proportion of the elderly increases there will be fewer workers, and they will be supporting more nonworkers. On the other hand, as resources become increasingly scarce, the productive elements in society may give the needs of nonproductive citizens very low priority indeed. As more sophisticated ways are devised of keeping people alive, children with heart, digestive, nervous, muscular, and blood defects, who would previously have died in infancy, will go on to become adults and have children of their own. However admirable the motives and ingenious the medical techniques, society faces the prospect of expending an increasing amount of its resources on endeavors that in the long run can only prove more and more expensive. The old, brutally high death rates ensured that, for the most part, only the strongest and most productive people would survive. This natural control is now seriously weakened, and it would seem that Western society is inadvertently beginning to breed a weaker and less productive population at an increasing cost in resources. As resources become scarce and the nonproductive section of the population grows, the pressure upon such important elements of Western society as humanitarianism and the work ethic may well become severe.

Changes in City Form: The Expansion of Suburbia

The swollen sprawl of suburbia that characterizes twentieth-century urban development is the product of the ambivalent relationship between modern man and his cities. Given the past history and current state of the technological urban economy, urban centers are a necessity in the modern world, for they are both workplace and marketplace for the majority of the population. Since the pace of industrial development quickened, more and more people have sought their living in the cities that industrialism created. Like the first immigrants into the early industrial cities, most of them have had little choice in the matter, for the alternatives of employment and unemployment leave no choice at all. From the earliest stages of development of the industrial city, however, those who could afford to do so attempted to compromise between their desire to live in pleasant surroundings and their need to live close to their urban jobs. Out of this compromise arose modern suburbia.

The early industrial city was an unpleasant living place; it was unsanitary, dirty, noisy, overcrowded, and crime rates were high even by twentieth-century standards. The mass of city dwellers might have preferred to live in a rural area or to make the rural-urban compromise in the suburbs, but they were financially unable to exercise much preference in the matter. The prosperous could afford to pay for the transport that enabled them to live almost in the country while going to work every day in the city, and those who could set their own working hours could also afford the time involved in long daily journeys. Moreover, the prosperous, educated, and socially ambitious segments of society were most affected by other considerations that encouraged the development of a prorural ethos among the nineteenth-century middle classes. Romantic writers who presented the city as a sink of vice and the country as the source of all virtues influenced them most. They were also aware of the fact that aristocrats and other leaders of society traditionally lived in country estates and kept only their "second house" in town. Since their social ambitions revolved around joining the top ranks of society, they strove to imitate the traditional leaders. The suburbs were, from the outset, the outgrowths of urban prosperity and social ambition.

The forms of transportation then available determined the patterns of early suburban growth. The rich who could afford horses and carriages could buy sizable parcels of inexpensive land alongside reasonably well-tended roads within driving range of the city where they could build large, comfortable homes. In the second half of the nineteenth century trams of various kinds were developed ranging from horse-drawn street railways to electric and motor-powered streetcars to such specially designed exotic forms as the cable cars of San Francisco. Tram and bus services that were within the price range of the modestly prosperous became more common in the latter decades of the century, their development coinciding with the period when real wages began to rise. They also enabled modestly prosperous people to emulate their economic and social superiors and move to the closer suburbs. Builders accommodated them with small, cheap, mass-produced houses on inexpensive land.

The railway, the great land carrier of early industrialism, played a considerable role in the development of the suburbs, especially around the major cities of Europe and along the eastern seaboard of North America. Railway companies found that many people were willing to pay for regular journeys between distant suburban homes and city workplaces and instituted special commuter services with frequent trains in the morning and early evening hours. Commuter services stimulated the growth of new communities around rural railway stations within acceptable traveling time of the city center. The railway station became the center of these communities, attracting shops and other service establishments to the nearby area. Since horses could not be parked outside the station and left there until evening, all but the wealthy who could afford coachmen to drive them to the station walked from their homes. This effectively concentrated community growth within walking distance of the station. Such railway communities provided their middle-class inhabitants with many of the things they were seeking. They were nucleated, semirural communities separated from the city and generally from each other by long stretches of countryside where trains did not stop. They grew up around the major urban centers like widely spaced beads on the strings of the railway lines leading to the city center.

Despite improvements in land transport, water transport remained of some importance and affected suburban growth in some places. Boats were often the easiest and cheapest form of transportation for people moving from riverside suburban communities to riverside city employment. Hence, services like the ferries of New York and the river buses of London played at least a small part in shaping the patterns of suburban growth.

Behind all suburban development lay the fact that in most parts of the Western world land prices and land taxes were lower outside the urban area. There people could buy more land for the same money and pay lower taxes than they would within the city limits. Speculative investors were able to build tracts of little suburban houses within the purchasing power of larger numbers of modestly prosperous people. This situation had always been possible, but before the development of cheap mass transport in the nineteenth century, few people could take advantage of it. In the twentieth century the mass-produced car would enhance the aesthetic and financial attractions of the suburbs and guarantee suburban sprawl.

The nature of early suburban transportation produced two basic forms of suburban development: the suburban community and the contiguous suburban area. Around their more distant commuter stations, the railways produced suburban communities, distinct, nucleated, clearly defined settlements that gathered around the station and its surrounding service establishments much as the medieval town had massed around the marketplace and the church. Contiguous suburban areas consisted of areas that were geographical extensions of urban centers and not separated from them by open stretches of rural land. Trams, buses, and urban railways created early suburban growth of this type, and the development of shopping centers and outlying business offices stimulated it. As more houses were built on what had been the fringes of the urban area, many small, independent communities were swallowed up and digested in the general metropolitan sprawl.

Although suburban development began to be a significant feature of urban configurations in the latter part of the nineteenth century, it did not present serious problems until the present century. In its early stages, the nature of the transport systems on which suburban growth depended imposed some restriction on urban sprawl. Railways could serve only a limited number of stations; otherwise the journey to work would take too long. Road passenger services, limited by frequent passenger stops and by the relatively slow speeds at which they could travel on public roads crowded with other vehicles, were only effective within relatively short distances from the city center. In addition, public transportation services were economically feasible only in densely populated areas that ensured an adequate supply of customers at each stopping place.

The transport machine of the new industrial system greatly expanded the growth potential of the suburban area. The automobile offered flexible, personal, high-speed transportation and added a new dimension to suburban prospects. By giving large numbers of people the opportunity to travel relatively long distances between home and work and to live "outside" the city, the automobile allowed masses of people to buy cheaper suburban building plots and to make their own compromise between the rural dreams of Thoreau and the urban necessities of IBM. The car, one of the major city-shaping forces of the twentieth century, is also the archetypal product of the current stage of mass-production industrialism, the creation of modern assembly-line methods of production; its production, care, and feeding require a complex economy and a sophisticated technology. The automobile consumes a vast variety and huge quantity of resources in an inefficient but convenient fashion. It produces considerable pollution in all stages of its manufacture and use. It is a product designed for consumption by the mass of the people, and its continued production and marketing is heavily dependent on mass advertising. In addition, its use by large numbers of people is common to all urbanized, industrialized parts of the world.

The car changed urban patterns by making private, as opposed to public, transportation available to large numbers of people. Indeed, the mass use of the automobile is such an important element in the making of the modern city form that it can be used as the distinction between the industrial and modern phases of development. Cities that have reasonably efficient and heavily used public transportation systems and relatively limited automobile use, such as Paris, London, and New York, are modified industrial cities. Cities in which public transportation facilities are meager and cars numerous are modern cities; the best examples are found in the western parts of North America: Los Angeles, Denver, Albuquerque, Phoenix. In the main, the two major characteristics of the car determine the characteristics of the modern city form: it is designed for individuals, and it has greater flexibility than public transportation systems.

Cities that developed in the early industrial phase collected at their centers many institutions that attracted people there: factories, docks, warehouses, offices, railway stations, shops, theaters, universities, libraries, and a whole host of other attractions. Initially, these "people magnets" collected in the center for convenience. As public transportation systems developed they focused on the center because that was where most people wanted to go. Later institutions located there in order to take advantage of the center-oriented public transportation systems and of the drawing power of other institutions already located there. Early industrial cities thus had well-defined centers around which the public transportation systems and the public life of the city revolved. The purest examples of the modern city, on the other hand, grew from relatively small settlements with few powerful central people magnets. In these developing cities where land was relatively cheap and where no city form existed to impose at least some predetermined patterns on general city development, the car had free rein to shape the form best suited to its own extensive use. Public road and railway transport systems evolved a spokes-and-wheel pattern with the central city as the hub, but the car could go anywhere there were roads. Once people could drive a few miles in their cars as easily as they could walk a few hundred yards, the people magnets no longer needed to be centralized. The car made it possible to drive comparatively great distances from home to work, from work to shopping centers, from shopping centers to restaurants, and from restaurants to theaters.

When people provided much of their own in-city transport by walking, cities were designed to some extent for human convenience; when people began to use cars for most of their in-city transportation, cities became convenient for cars. Because cars required more space than people, land values became a major consideration in the siting of people magnets. Land was generally cheaper on the outskirts of the built-up area than it was at the center, and as a result, the people magnets were decentralized and scattered around. The characteristically modern city lacks a high-density, multi-functional center and more closely resembles a vast contiguous suburban area than any previous city form. In its purest state, car city is a nonnucleated city, a city with no single, well-defined center.

Established cities with well-defined centers and effective public transportation systems retained their basic form because they were sufficiently established to resist some of the challenges presented by cars, but even these cities began to experience denucleating trends. In some cases, "new towns" were built around them, as they have been built around London as industrial and commercial firms, presuming that their employees have personal transportation, tended to locate new plants and offices on cheaper land on the outer fringes of the cities. In most "old" cities, the central people magnets and the public transportation systems oriented toward the city center remain vital enough to keep old urban patterns alive, but from the middle years of the twentieth century the pressure of cars upon them became increasingly severe and more modifications had to be introduced.

The modern city is typically less densely built up than the earlier city forms, and the urban fabric is full of holes of various kinds. Because the majority of people are highly mobile, at least over medium distances, and are functionally "auto-centaurs," half car and half human, land developers no longer think it imperative to make optimum use of land, particularly within built-up areas. Few people in car city travel far on their own feet; few are tied to public transportation routes and stopping places. The human convenience that tends to lead to maximum land use does not, therefore, operate in the development of the modern city. Relatively minor problems or differences in price are enough to make

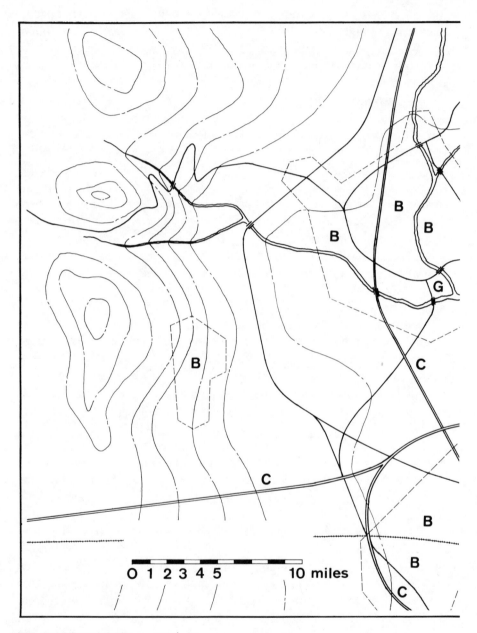

THE MODERN CITY c. 1974

The old industrial center declined as the nature of industry and the whole economic system changed. Internal combustion engine vehicles began to dominate transportation, and both residential areas and some light industries moved to the outer edges of the urban area. Sprawl became the major characteristic of city development.

A Old industrial-residential area declined; urban renewal began in some sections of the old city center.

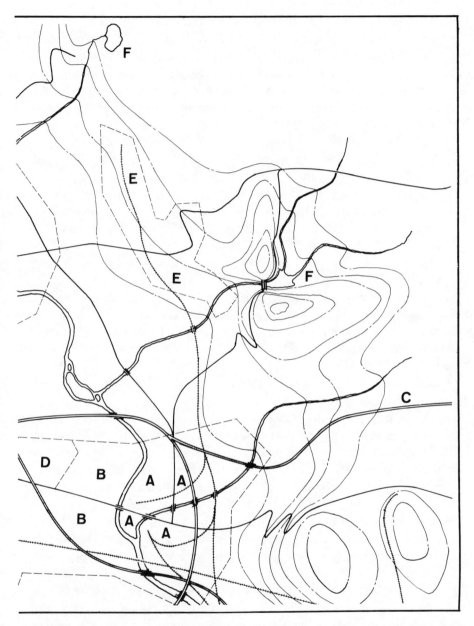

B Development of suburban sprawl promoted by the automobile and by private land and home ownership.

C Freeways.

D Airport.

E Exclusive suburbs close to forests and recreation areas.

F Recreation area developed around reservoirs.

G Old urban centers redeveloped as historic sites and tourist attractions.

(MAP DRAWN BY SATHIT CHAIYASIN)

builders pass over more central locations in favor of cheaper or more easily developed ones on the fringes of the built-up area. A slightly overpriced parcel of land may remain undeveloped for years in a modern city and become a curious refuge for weeds and small wildlife or an unofficial playground surrounded by banks, professional buildings, and houses. Land that has special drainage, access, or other problems that might involve additional expense in development are similarly neglected as the tide of city growth sweeps around and past it.

Inevitably, a high percentage of the surface area of car city is devoted to the car and its needs. In terms of the volume of passengers or goods delivered per foot of ground space occupied, cars and trucks are extremely inefficient carriers compared with railways, subways, and other forms of public transportation. Hence, any city that relies heavily on cars for transportation will devote a large portion of its ground area to cars. The vast highways necessary to move thousands of people regularly and frequently from place to place consume considerable quantities of land; over half of Los Angeles is covered with highways, streets, and parking lots. High-speed interchanges, ramps, medians, paved shoulders, and safety easements also render large pieces of land unusable by making them inaccessible, unpleasant, or dangerous. The large spaces within and around cloverleaf interchanges, for example, could be put to some useful purpose, but building subways or bridges to reach them would be expensive and car city always has cheaper, problem-free lots farther out on the fringes of the city.

Mass private transportation requires many other land-consuming facilities. Garages and gas stations must be allowed to proliferate to provide for the upkeep and fueling of cars, and parking lots must be available at points at which the auto-centaur is apt to convert into human being. Because people magnets are scattered throughout the modern city and the only practicable way to get from one to another is by car, each people magnet must have a parking lot. The interests of business dictate that each lot, whether for office, factory, store, or theater, should be big enough to accommodate the largest crowd ever likely to appear. In Anaheim, California, the parking lot of Disneyland alone can accommodate ten thousand cars. As a consequence, a large proportion of the land in many modern cities is devoted to large parking lots that are in use for only a few hours each day. Even the people magnets that do not require conversion from auto-centaur to human, such as drive-in banks, restaurants, and movies, require much larger spaces than comparable human facilities because the car is bulky and difficult to maneuver.

The changes that the industrial city form made to adapt to the automobile involved the enormous consumption of space. The result is a centerless, car-sustaining expanse of suburb with people magnets scattered according to no particular pattern. Because it sprawls over huge areas in a relatively short time, car city and the car-city fringes around established urban centers tend to fill up open spaces between settlements rapidly and to produce a "megalopolis" or giant city in which expanses of suburban growth connect urban settlements. "Los Angeles" reaches north into Santa Barbara and south into San Diego; great stretches of car city more or less connect Boston with Baltimore as well as Philadelphia, New York, and other cities between; for all practical purposes, San Francisco, San Jose, and Oakland have become one great "Bay Area" city; Aachen, Bonn, Cologne, Dusseldorf, and Essen have formed the Rhine-Ruhr conurbation; growth around Liverpool and Manchester has linked these cities and swallowed up many smaller towns in the process.

On the basis of the evidence of the past, it seems unlikely that present trends in city development will change as long as the unrestricted use of the automobile and uncontrolled land development continue to be central parts of the life-style of the industrialized West. The car has become the major city-shaping force of the twentieth century, and without it, many other important phenomena, such as the widespread use of cheap suburban land, would not operate with such vigor. Unless something is produced to supplant the car, it will continue to shape urban development as the most powerful forces in the economy have always shaped cities. Even if mankind objects to the city form dictated by the car and imposes artificial restrictions on its use, some changes, like the expansion of the suburbs, seem irreversible as long as some car use continues. Unless the world runs out of fuel, steel, or other resources, it is probable that car city will continue to be the viable city form and that both old and new urban settlements will more closely resemble car city as time passes. Departures from the car-city form, such as Reston, can resist automobile domination only as long as its powers and effects are recognized and manipulated by effective restraints on its use.

Modifications of the City Center

Although the automobile has been the major and most dramatic shaper of the modern city form, others have acted to change the centers of established cities in the twentieth century. As the population of cities increased in the later nineteenth and twentieth centuries and as commercial functions became more numerous and intricate, commercial and industrial demand grew for office space at prestigious locations in established city centers. Some central areas like Oxford Street in London, Union Square in San Francisco, and Fifth Avenue in New York acquired a reputation for elegance from the establishments that grew up in and became associated with them. This "name" attracted other concerns anxious to gain prestige by association. The excess demand for the land within and around such areas caused land prices to rise. Coupled with innovations in building technology, this economic pressure produced high-density use and vertical growth, a trend running counter to the diffusion and horizontal sprawl created by the car. The vertical counter-trend operated most effectively on the centers of established settlements with some decades of precar building. While its effects on places such as Manhattan and central London were spectacular, its effects on new suburbs around old cities and on new cities with no well-established prestige centers were minor.

The invention and development of the Bessemer process of steelmaking in the latter half of the nineteenth century made it possible to produce cheap steel in large quantities. Load-bearing steel beams became an important building material that permitted construction of buildings of a hitherto impossible height. Offices or apartment blocks with enormous floor spaces could be built on small pieces of expensive central-city land. Before skyscrapers could come into general use, however, a new form of vertical transportation had to be mass produced. The passenger elevator, invented by Elisha G. Otis in the 1850s, provided the new form of transportation suitable for the job. The steel building beam, elevators, and the price of prestigious central building sites combined to produce distinctive skylines such as those of New York, Chicago, and San Francisco. As the centers of established cities throughout the Western world succumb to the pressures of "prestige" building, the "bed of nails" skyline becomes more common.

The vertical growth of the central business section accelerated in the twentieth century as the pressures upon commercial prestige land increased and as more sophisticated building techniques employing such things as prestressed concrete and curtain walling were introduced. By the mid-twentieth century, verticality was a major characteristic of virtually every long-established city. The relationship between spaces and buildings within these areas was dramatically different from what it had been a century earlier. Many of the wide, light, open thoroughfares constructed in the centers of nineteenth-century cities became the dark, narrow floors of the great steel, cement, and glass canyons created by the multistory buildings of the twentieth century. Before the advent of modern industrialism, the highest building in most cities, the one most obvious to a newcomer and the clear focus of the urban area, was the church. In the nineteenth century the tallest structures in the dynamic, growing city were the smoke-spewing factory chimneys and the tallest spires of some central building born out of new prosperity and civic pride. Until the middle of the nineteenth century, however, it was not possible to construct buildings that were abnormally taller than anything that had been built before, and churches and palaces were able to hold their own with town halls and chimneys. The twentieth-century skyscraper, however, destroyed the previous rough equality between city landmarks, and the great vertical shafts of glass and steel overwhelmed churches and palaces alike. The dramatic changes in the skyline and the radical shift of the focus of central urban areas reflected the dramatic changes in economy, technology, and society that evolved in the second "industrial revolution." The most obvious buildings and clear focal points were the great towers constructed by banks, insurance companies, industrial corporations, conglomerate companies, and real estate developers. Urban man has always devoted his tallest structures, from ziggurat to cathedral to chimney, to whatever gods dominated his life. By his skyscrapers, twentieth-century man demonstrated that he had changed little but that his gods had changed much; technology and finance had clearly supplanted spiritual gods.

Mid-twentieth-century urban centers have characteristics other than verticality, many of which are curiously at odds with each other and with previous notions of typical city features. In general, the commercial center of the city, which usually contains the tallest buildings, has a minute resident population. The offices, retail stores, and sandwich shops that are hives of activity during the day and fairly busy in the early evening are totally empty at night except for a service population of cleaners, security guards, and policemen. The few residents who remain live in old apartments and houses that have temporarily escaped the developers. This pattern of central nonresidence is broken only in the few exceptional and almost experimental cases in which high-rise apartments, such as the hundred-story John Hancock Center in Chicago, have been constructed for prosperous residents. Medium-distance mobility, which the automobile makes possible, in conjunction with competition between business firms for central status addresses, has forced people out of the central city. Commercial competition for desirable central locations has pushed up land prices making central-city rents too high for most individuals and families. At the same time, these central offices employ large numbers of white-collar workers who must, of necessity, go to the center of the city during the day to earn their living. As a consequence, for most central-city workers quite considerable distances that must be covered twice a day separate home and work. Although the car has made it possible to traverse them, commuting has had serious consequences both for the city and its people.

The central city fills up during the day and empties at night in great ebbs and flows of humanity. In old cities with well-defined centers and extensive public transportation systems, such as London and New York, public transportation carries a large part of the rush-hour traffic. Even in these cities, however, enough car commuting is done to produce traffic problems and make adjustments such as one-way streets and expressways necessary. Traffic congestion and accidents in central cities have forced other traffic control schemes, such as road widening and extra traffic light installation, on civic authorities, but each improvement in the traffic flow seems to encourage more people to commute by car and even more congestion on an even larger scale results. In many major cities, improvements like highway interchanges and street widening are more than offset by heavier traffic even before they are completed. Heavy traffic flow generates other serious problems within the central area. For example, many cities have been forced to build freeways, expressways, and giant central parking stacks on valuable land, filling their centers with concrete and reducing the land area from which land taxes can be expected. Until a city has enough road space to allow all its car population to be on the move at once and has enough central-city parking to also allow that population to be all parked at once, it must expect traffic problems to continue, unless an effective alternative to personal transport is developed.

If cars have been in large part responsible for central-city verticality and outer-city sprawl, it might be presumed that a refusal to accommodate the car would result in a more homogeneous urban fabric with a more dynamic, multi-use center. Although some new cities, such as Reston, have deliberately ostracized the car from the city center, few established cities have been able to resist the pressure of the automobile. A truncated section of unfinished elevated freeway that hangs over part of the central area symbolizes resistance in San Francisco, but most cities have been unable to resist even this far. In any event, outright rejection of the car by refusing to accommodate it seems to kill cities rather than sustain them because cars, businesses, and people simply go elsewhere. Merely ignoring the car does little for urban development for the tide of dynamic city growth sweeps around apathetic communities and goes on to generate growth elsewhere.

Despite the trend toward verticality and high-density commercial use of the center, most cities are experiencing a contrapuntal trend that leads to inner-city decay. Adjacent to the commercial core and its tall buildings are often old residential and small business districts that range from appalling slums to districts that are seedy and dilapidated and on their way to becoming slums. Often these border on industrial plants and docks that provide employment for unskilled and semiskilled manual workers. These districts are the no-man's-land in the current stage of the struggle of mankind to live in cities. Although they are often close to the prosperous business sections, developers are reluctant to invest in them because their names have slum associations and their cluttered and decaying streets have no status value. People who work in the central-city blocks could shorten their journeys to work markedly if they lived in these districts, but the slum reputation that discourages business also discourages residence. Few prosperous individuals are willing to tolerate lack of prestige and cope with problems like crime, vandalism, dirt, and poor urban services that typically plague these areas, especially when they can travel by car to some desirable suburb.

These districts, apparently ripe for redevelopment, are neglected because no one, individual or business, wants to live in an inner-city slum. People who have a choice live in the suburbs, and successful businesses prefer to use space in the central office buildings. The decaying penumbra of the inner city is thus left to people and businesses that have no choice. The poor, the undereducated, the manual laborers, the black, the brown, or whatever group of people happens to be lowest on the socioeconomic totem pole inhabit the inner fringes. The situation of the inhabitants does nothing to help improve the district. The people are poor and do not contribute much to the city in taxes, nor are they able to demand many decent urban services in return. Often small-time criminals make up a proportion of the population, and the poorly policed houses and apartments invite petty theft in spite of their poverty. The frustration of living in substandard surroundings in an affluent world breeds anger among the residents that can lead to vandalism and riots. Thus, the area suffers a high crime rate and a worsening reputation. As crime, neglect, and notoriety spill over into surrounding areas, the decay eats deeper and the rot spreads.

National and city governments have become concerned about the decay of the inner city and its accompanying problems of low tax income, high crime rates, and waste of space, but operations designed to revitalize the inner city have not generally produced much long-term success. The demolition of dilapidated buildings to make room for parking lots, convention centers, and office buildings removes the symptoms of urban blight from the specific areas treated but it does not cure the disease any more than the clearing of slums for the building of railways and new streets ended slums in the nineteenth century. Indeed, such "cures" tend merely to spread the blight and to create new slums outside the cleared areas, for the poor do not vanish with their old homes. They simply move to the next-cheapest and hence least desirable areas in town, creating new slums in areas that before were only dilapidated.

In some cities attempts have been made to create low-cost housing for the displaced slum dwellers to move into, offering the poor an alternative to moving to another decaying area. All too often, however, "low-cost housing" has proven to be a polite euphemism for newly built slum. Small, cheaply built housing units offer no attractions to people with enough income to support a really comfortable home, and therefore the new units tend to be as clearly identifiable as ghettos for low socioeconomic groups as were the old slums. The new buildings change little, except that new low-cost housing tends to be high-rise and slums become vertical instead of horizontal. Also, low-cost housing generally means low-cost building and maintenance. Cheap materials, shoddy workmanship, inadequate heating and cooling systems, small rooms, and unkempt community areas such as stairways and halls ensure that low-cost housing soon becomes high-density slum. Broken windows are not repaired, numerous building and service system defects go uncorrected, and the "new" housing ages even more rapidly and dramatically than the old. Little long-term change is effected in the environment of the inhabitants who have no more incentive to self-improvement or cause for self-respect than they had in their old homes.

The main reason for the failure to find a satisfactory solution to inner urban problems lies in the fact that so far they have been approached as isolated problems peculiar to the inner city and not as facets of general problems spawned by the operation of the urban mechanism as a whole. Central decay and suburban sprawl are related phenomena generated by the nature of the operations of the modern city. The cure for both lies not in the intensive treatment of the worst symptoms, but in the readjustment of the forces that create modern urban operations and patterns. Given the nature of the operations of the urban mechanism, it is clear that as long as the forces that currently determine city form continue to dominate, the city will both rot around its center and sprawl at its outer edges no matter what delaying palliatives are employed.

THE
MODERN
CITY 7 The
Divided
Society

Given the shapeless, sprawling, unformed character of the modern city and of modern additions to old cities, it is no surprise that modern urban society is also, to a large extent, shapeless, unformed, and difficult to define. Even before the modern city began to develop, society had not completely adjusted to the pressures and demands of the early industrial city. Adjustments were beginning to be made, such as improved urban services and better planning, but all urban problems, especially social ones like poverty and prejudice, had by no means been solved when yet another phase of urban development brought further changes. People had not completely adapted to the demands of the railway train, the factory, and the steam engine when they faced the far greater demands of the electrical generator, the internal combustion engine, and the assembly line.

Adjustments to new urban forms have always been difficult to make, but the process is incredibly difficult when changes occur as rapidly as they have in the twentieth century. In the past, people's lives changed infrequently and major social adjustments occurred over generations without causing too much pain and turmoil. The rate of change and the number of necessary social adjustments began to increase rapidly with the advent of industrialism, when it became more dramatic and more painful. Nevertheless, the pace of change in the nineteenth century was comfortably slow compared with that of the twentieth century. In the present century the list of innovations that people have accepted as part of their daily lives is staggering. Radio, television, cars, telephones, jet planes, rockets, terrifying weapons of war, orbiting satellites, space laboratories, computers, and a host of other inventions have appeared with breathtaking rapidity. At the same time, people had not yet fully come to terms with phenomena like urban expansion and exploding population that began in the nineteenth century. It is not surprising that Western man has not yet developed a rational reaction to his problems, let alone an effective program for their solution. While individuals have to adjust to the modern world as best they can, society as a whole confronts innumerable problems for which there is no single solution. Suburban sprawl, inner-city decay, pollution, crime, civil disorder, poverty, racial prejudice, and the myriad ills of the modern world have so many facets that national and local government bodies so far have been able only to react to the more extreme and troublesome manifestations and hope that some alleviation results.

Society in the Suburbs

Vast, sprawling suburbs now make up most of the urban landscape, and their social forms are therefore a significant, if not a dominant, element in modern urban society. The railway, the tram, the bus, and above all the car provided people with the mechanical means to move to the suburbs. The suburban migration of the twentieth century resulted from the same motivations as in the nineteenth century: escape from the noise and dirt of the city, the opportunity to use cheaper land, the avoidance of the distressing necessity of always being near poor people, and the means of gratifying latent territorial instincts by owning a piece of land and a house. In the past, urban people had lived happily enough with dirt, noise, and the poor and had exhibited few symptoms of personal territoriality. Medieval city people, for example, had attached great importance to property, but paid very little attention to the personal ownership of nonagricultural land. City man has little real need for territory. His need for living and working space is for floor space, not acreage. Theoretically, an apartment of suitable size should fully satisfy his needs. An open balcony, a few flowering plants, access to a public park, and transportation to wilderness areas should satisfy whatever urges he may have to commune with nature. The suburban lot with its one-family home bordered by narrow strips of land is clearly neither a necessity for survival, nor an absolute economic asset, and is not even particularly aesthetically appealing. Land ownership is a fundamental economic and social asset only in farming communities in which land represents potential income and hence social standing. Nevertheless, the desire to own land has been one of the basic forces shaping the modern city. The grandparents of most modern city people, especially those in the United States where the modern urban pattern is set, were born in rural communities and hence had deep and legitimate feelings about land ownership. Many of these were passed on to their immediate descendants in some form, even if only through the vague notion that land ownership represented economic stability and social standing. The territorial drive of the modern suburbanite illustrates the fact that the world has changed radically in the past hundred years, while personal value systems have in very many ways remained relatively static.

Before the eighteenth century, the relatively few countrymen moving into urban areas were anxious, for a variety of reasons, to fit into the urban community, so they adjusted to the values and attitudes of the established townspeople. With population growth and industrialism, hundreds of thousands of people who were born and spent their early years in the countryside flooded the towns and cities, destroying the traditional predominance of town-born over country-born people in urban areas. People educated in rural values eventually predominated. This new majority with an essentially rural value system carried rural territorial drives with them into an urban setting and transmitted them to succeeding generations in somewhat modified forms. Twentieth-century suburbanites compromised between their rural longings for land and economic realities by buying one-family homes on suburban lots that they could eventually call their own.

Bound up in the move to the suburbs was the desire to get into the country where children would have pleasant places to play and where adults could relax. The economic realities of developing suburban tracts, however, dictated that not too much provision be made for open wild spaces or parks. In addition, the amount of land attached to each house was restricted. If a large piece of land surrounded each house, the price of the whole unit would prohibit mass sales and reduce the developer's profit. The suburban dream was "country"—trees, grass, streams, and flowers— but the reality was relatively large houses on relatively small lots, garages, expanses of concrete paths and driveways, barbecues, houses packed closely together, and comparatively few patches of raw, "undeveloped" earth where things could grow. Because "nature" is untidy, wasteful of space, and occasionally dangerous, hills, streams, fields, and forests were bulldozed into oblivion. In the end, the desire to be in the country was expressed in artificially tidy lawns and flower beds to whose care and feeding all the resources of modern industrialism were applied: motor-driven lawn mowers, electric hedge clippers, chemical fertilizers and pest destroyers, hybrid plants, garden furniture, cement statues and bird baths, and a host of other "outdoor" mass-production items. Far from finding life in the suburbs relaxing, many homeowners found themselves in bondage to their houses and tiny gardens.

In addition to exercising rural instincts and pursuing bucolic dreams, people found practical reasons for moving to the suburbs. Lack of good planning had resulted from the earliest stages of industrialism in the unpleasant inner-city conditions that people in the nineteenth century moved to the suburbs to escape. For the same reasons—to escape dirt, noise, overcrowding, disease, and crime—people left the city in the twentieth century. These problems were not exclusive to the central city, however, and failure to solve them tended to promote their spread to suburban refuges. Many people moved to the suburbs "for the good of the children"; pictures of urchins playing in grimy city streets haunted parents. Although the country may indeed be a better place to raise children than the city, the suburbs are by no means country. Suburban lawns may have some advantage over sidewalks or city parks, but a move to the suburbs may produce individual and family strains that more than offset these advantages. Suburban children often have to commute to school, which reduces their time for play. Parental commuting to work in the city reduces the time that parents can spend with their children. Although suburban living may give children more time for playing on a lawn, it generally gives them less time, especially early in their lives, with their fathers. The value of this exchange is open to question.

Another frequently cited reason for the mass exodus to the suburbs was a desire for privacy, which the appearance of nineteenth-century suburban houses certainly suggests. Fences or hedges enclosed many front as well as back gardens, and houses were set well back from the road and away from prying eyes. Windows were relatively small and heavily curtained to shield the occupants from the view of passersby. In short, the occupants made real efforts to be well concealed from both neighbors and people in the street. By contrast, modern suburban housing styles suggest that their occupants are less than devoted to the preservation of their privacy. The modern lot is very small, and people find themselves living cheek by jowl with their neighbors. In spite of this, the hedge and the fence have gone out of style in favor of unfenced front yards, in many parts of the United States at least. In addition, the mass production of sheets of plate glass has made picture windows standard equipment in many suburban houses. Although they are sometimes heavily curtained, they obviously exist to give the occupants of the house a panoramic view of the street and their neighbors. At the same time, they function as shop windows displaying the occupants of the houses and many of their possessions. If a desire for privacy is indeed one of the motivating forces in the drift of people to the suburbs, most mid-twentieth-century architecture and landscaping certainly does not reflect it.

Initially only the wealthiest urban people could afford to maintain houses in the suburbs. In the nineteenth century ambitious people who moved to the outer edges of the city created their own version of the country estates owned by the "top" people in society and aped the established social rulers as closely as they could. The design of these early suburban houses reflected rising social aspirations. They were as spacious and sprawling as their owners could afford, sporting pillars, gables, gardens, and entrance halls in imitation of castles and mansions. The connection between suburban residence and social status as ambitious nineteenth-century townsmen perceived it became embedded in Western social thinking and lasted into the twentieth century.

By the time the automobile was introduced and mass-production–mass-consumption society developed in the twentieth century, the notion that prosperous people lived in the suburbs was widely accepted. The growing number of people whose rising incomes indicated success began to move to the suburbs to mark their increased affluence and impress it on themselves, their friends, and society in general. The fact that such a move coincided with the vague desire to own land merely added to its attractions. As more people followed this pattern, the more solidly established the pattern became. By the mid-twentieth century it was the general rule that, apart from a few rich eccentrics, only the poor lived near the center of the city. The association between the area of residence and social status is now so firmly established that probably only dramatic changes in the distribution of socioeconomic groups in urban areas and in the forces that determine current urban patterns can break it.

The new industrial system has shaped many of the social forms of suburbia. Not only has modern industry provided the means for ever-larger numbers of people to become suburbanites, but it has also supplied the consumer goods that form the basis of suburban social structures. Before mass production, almost every item for domestic use had to be made by hand, and only the wealthy could afford to buy many nonessential or nondurable goods. The average person had few possessions, and these were primarily utilitarian in nature. Mass production not only made goods available to people of average incomes but also increased the number and variety and changed the very nature of their possessions. The novelty fascinated people of the later nineteenth century; the ability to own so many things and thus emulate the social leaders of the past charmed the prosperous. Accumulation of possessions was so delightful and the social rewards so gratifying that the goals of acquisition and ownership were pursued in earnest, especially in the suburbs where the most prosperous townspeople lived; the competition was for status in terms of personal possessions rather than personal achievements. This suburban game was well established by the turn of the century. As the new industrial system of the twentieth century increased the number of suburban dwellers, the number of objects that they could own grew, and advertising stimulated competition as the economy became more dependent on high consumption levels.

The economic changes that took place in the late nineteenth and the twentieth centuries also influenced the social makeup of suburbia. The early suburbanites of the nineteenth century were a small group of property-owning, capital-owning, entrepreneurial, middle-class people who owned and managed industries and commercial enterprises, employed workers, and derived their income from property and capital. Toward the end of the nineteenth century a new group began to emerge that was neither established middle class nor working class, the forerunner of the twentieth-century middle class of white-collar workers. They were administrators, managers, bureaucrats who issued orders and shuffled the papers created by the increasingly sophisticated operations of the new industrial system. This group, whose members generally owned little or no property or capital at the beginning of their adult lives, worked for other people, but since they did not get dirty or perform physical labor during the course of their work, they did not think of themselves as working class. The group expanded rapidly in the first half of the twentieth century as business operations required more managers, organizers, technicians, administrators, and office personnel. By the middle of the twentieth century this group had become extremely large and had usurped the role of social standard setting in suburban areas that had once been filled with the entrepreneurial middle class.

As a result of its rapid growth and its amorphous nature, the new middle class lacked a specific character of its own. Many of its members came from rural or working-class backgrounds that they had left behind but had not quite forgotten. Although in appearance and training they resembled the traditional nineteenth-century middle class, they were, nevertheless, hired workers who were just as dependent on their employers as working-class people, and their incomes were closer to working-class than to established middle-class standards. They belonged fully to neither group. While they admired and tried to copy the life-style of the established middle class, its prosperity, its leisure, and its possessions, they lacked for the most part the solid economic foundation and financial independence from which this life-style had grown. They were therefore less sure of themselves and more inclined to accept established patterns and norms than the old middle class had been. The expansion of the white-collar middle class in the twentieth century and its adoption of a modified version of the customs of the old middle class have played a major role in determining the social composition of modern suburbia.

The mass production of the new industrial system is important to the development of mass society in the urbanized West. The mass consumption of identical or very similar items inevitably produces a feeling of uniformity and an expectation of standardized appearances. For example, suburban families live in houses made up of a number of mass-produced units such as doors, windows, draperies, carpets, and furniture. A growing number of people live in houses that are almost entirely mass-produced modular units. Houses built from local materials like stone or adobe and of individualized architectural style are becoming less common as they become more expensive. Mass-produced building components are easier to work with, and mass-produced designs that use them are cheaper. Thus, cities and suburbs throughout the Western world are beginning to look increasingly alike. Housing units within any given area of development tend to be so alike that visitors and even residents sometimes become confused. Mass-produced clothing has made people look more and more alike. Standardized food-processing machinery and modern distribution systems have produced a host of foods that always taste the same, wherever they are consumed. Furthermore, mass advertising has succeeded in producing a high level of uniformity in the needs and aspirations of urban people everywhere.

Most mass-communications systems and mass advertising are now aimed at suburbanites. They are numerous; they have both the leisure and the money essential to maintaining the new economy; hence they constitute the main market for most mass-produced goods. As a result, a major characteristic of suburban society is its gadget orientation and the emphasis it places on possessions. As suburbanites have acquired more

TOMBSTONES, *by Jacob Lawrence* Among twentieth-century urban migrants are the large numbers of black Americans who have moved from the agricultural South to the inner slums of large northern cities. This work by a black artist captures the spiritual as well as the economic deprivation experienced by inner-city residents.   Jacob Lawrence. *Tombstones*. Gouache. 28¾ x 20½″. Collection of the Whitney Museum of American Art

Riot damage, Albuquerque, New Mexico This liquor store, looted and burned during summer riots in this southwestern city, typifies the property destruction that horrifies suburbanites. Inner-city riots and high crime rates have not only driven the middle classes away from the central city but have also closed many of the businesses serving and employing the poor.   Photograph by the author

Assembly line The modern assembly-line economy is enormously productive but lends itself to uniformity and monotony. Line workers perform one small, routine task and act as replaceable parts in the great production machine; boredom is a common complaint. Mass consumption is a necessary part of mass production, and even children play an important role in the standardized consumer society.   Ideal Toy Corporation

Subdivision in Rockland County, New York Suburban housing typically makes adequate provisions for cars but often unsatisfactory provisions for people; for example, the absence of sidewalks discourages walking and the use of front yards as playgrounds for children since there is nothing to prevent them from running into the road. While there appears to be a good deal of open space, it offers no privacy and not much of it is useful. The basic similarity of the housing units and their raw, bleak surroundings do little to foster a sense either of personal identity or of community.

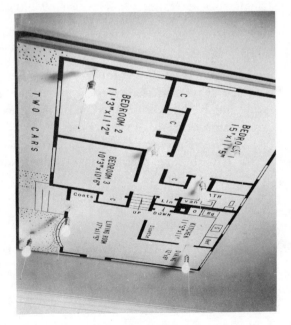

DOORSTOP, *ceiling piece by James Rosenquist* The modern prosperous ideal: a suburban house with three bedrooms and two cars. Mass-produced housing has combined with growing prosperity and increased leisure to make a great contribution to the "identity crisis" in modern mass culture.
Collection of Mr. and Mrs. Robert C. Scull

things, man-made objects have increasingly shaped the pattern of human life in the suburbs. For example, cars are essential in the suburbs and multiple car ownership is becoming the rule rather than the exception, especially among families living in the suburbs of the most dynamic modern cities. In the archetypal car city, Los Angeles, people walking along thoroughfares are objects of curiosity for the majority of people passing by in cars, who look sympathetically for the broken-down automobile whose failure has produced this unfortunate and unusual activity. Father goes to work in his car, mother to work or shopping in hers, and often the older children go to school in theirs. Very few daytime hours are spent in the company of other members of the family unless there are not enough cars to go around. The car has made recreation outside the home readily accessible to both parents and children. Family members who stay at home tend to find their evenings and weekends shaped not by other family members and friends, but by the programs offered on television. In many ways the pressures created by industrialism continue, as they have already done, to isolate individuals and to make close groupings, including family groupings, more difficult to sustain. The desirability of the traditional family grouping as a social ideal persists despite the pressures that tend to separate families into individuals living essentially separate lives while sharing a few common interests, possessions, and the same address. No way has yet been found of adjusting the social ideal of the family to fit the realities of modern life or of deliberately changing those realities to produce conditions that would support the family ideal.

A vitally important facet of mass urban society is its scale. It encompasses not just hundreds or thousands of people, but millions. Vast numbers have been drawn into ever-expanding urban areas that function in similar ways and share similar problems. The enormous number of people involved has combined with the great speed of change in the present century to make urban problems extraordinarily difficult to solve, for people have no time to think, governments have no time to plan, and society has no time to make harmonious adjustments along the way. Given that the pace of innovation and change seems to be accelerating, not slowing, members of urban society will undoubtedly find even less time to adjust to new situations in the future and less opportunity to solve problems before they become crises. Since the rate of change seems unlikely to slow down of its own accord so that individuals and society can cope with it, it may well be that the only solution is to do what has not been done before: to slow the rate of change deliberately by conscious intervention.

The Central City

As the suburbs have spread, central cities have been depopulated. The rate of population decline seems to depend on when the center was founded. Long-established city centers, like those of Paris and New York, appear to have less trouble retaining residents than those of cities like Denver and Los Angeles that had achieved only a rudimentary stage of development before the advent of the automobile. However, city centers everywhere in the West have been losing rather than gaining resident population. The centers of most cities are commercial and administrative centers with few permanent residents. Furthermore, prestigious retail organizations tend increasingly to close their outlets in central areas and follow the population to the suburbs. As city centers lose residents and market functions, they increasingly become merely areas that are subordinate to the suburban social pattern rather than independent social milieus. City centers contain the offices and other institutions employing white-collar workers to which many suburbanites must commute, but a trend toward the decentralization of white-collar employment is also growing and promises a further depletion of the functions of the central city.

Since industrialism began to influence city patterns, only the poor, with few exceptions, have inhabited the districts in the immediate vicinity of the industrial-commercial urban core. Most inner-city houses are comparatively old; they lack modern conveniences and are very often unsafe. Their owners generally have neither the money nor the inclination to make improvements since they know that better plumbing or heating will tempt few prosperous people back to the inner city, so they allow these older houses to deteriorate even further. Whole areas become slums, or when poverty and race coincide, ghettos. Virtually their only inhabitants are the poor, the undereducated, and the unskilled.

The Western urban poor live in inner-city residential areas primarily because they do not have the money to move to the suburbs, where housing is expensive compared with slum housing. While many of the modern amenities suburban houses offer are desirable, they are generally not optional. Houses come already equipped with expensive built-in appliances, two bathrooms, landscaping, carpeting, and garages, with no provision for people who cannot afford what the prosperous desire. In addition, people in the suburbs normally need reliable cars for commuting to work, for public transport is meager or unavailable and too many car breakdowns and late arrivals mean lost jobs. Gasoline, oil, tires, and servicing are also a heavy burden on inadequate incomes. Suburban people are expected to keep up with neighborhood standards in such matters as house maintenance, lawn and garden care, and gadget ownership. These overt and implicit expectations involve time, labor, and money, and poor people relocated in suburbs who cannot afford all three are likely to find that community acceptance is minimal at best and that suburban life is socially uncomfortable. Suburban housing is middle class by definition. That efforts to relocate the poor by moving them to suburbs have failed is therefore not surprising.

Two main types of inner-city housing provide accommodation for the urban poor. Houses built by the rich in an earlier era when the neighborhood was respectable are one type. When the rich moved away, these houses were often converted into low-rent apartments. A second type consists of apartments and houses designed for the poor from the outset. In these buildings, rooms are relatively small, services and comforts minimal, and construction materials of low quality and durability. In a few cities there is a third type of low-rent housing. Decades ago, some poor people managed to build their own little houses on land in some cities which, for one reason or another, was then available and cheap. Modern urban growth swept around these poor settlements, however, leaving them among the dirtier processing plants, the city sewer works, and small, nonprestigious factories.

Many of the problems of the inner city are essentially the problems of poverty, which is an elusive condition to describe. In the past, the poor were easily identifiable because they lived close to the margin of survival and vast economic distances separated them from the prosperous. Along with the general rise in living standards in modern times, however, there has been a rise in the standard of living of the poor. There are few places in the West where the poor are as close to starvation as in the past. Modern Western urban poverty can perhaps be described as income insufficient to maintain the appearance of what is popularly accepted as modest prosperity. This is tantamount to saying that being poor is being something less than lower middle class in appearance, but it is a definition that emphasizes the importance of appearances as opposed to the realities of income or net assets. In modern society people are generally classified by their overall appearance rather than by their actual financial standing; although deceptive, appearances are the main yardstick modern Western society uses to make practical, everyday social judgments. Perhaps most importantly, appearances are generally a good indication of how people classify themselves.

Poverty springs from a variety of sources, many of which are directly traceable to the new industrial system. Many poor people lack marketable skills; as industry became more sophisticated, education and special skills became more necessary for people who hoped to earn a decent living. Physical strength and willingness to work long hours generally assured a worker of a job of some kind in the nineteenth century, but in the twentieth century there is no guarantee that an unskilled worker, however strong and willing, can find employment. Programs to teach marketable skills to the poor have been initiated in many areas, and although some have met with success, the rapid pace of change has defeated many. For example, unskilled laborers trained for specialized jobs in coal mining have often found their skills useless on the labor market because of the transition to more mechanized mining and to the use of oil and electricity as power sources; secretaries find shorthand skills less in demand as more offices begin to use dictating machines; the operators of specialized business machines like comptometers have often found the market in their home district flooded with hundreds of people who have taken the same intensive training course. In addition, many training courses are based on unrealistic assessments of demand. For example, many of them teach commercial and technical skills although skilled carpenters and plumbers earning middle-class incomes may be in great demand; as a result the market is glutted with low-grade office and technical workers who are thus relatively poor.

Poverty is just as transmissible in the modern industrial system as it was in the past. As in the early industrial system, a far higher proportion of the children of the modern poor are themselves poor than are the children of prosperous parents. Poor families lack the money to educate their children; even when the state fully subsidizes the tuition, they may not have enough money to buy the kind of clothing accepted by the children's peers in school or to pay for additional educational advantages like extra books and field trips. The need for money also tempts poor children to leave school as soon as they are able to find a job. Although having children working and contributing to the total family income may have short-term advantages, it does tend to condemn the children of the poor to adulthoods in low-income, unskilled jobs.

The population of the inner city in all parts of the industrialized West includes a disproportionate number of people from minority groups. For some time, Western people have seen poverty not only as an uncomfortable and undesirable state, but also as a morally shameful and socially contemptible one. Where certain groups of people have become associated with poverty, mere membership in that group has brought social downgrading. The nature of the socially deprecated groups varies from country to country. Some minorities are determined by surnames, some by accents, some by skin color, but the basic forces that result in the low status of a minority group are generally similar. An individual who belongs to a minority is more likely to have poor parents, and hence he is more likely to be undereducated and poor himself. If he has managed to acquire a good education or a marketable skill, he is more likely to have his applications for jobs rejected than are similarly qualified nonminority people. If he finds a job, he is more likely to be confined to the lowest ranks, to be given unpleasant work, to be passed over for promotion, and generally to be less well paid than he should be. Social injustice of this kind is now widely recognized as a problem, and many countries have initiated programs to alleviate the situation. In many cases, however, social prejudice has deep roots and is as difficult to overcome and eradicate as poverty itself.

The urban poor tend to congregate in the cheap, run-down areas in the inner city while the prosperous flock to the suburbs, producing sharply defined patterns of socioeconomic division within metropolitan areas. Whether or not such economic segregation is socially desirable, it certainly accounts in large part for a variety of urban problems. The most lucrative sources of public income are the prosperous people in the suburbs, while the most exhausting drain on public funds is the inner city, where poor inhabitants need more welfare payments and more publicly financed health care and other services. In addition, education, police protection, and other public services are comparatively costly in the inner city although the residents pay only a small part of the local and national tax bill. As the socioeconomic divisions within the city become more pronounced, inner-city government authorities are faced with mounting costs and declining income. Whenever civic expenditure is reduced in an effort to balance the budget, the inner city is most severely affected. Loss of funds for civic services leads to even more rapid deterioration of the inner city and reinforces the determination of the prosperous not to live there. It also increases the burdens of poverty on inner-city inhabitants. The quality of education available is reduced, police services are spread more thinly, streets are cleaned less often, and in general the inner city becomes a poorer place to live.

Inner-city areas also tend to have high crime rates. Dark streets lined with overcrowded houses, often underpatrolled by police forces, are perfect settings for acts of violence and robbery, and the poor are particularly vulnerable to petty crime. Small-time criminals, drifters, alcoholics, and drug addicts gravitate toward the inner city where rents are low and law enforcement is lax. Criminal profits are undoubtedly higher in suburban areas, but small-time criminals lack the expertise to overcome the security precautions in suburban homes and to evade the police action that generally results from an articulate complaint made by a prosperous citizen. It is both easier and safer to rob the poor; the pickings are sufficient to satisfy the unambitious criminal. To some extent, poor areas also generate their own crime problems. Poverty, unemployment, and squalid surroundings make the slums and ghettos breeding grounds for envy and frustration which, especially when coupled with real deprivation, lead to crime. The crimes typical of the inner city, such as robbery and personal violence, are also more sensational and less acceptable in respectable society than the typical crimes of the suburbs, such as tax evasion and drunken driving. This ensures that the deserved reputation of the inner city as a high crime area is both widely publicized and much deplored. Furthermore, people have found it convenient to classify the poor, already social pariahs because of their poverty, as criminals as well and thus to package all undesirable elements together in one tidy and identifiable group.

Once an area acquires a reputation as a high crime district, its reputation sinks even lower. The affluent people living in nearby districts are frightened into moving away, thus abandoning new neighborhoods to the poor. High crime rates have a bad effect on police morale and reduce the effectiveness of other civic employees who provide services essential in slum districts. Garbage collectors and sanitation workers are reluctant to enter many inner-city areas, and firemen, disillusioned by innumerable false alarms and frequent attacks by malicious crowds, have sometimes refused to answer alarms from these districts. High crime rates thus tend to increase official wariness and neglect of inner-city slums, and as a consequence, their already poor services worsen.

As the unofficial boundaries of the poor inner city and the prosperous suburbs become more clearly defined, less personal contact takes place between the prosperous and the poor. The modern city of great geographical distances is also the city of great social distances. Slum dwellers, feeling that the prosperous have everything while they have nothing, become frustrated and angry and occasionally resort to arson and riot. Slum dwellers tend to equate suburbanites with "the system," an economic and social structure that has not allowed them to reap many of its rewards. Their frustrations at being poor in a prosperous world are thus often directed not only at the government and authority figures who personify the system, but also against prosperous people who benefit from it. Lack of money and lack of education has made it difficult for the poor to organize, despite their shared frustrations. Some poor groups, however, such as American blacks, whose identifying characteristics have long made them targets of discrimination, are now beginning to use those characteristics to build a sense of community that extends beyond the inner city.

For their part, many suburbanites are also becoming frustrated and angry and are helping to intensify tensions between the prosperous and the poor and between majority and minority groups. They feel, for example, that the taxes they pay are higher than services warrant. Many conclude that they pay for ill-advised, expensive schemes that support lazy welfare swindlers in poor districts. They suspect that the people who do not work or pay taxes are the same ones who steal and destroy property and that their taxes subsidize thieves, vandals, and undeserving riffraff. In addition, many suburbanites feel extremely threatened by rising crime rates and juvenile delinquency. They frequently attribute stolen cars, burglarized houses, robbed and looted stores, and vandalized schools entirely to whatever minority group happens to inhabit the local slum. Thus, when local officials ask for tax increases to build more and better schools, to hire special teachers for slum areas, to finance social welfare programs in the inner city, or to pay for more firemen and policemen in high-crime areas, taxpayers are increasingly prone to resist. Many conclude that the poor are personally expensive to them, ungrateful, idle, destructive, and undeserving of the special treatment they have received. Some feel that public charity should be abandoned and that hard work, discipline, and punishment when appropriate should be substituted for it. To the poor, such ideas sound like threats to deprive them of the little they do have.

If the poor could see that the glittering version of the good life as represented by the mass media is far from the truth and that the typical middle-class family suffers from financial problems, personal frustrations at work, and family problems at home, they might be less apt to imagine that the whole of society has conspired against them and given every possible hardship to them alone. If the prosperous could see that willingness to work was no guarantee of a job, that hard and devoted work may well yield miserable wages, and that the general level of life sustained by welfare payments is degradingly poor compared with their own, they might feel less hostile to the poor. As long as the prosperous avoid contact with the poor by living in different neighborhoods, and as long as the poor have no opportunity to see firsthand the realities of prosperous life in the suburbs, there is little hope of better understanding. Modern urban society is rapidly dividing into two societies, and each section has as little knowledge of and personal acquaintance with the other as it has acquired of life in China or Africa from TV travelogues.

Urban social tensions are, of course, more complex than any brief presentation such as this can suggest. Indeed, each year seems to give birth to new tensions or revive old ones. Racial problems in the United States have become temporarily less violent but far more complicated; racial problems in Britain are mounting and there is a movement to compel black Commonwealth immigrants and their children to "go home"; the protests of the young against the old and the world they seem to have made have become commonplace; Catholics and Protestants have turned the urban areas of Northern Ireland into a battlefield. The basic patterns of these and many other manifestations of social tensions are, however, remarkably similar. In the background of each is the increasing social distance generated by the nature and form of the modern city.

Confronting Urban Problems

Since the majority of people in Western nations are now urban residents, urban problems inevitably affect the lives of every citizen. Because the majority of voters also live and work in urban areas, urban conditions are included among the major political issues of the twentieth century. Urban problems have also acquired an additional edge of urgency because the drift of people into towns and cities continues, promising an intensification of urban problems in the future. Despite the widespread concern about these problems and their enormity and multiplicity, surprisingly little effective action has been taken to solve them. For the most part, the lines of approach have been variations of those taken in the nineteenth century, and not many advances have been made in understanding the basic causes of the problems.

Attempts continue to be made to establish utopian communities.

Settlements born out of a utopian drive that have survived and succeeded
have done so generally only by arriving at a compromise between utopian
ideals and urban realities, but in accepting the compromise they have
acquired many of the problems of the nonutopian world. Salt Lake City,
for example, was the product of the ideals of the early Mormons. While
some of its problems may be less acute than those experienced in other
major cities, it has not avoided the characteristic ones such as pollution and
urban sprawl. A much more common approach taken by utopians, from
the Amish to "counterculture" farming-commune members, has been to
solve the problems of urban industrialism by simply abandoning it. This
approach has dealt with urban problems no more effectively than living
beside Walden Pond did in the past. The "ideal society" utopias can work
on a large scale only if human nature is reshaped and cooperation is raised
to hitherto unprecedented levels. Agrarian-based utopias bear little
relevance to the conditions and problems the majority of Western
humanity faces now and will continue to face in the future. Unless there
is a dramatic reduction in the population or the Western economy reverts
to a much more primitive stage, the forces of urban industrialism will
continue to shape society and utopias will make little contribution to
solving the problems that confront most people.

The charitable impetus that generated social reform in the nineteenth century continues to operate in a slightly amended fashion in the
reform movement of the present century. There is less direct, overt,
individual "charity" visible in the twentieth century, but the evident
concern of many prosperous people for the general condition of
humanity, for human rights, and for equal opportunities for all citizens
springs from sources similar to the philanthropy of the nineteenth
century. The diffuse humanitarianism of today also fulfills similar
purposes, although it operates less at a personal and more at a
governmental level. The replacement of private social reform programs
with government ones has had a variety of consequences, including a less
visible and direct transaction between the rich and the poor in the
donation of financial support and a more even distribution of national
wealth among the population of some Western nations with very highly
developed social welfare programs.

The most powerful impetus toward reform in the twentieth century,
as in the nineteenth, is a consequence of the immediate, practical impact
of urban and social problems on the lives, homes, and families of the
prosperous and politically active segments of the population. If the
diseases of the poor can spread to the homes of the prosperous, then the

poor must have health and sanitation services; if poverty drives people to crime and the crime spreads into prosperous districts, then poverty must be alleviated. The realization that undesirable conditions and activities cross the barriers between poor and prosperous districts has resulted in attempts to treat many of the symptoms of disorder in modern cities, such as through social programs that ensure that the poor are fed, educated, and given some medical care. While many such programs have succeeded in attaining relatively limited goals in some countries, they have also generally succeeded in raising the expectations of the poor without giving them the means of gratifying their wants fully or allaying their frustrations and aggressions.

The fact that problems persist and even increase despite reform schemes has generated disillusionment and frustration in the would-be reformers, the would-be reformed, and in those whose taxes finance the reforms, but the lack of resounding success is entirely understandable and even foreseeable. To date, the problems of the modern city have been dealt with by making piecemeal attempts to treat various isolated symptoms, not the disease. Schemes such as model cities and urban renewal are the best practical treatments yet devised, but they have proven no more effective in the treatment of the problems of the modern city than scraping off the scabs and applying cheap makeup would be in the treatment of smallpox. If a cure is to be effected, the treatment must act upon the disease, not its symptoms alone.

Because of the nature of the urban mechanism, as long as the forces that currently determine city form continue to dominate, the city will clearly continue to rot in its center and sprawl at its outer edges. This pattern is undesirable for it seems directly linked to slums, crime, automobile accidents on overcrowded highways, waste of natural resources, and pollution from too many cars used too often in too small a space. The excessive consumption of land by suburban growth is especially serious when suburban sprawl swallows up the fertile farmland needed to feed the still-growing population. If individual communities ignore the car, urban growth passes them by and goes elsewhere. On the other hand, cities that make good provisions for cars exhibit all the worst urban problems and are beginning to strangle in a web of highways.

There are few basic alternatives available to those who would try to solve the problems of the modern city. The Western world can simply live with them and hope for new innovations to emerge that will automatically change city shape as dramatically as the new industrial economy and the car reshaped the first industrial city and hope that these alterations are desirable. Alternatively, reformers can attempt what has not so far been done very successfully on a large scale, that is, to analyze the forces that make the city work the way it does and then deliberately manipulate them to produce the most desirable urban form. With few sophisticated tools at their disposal, the people of nineteenth-century cities used civic government to modify their city form sufficiently to keep the city from being a death trap. The best hope for future manipulation, short of waiting for a piece of economic or technological luck, seems to lie in similar popular and governmental initiatives that make use of the many sophisticated tools of modern technology. The ramifications of such actions would be significant and numerous, but legislation could be passed to regulate the use of the automobile, to make cars too expensive to use in cities, to make suburban land more expensive to use than inner urban land, and generally to use economic incentives to revitalize public transportation and bring coherence back to the urban form. The people of the nineteenth century adjusted only after tens of thousands had needlessly died and when their cities were on the verge of becoming totally unacceptable living places. Modern cities have not yet provided twentieth-century people with a similar incentive to act.

EPILOGUE

Mechanisms of Change

The city has acted as an agent of social change because it has continually operated as an environment for the generation and practice of innovations of all kinds. The city is like a huge translating machine in which economic pressures and technological innovations are converted into social structures. The economic pressures that individuals exert within society are generally highly complex, but in the simplest terms they boil down to the individual's desire to survive. To this basic economic imperative people have appended a variety of additional goals: to secure a future free from want, to gain rest from labor, to achieve an optimum degree of material comfort, to provide for the welfare of the next generation, and to attain spiritual satisfaction. From the first experiments with fire to the latest applications of atomic energy, mankind has reshaped social forms and functions through technology to better attain basic economic goals. The combination of the current manifestations of economic drives and of current technical capacity at any given time produces the city form "typical" of that time. For example, the needs of trade, defense, and church organization, combined with a technological capability that included transport using wheels and sails and a production system that relied heavily on individual skill and handwork with a few comparatively elementary tools, determined the form and character of the medieval city. It functioned within the wider framework of a predominantly agrarian society whose upper levels were still engaged in a struggle for regional or national political and legal power. The form that resulted was the nucleated walled city with a marketplace and church at its core.

The pressures of the enormously productive, mass-consumption economy, combined with a complex and advanced technological capacity perhaps best symbolized by the family automobile, determine the character of the modern city. The city form produced is the giant suburb city composed of an unprecedented number of highly mobile people with a high material standard of living who perform a wide variety of specialized tasks.

The form and functions of the city at any given time impose conditions on the people who live in it. They must shape their lives to suit the demands and requirements of the city if they are to survive and prosper within it. For example, the familial or tribal organizations suited to a small farming community with a primitive technology became inadequate after the invention of the wheel and the sail when extensive trade became possible. As trade became a major economic factor within the community, its need for surplus production and specialists grew. The farming village thus developed into a trading, manufacturing, and marketing town, and needed new social forms to provide for new situations such as the incorporation of alien traders and craftsmen without kin or tribal connection with any of the original inhabitants. If the community was to prosper and grow, it had to produce a social structure flexible enough to cope with the new pressures imposed by increasing specialization of function and with more frequent and broader contacts with the outside world. It eventually had to be complex enough to organize people so that the community could build large and expensive civic, military, and religious structures. Many centuries later, the corporate social organizations that developed in response to the needs of medieval trading and manufacturing cities proved inadequate when technological innovations made powered machines, faster methods of transport, and larger markets available. The product of these innovations was an industrial economy in which efficient production for a large market became the dominant economic drive. The urban community faced problems of unprecedented expansion in the age of industrialism. It had to develop a new kind of working system suited to the capabilities of industrial machines and to evolve a new social value system in harmony with the increased wealth that accompanied expanding production. The larger urban community also had to change the habits of its citizens and the machinery of government in order to make the improvements that would reduce the epidemic diseases and high death rates threatening its existence.

The need of the city for food and the raw materials necessary for manufacturing and trading has always had a profound effect on surrounding rural areas. As cities grew, they imposed an increasing pressure on agricultural society to produce larger surpluses of food and raw materials. Rural people responded to these pressures by cultivating more land and by using more efficient farming methods. Exceptionally high demands occasionally led to urban intervention in rural affairs by military occupation, the introduction of slave labor, the imposition of taxes payable in food and raw materials, or by a combination of methods designed to increase the surpluses available to the urban population. Generally, however, the profits that could be made by meeting the urban demand for rural commodities provided sufficient incentive to change the rural economy, and technological innovations provided the means by which farmers could increase their efficiency and the size of their surpluses. In short, the needs of the cities imposed conditions on countrymen that caused them to adjust to changes in urban areas. Although rural change took place more slowly and took less extreme forms than in urban society, the cities' demand for food, raw materials, and trade goods eventually transformed Western rural society completely by leading it away from subsistence farming and self-sufficiency to cash-crop production and, hence, to a symbiotic relationship with the city.

Although the needs of the city have had profound and direct effects on the development of Western society, society generally has been unable to shape its cities to accord with philosophical or social ideals. In their direct, day-to-day relationship with the city, people act as selfish economic units and not as wise, farsighted, idealistic members of a community. People find jobs that will pay for food, shelter, and clothing for themselves and their families, and they take houses they can afford, regardless of the philosophical or social ideals of society. Only when basic needs are satisfied do people begin to operate at a second level, as members of the urban community. A highly skilled, educated, modern city dweller, for example, may be deeply concerned about the problems of cities, the consumption of resources, and the destruction of the natural environment, but his first priority is to find a job for himself and a comfortable home for his family. He often finds that the only demand for his particular skills is in the central business district, while the most desirable homes are in the suburbs. Consequently, he commutes from his suburban home to his job in a central office block. He may at the same time demand that "something be done about" inner-city decay, suburban sprawl, traffic congestion, and air pollution. If he acted unselfishly on the basis of his ideals, he would live in the inner city within walking distance of his job, thus reducing traffic congestion and pollution, adding a prosperous voice to the clamor for better inner-city services, and helping to bridge the gap between rich and poor societies. Few individuals, however, can flaunt social convention in this way, and even fewer wish to do so when such actions would merely add to their personal discomfort. As long as the city dictates that homes are in the suburbs, that white-collar jobs are in the central city, and that transportation is by automobile, all but eccentrics or renegades shape their lives to fit the established patterns. The mass of the people, restricted by their basic personal desires to survive, get jobs, and do their best for themselves and their families, are relatively powerless to exert any pressure to change the city by direct personal action.

People react primarily as individuals to the demands currently imposed by city forms and functions, which in turn are created by current economic pressures and technological capacities. In some senses, human beings determined these city-shaping forces; it might be supposed that humans, therefore, ultimately shape the urban environment. In practice, however, people have been able to exercise little deliberate and effective control over the city-shaping forces because these tend to act as if they had no human connection at all. Reduced to the simplest terms, economic pressures are the sum total of all individual human material needs; technological capacity is essentially the sum total of human efforts in problem solving. A massing of the needs of multitudes of people to survive, to acquire possessions, and to provide for the future ceases to be a collection of individual activities and becomes a monolithic entity called the economy. The trading economy of the medieval city comprised a combination of such individual drives as the need of the shoemaker to sell shoes to support himself and his family, the desire of the weaver to get a dowry for his daughter, and the longing of the spice merchant to be the most powerful man in his city. Similar individual drives compose the modern industrial economy: the need of the lathe operator to support his family and his desire to send his children to college, the desire of the engineer and his teacher wife to own prestigious cars in which to commute to work from the suburbs, and the drive of the stockbroker to amass enough money to enter the social circle of the very rich whose position and material possessions he envies. At the level of the particular shoemaker or engineer these drives are under human control, and in the twentieth century, at least, a variety of techniques are available by which some central agency might manipulate them. Society has been reluctant, however, to attempt to overhaul the economy according to some carefully drawn plan by tampering with the human drives that make the economy work.

Technology has proven similarly difficult to control. Individuals generate innovations and inventions and others put them into operation for individual purposes; once in operation, however, they become part of the technical capacity of the age and they, too, slide out of human control and become part of a monolithic, extrahuman force. The first efficient steam engine was truly within human control only when it existed solely as an idea of James Watt, as was the cotton gin when it was an idea of Eli Whitney, and the assembly-line production of automobiles when it was merely a concept of Henry Ford. The innovators transformed their ideas into real machines, and they and others put those machines to use in order to make a better living. As more people bought Watts's engines, used Whitney's gins, and adopted Ford's production techniques, the innovations became part of the economic system of their day.

Society cannot simply decide to change the form and character of cities to make them conform to rationally determined aims and orders of priorities because these basic forces that shape cities are neither conscious nor rational at the operational level. Social agencies that tinker with the form and character of the city cannot, therefore, produce much except a city that has been changed in minor and superficial ways for short periods of time, for the force behind such readjustment plans is pathetically small compared with the tremendous pressures exerted by the economy and technological capacity. Profound changes in the character of the city can only come from the sources from which they have always come, changes in economy and technology.

Although this conclusion may appear to undermine the whole notion of urban planning, in reality it merely places it in its proper context. Cities have been "planned," that is, their sites, streets, buildings, parks, and public facilities have been designed and arranged in a preconceived development pattern, from the earliest stages of urban development. Planning can produce more orderly, more pleasant, and healthier cities, but planning in the conventional sense can do no more than effect modifications of the current city form or give full expression to its character. The current economy and state of technology make cities viable and determine their basic character. A city planner who lays out a city without functions, with no factories, offices, sources of raw materials, transportation facilities, or services, may create an aesthetically and socially desirable urban environment, but no one will build his city and even if some impractical benefactor should do so, no one would live there.

Any planner who designs a carless city while cars are still the most convenient and cheapest form of transportation will find his city plagued with automobile problems until an attractive and cheap substitute for the private automobile is found and installed. Simple physical planning of the city can do many useful things, but alone it cannot effect a transformation of city form. To expect or to hope for it is unrealistic and unfair to both the planner and the planned-for.

The problems that beset modern cities are legion and range from pollution to poverty to parking problems, from alienation to education to drug addiction. They are, however, all part of the general problem of making cities into places in which the mass of humanity can live harmoniously. At the root of most of the problems lies the fact that innovations have been developed and introduced and have passed into the uncontrollable, autonomous stage of operation more rapidly since the beginning of industrialism than ever before. The pace of change in the twentieth century has become dizzying. In the past, people were able to adjust to small changes in the traditional way of life because they occurred slowly. Over a century or two the sum of the changes was sometimes dramatic, but the adjustments that had to be made over one or two generations were few enough to cause no severe dislocations. Now the rate of change has accelerated to a point at which its pace outstrips human and social abilities to make comfortable adjustments and sound judgments. In many ways, the city has ceased to be the place in which mankind is in closest contact with the future and has become instead the place where the future arrives before mankind has finished coping with the immediate past. The advent of the automobile changed the city before people had fully understood the city of the railway and the subway; very often cities abandoned the latter and poured money into highways only to discover, about half a century later, that they should have spent the money to improve forms of mass transit in the first place. Mass telecommunications arrived before personal and social adjustments had been made to the telegraph and telephone. The full effects of compulsory mass education had not been worked out when education was reduced to a patchwork quilt arrangement based on guesses about future needs.

If Western urban society is indeed being swept toward a future of confusion, disorientation, and social crises, as now seems to be the case, can society get a grip on the forces that shape cities and manipulate them in such a way as to cause them to create a more beneficial urban environment? Meaningful adjustment of the urban mechanism can be made only if the operations of that mechanism are understood and more knowledge is gained about the points at which mankind can interfere in its operations with positive and lasting results. If a disease is to be cured, its pathology must be understood before an effective treatment can be devised. Rarely can simply treating the worst of the symptoms effect a cure. For example, feeding the hungry may actually aggravate the social disease of poverty by raising the number of live births, prolonging life, and hence increasing the population of the poor. Under such "treatment" other symptoms of poverty, such as inadequate housing, are likely to grow worse. In addition, as the disease itself remains uncured, malnutrition will appear again when the gifts of food are withdrawn. Similarly, inner-city slums are not diseases but symptoms of the breakdown of cohesion in modern urban centers. The symptom may be treated by tearing down old slums and building office blocks or low-cost housing in their place, but such physical renovations do not touch the forces that create slums and they will therefore continue to operate. The treatment does not lie in putting old, undesirable conditions into new packages but in doing what has so far rarely even been attempted: to adjust, redirect, or replace the economic and technical forces that cause urban decay in the first place.

Three avenues of approach to the practical solution of the problems of modern cities seem open. The first is to recognize the difficulties involved and do nothing. Bearing in mind that much of what has been done so far has accomplished as much harm as good, this approach is not as unattractive as it might seem at first. It would at least have the virtue of conserving the energy and resources now being spent on programs doomed to failure. The second alternative is to continue the approach of the past, that is, to take palliative measures, to attack the worst symptoms of the disease, and to allow the urban mechanism to operate and develop in response to uncontrolled technological and economic forces. If this is done, urban conditions will undoubtedly get worse before they get better. Cities will continue to sprawl, their centers will sink deeper into decay, and the social cleavages will open wider. With this alternative, as with the first, there is always the possibility that the next group of innovations or the next great economic change will produce forces that will automatically solve the problems and bring cohesiveness and vitality back to the cities. As most of the operations of the city have yet to be completely analyzed or understood, problem solving by this means is clearly a matter of luck. Economic and technical change could just as easily plunge the city into even deeper trouble

The third choice is to use the vast potential for problem analysis provided by modern industry and technology to define the operations and problems of the city in more precise terms. Groups of specialists and sophisticated computers could undertake this task, but much would depend on how well society was prepared to follow their prescriptions. This approach would involve something new: the deliberate manipulation of city-making forces with the aim of creating an urban pattern and environment predetermined as the one most likely to produce socially desirable effects. The basic outlines of some possible measures are already evident. For example, if suburban sprawl and inner-city decay are undesirable, the forces that make cities rot around the center and sprawl at the edges must be altered. The changes recommended might include vast investments on mass-transit systems followed by the closing of freeways in cities to all local traffic, regulating the use and size of cars and trucks within city boundaries, the elimination, or at least reduction to a nominal fee, of fares on public transportation, and the manipulation of land prices and taxes in order to make land inside city boundaries more desirable for development than land at the fringes. If residential areas segregated by income and status cause great social problems, adjustments must be made to produce nonsegregated housing throughout the city and its suburbs, perhaps by requiring that all housing projects contain some houses for the very poor and the very rich and that all houses be built to the same high standards. It might be done by redistributing incomes on a national scale to minimize inequality of wealth, or by providing for rent subsidies for low-income people. Most of these possibilities involve increased national, regional, and civic government controls on almost every aspect of life, which many people will undoubtedly find unpalatable. The manipulation of land prices and taxes to limit suburban expansion and the imposition of economic controls that make public transit virtually free to everyone while also making it financially impossible for the average person to use a car to commute from the suburbs to the central city will outrage many suburbanites and bring up questions of individual freedom of action.

Nothing is without its price and it may well be that the price of better cities is a dramatic, enforced change in the style of life of urban people throughout the West. Alternatively, the price of the modern urban way of life is a battery of urban problems. The great difficulty lies in choosing, and there is no doubt that many will echo the protest of the *London Times*, when confronted with urban reform in the nineteenth century, that it would rather take its chances and die of cholera than be bullied into health.

Bibliography
Index

Bibliography

A reasonable bibliography would require at least one additional volume, and a short reading list adequate for all purposes is impossible to construct. The following list is inadequate and is intended merely to suggest the wide range of materials that are readily available. The chronological breakdown is by no means precise, since not all authors follow the same chronological framework, and some overlapping is inevitable.

General

Ariès, Philippe. *Centuries of Childhood: A Social History of Family Life.** New York: Random House, 1962.

Barnett, Homer G. *Innovation: The Basis of Cultural Change.** New York: McGraw-Hill, 1963.

Cipolla, Carlo. *Economic History of World Population.** Baltimore: Penguin Books, 1962.

Derry, T. K., and Williams, Trevor I. *A Short History of Technology from the Earliest Times to A.D. 1900.* New York: Oxford University Press, 1961.

Dickinson, Robert E. *The City Region in Western Europe.** New York: Humanities Press, 1967.

————. *The West European City: A Geographical Interpretation.** 2nd ed., rev. London: Routledge & Kegan Paul, 1968.

Dyos, Harold J., ed. *The Study of Urban History.* New York: St. Martin's Press, 1968.

* Paperbacks are starred throughout.

Gilmore, Harlan W. *Transportation and the Growth of Cities*. New York: Free Press, 1953.

Gras, Norman S. *A History of Agriculture in Europe and America*. 2nd ed. New York: Johnson Reprint, 1968.

Gutkind, Erwin A. *International History of City Development*. 7 vols. New York: Free Press, 1964–72.

Handlin, Oscar, and Burchard, John, eds. *The Historian and the City*.* Cambridge, Mass.: MIT Press, 1963.

Hollingsworth, T. H. *Historical Demography*. Edited by R. Elton. Ithaca: Cornell University Press, 1969.

Mumford, Lewis. *The City in History: Its Origins, Its Transformations, and Its Prospects*.* New York: Harcourt Brace Jovanovitch, 1968.

———. *The Culture of Cities*.* New York: Harcourt Brace Jovanovitch, 1970.

———. *Technics and Civilization*.* New York: Harcourt Brace Jovanovitch, 1963.

Toynbee, Arnold J., ed. *Cities of Destiny*. New York: McGraw-Hill, 1967.

Usher, Abbott P. *A History of Mechanical Inventions*. Rev. ed. Cambridge, Mass.: Harvard University Press, 1954.

Weber, Max. *The City*.* Translated and edited by Don Martindale and Gertrud Neuwirth. New York: Free Press, 1958.

Wrigley, E. A. *Population and History*.* New York: McGraw-Hill, 1969.

From Community to Empire

Adams, Robert M. *The Evolution of Urban Society: Early Mesopotamia and Prehispanic Mexico*.* Chicago: Aldine-Atherton, 1966.

Africa, Thomas W. *Rome and the Caesars*.* New York: John Wiley & Sons, 1965.

Balsdon, J. P. *Life and Leisure in Ancient Rome*. New York: McGraw-Hill, 1969.

Bottero, Jean; Cassin, Elena; and Vercoutter, Jean, eds. *The Near East: The Early Civilizations*. New York: Delacorte Press, 1967.

Braidwood, Robert J., and Willey, Gordon R., eds. *Courses toward Urban Life: Archaeological Consideration of Some Cultural Alternates*. Chicago: Aldine-Atherton, 1962.

Carcopino, Jerome. *Daily Life in Ancient Rome: The People and the City at the Height of the Empire*.* New York: Bantam Books, 1971.

Childe, V. Gordon. *What Happened in History*.* Baltimore: Penguin Books, 1954.

Clark, Grahame. *Archaeology and Society*.* New York: Barnes & Noble, 1960.

Ferguson, William S. *Greek Imperialism*. New York: Biblio & Tannen, 1941.

Forrest, William G. *The Emergence of Greek Democracy*.* New York: McGraw-Hill, 1967.

Frankfort, Henri. *Kingship and the Gods: A Study of Ancient Near Eastern Religion as the Integration of Society and Nature.* Chicago: University of Chicago Press, 1948.

Frost, Frank J. *Greek Society.** Lexington, Mass.: D. C. Heath, 1971.

Glotz, Gustave. *The Greek City and Its Institutions.* Translated by N. Mallinson. New York: Barnes & Noble, 1965.

Gruen, Erich S., ed. and comp. *Imperialism in the Roman Republic.** New York: Holt, Rinehart and Winston, 1970.

Hammond, Mason. *The City in the Ancient World.* Cambridge, Mass.: Harvard University Press, 1972.

Hodges, Henry. *Technology in the Ancient World.* New York: Alfred A. Knopf, 1970.

Lampl, Paul. *Cities and Planning in the Ancient Near East.** Edited by George R. Collins. New York: George Braziller, 1968.

MacMullen, Ramsay. *Soldier and Civilian in the Later Roman Empire.* Cambridge, Mass.: Harvard University Press, 1963.

Moscati, Sabatino. *The World of the Phoenicians.* Translated by Alistair Hamilton. New York: Praeger Publishers, 1968.

Rostovtzeff, Mikhail I. *Social and Economic History of the Hellenistic World.* New York: Oxford University Press, 1941.

———. *Social and Economic History of the Roman Empire.* 2 vols. Edited by P. M. Frazer. New York: Oxford University Press, 1957.

Saggs, H. W. F. *The Greatness That Was Babylon: A Sketch of the Ancient Civilization of the Tigris-Euphrates Valley.** New York: New American Library, 1968.

Sjoberg, Gideon. *The Preindustrial City: Past and Present.** New York: Free Press, 1965.

Storoni Mazzolani, Lidia. *The Idea of the City in Roman Thought: From Walled City to Spiritual Commonwealth.* Translated by S. O'Donnell. Bloomington: Indiana University Press, 1970.

Wheeler, Mortimer. *Roman Art and Architecture.** New York: Praeger Publishers, 1964.

White, Lynn, Jr., ed. *The Transformation of the Roman World.* Berkeley: University of California Press, 1966.

Wilson, John A. *The Culture of Ancient Egypt.** Chicago: University of Chicago Press, 1956.

Wycherley, R. E. *How the Greeks Built Cities.** New York: Doubleday, 1969.

The Medieval City

Adelson, Howard L. *Medieval Commerce.** New York: Van Nostrand Reinhold, 1962.

Bloch, Marc. *Feudal Society.** 2 vols. Translated by L. A. Manyon. Chicago: University of Chicago Press, 1968.

Boissonnade, P. *Life and Work in Medieval Europe: Fifth to Fifteenth Centuries.* San Francisco: William Gannon, 1927.

Brucker, Gene A. *Florentine Politics and Society, 1343–1378.* Princeton: Princeton University Press, 1962.

Burke, G. L. *The Making of Dutch Towns: A Study of Urban Development from the Tenth to the Seventeenth Centuries.* New York: Simmons-Boardman, 1960.

Carus-Wilson, Eleanora M. *Medieval Merchant Venturers.** 2nd ed. New York: Barnes & Noble, 1967.

Duby, Georges. *Rural Economy and Country Life in the Medieval West.* Translated by Cynthia Postan. Columbia: University of South Carolina Press, 1968.

Lane, Frederic C. *Andrea Barbarigo, Merchant of Venice, 1418–1449.* New York: Octagon Books, 1967.

Lopez, Robert S., and Raymond, Irving W., eds. *Medieval Trade in the Mediterranean World: Illustrative Documents.** New York: W. W. Norton, 1967.

Lucas-Dubreton, J. *Daily Life in Florence in the Time of the Medici.* Translated by A. Lytton Sells. New York: Macmillan, 1961.

Luzzatto, Gino. *An Economic History of Italy from the Fall of the Roman Empire to the Beginning of the Sixteenth Century.* Translated by Philip Jones. New York: Barnes & Noble, 1961.

Mundy, John H., and Riesenberg, Peter. *The Medieval Town.** New York: Van Nostrand Reinhold, 1958.

Parkes, James W. *The Jew in the Medieval Community: A Study of His Political and Economic Situation.* London: Soncino Press, 1938.

Pierenne, Henri. *Early Democracies in the Low Countries: Urban Society and Political Conflict in the Middle Ages and the Renaissance.** Translated by J. V. Saunders. New York: W. W. Norton, 1971.

——. *Medieval Cities: Their Origins and the Revival of Trade.** Translated by Frank D. Halsey. Princeton: Princeton University Press, 1969.

Robertson, Durant W., Jr. *Chaucer's London.** New York: John Wiley & Sons, 1968.

Rörig, Fritz. *The Medieval Town.** Translated by D. J. Matthew. Berkeley: University of California Press, 1967.

Russell, Josiah C. *Medieval Regions and Their Cities.* Bloomington: Indiana University Press, 1972.

Sapori, Armando. *The Italian Merchant in the Middle Ages.** Translated by Patricia Ann Kennen. New York: W. W. Norton, 1970.

Strauss, Gerald. *Nuremberg in the Sixteenth Century.** New York: John Wiley & Sons, 1966.

Thrupp, Sylvia L. *The Merchant Class of Medieval London.** Ann Arbor: University of Michigan Press, 1962.

Waley, Daniel. *The Italian City-Republics.** New York: McGraw-Hill, 1969.

White, Lynn, Jr. *Medieval Technology and Social Change.** New York: Oxford University Press, 1966.

The Early Modern City

Barbour, Violet. *Capitalism in Amsterdam in the Seventeenth Century.** Ann Arbor: University of Michigan Press, 1963.

Blunt, Anthony. *Art and Architecture in France, 1500–1700.* Baltimore: Penguin Books, 1953.

Bridenbaugh, Carl. *Cities in Revolt: Urban Life in America, 1743–1776.* New York: Oxford University Press, 1970.

Chrisman, Miriam U. *Strasbourg and the Reform: A Study in the Process of Change.* New Haven: Yale University Press, 1967.

Cipolla, Carlo M. *Guns, Sails and Empires: Technological Innovation and the Early Phases of European Expansion, 1400–1700.** New York: Pantheon Books, 1966.

Clark, Peter, and Slack, Paul, eds. *Crisis and Order in English Towns, 1500–1700.* Toronto: University of Toronto Press, 1972.

Dickens, A. G. *Reformation and Society in Sixteenth Century Europe.** New York: Harcourt Brace Jovanovitch, 1966.

Dobb, Maurice. *Studies in the Development of Capitalism.** Rev. ed. New York: International Publishers, 1964.

Ehrenberg, Richard. *Capital and Finance in the Age of the Renaissance: A Study of the Fuggers and Their Connections.* Clifton, N.J.: Augustus M. Kelley, 1928.

Forster, Robert, and Forster, Elborg, eds. *European Society in the Eighteenth Century.** New York: Harper & Row, 1969.

Herlihy, David J. *Pisa in the Early Renaissance: A Study of Urban Growth.* Port Washington, N.Y.: Kennikat Press, 1973.

Lamb, Harold. *The City and the Tsar: Peter the Great and the Move to the West.* New York: Doubleday, 1948.

Marshall, Dorothy. *Dr. Johnson's London.** New York: John Wiley & Sons, 1968.

Martines, Lauro. *The Social World of the Florentine Humanists, 1390–1460.* Princeton: Princeton University Press, 1963.

Monter, E. William. *Calvin's Geneva.** New York: John Wiley & Sons, 1967.

Nef, John U. *Western Civilization since the Renaissance: Peace, War, Industry, and the Arts.** New York: Harper & Row, 1963.

Parry, J. H. *Europe and a Wider World, 1415–1715.* London: Hutchinson, 1949.

Ranum, Orest A. *Paris in the Age of Absolutism.** New York: John Wiley &
    Sons, 1969.
Saint-Simon, Louis. *Louis XIV at Versailles.* Translated by Desmond Flower.
    Chester Springs, Pa.: Dufour Editions, 1954.
Soboul, Albert. *The Parisian Sans-Culottes and the French Revolution, 1793–94.*
    Translated by Gwynne Lewis. New York: Oxford University Press, 1964.
Tapié, Victor L. *The Age of Grandeur: Baroque Art and Architecture.** Translated
    by A. Ross Williamson. New York: Praeger Publishers, 1961.
Tawney, Richard H. *Religion and the Rise of Capitalism: A Historical Study.**
    Gloucester, Mass.: Peter Smith, 1963.
Walker, Mack. *German Home Towns, Community, State, and General Estate,
    1648–1871.* Ithaca: Cornell University Press, 1971.
Weber, Max. *The Protestant Ethic and the Spirit of Capitalism.** New York:
    Scribners, 1930.

The Industrial City

Anderson, Nels. *The Industrial Urban Community: Historical and Comparative
    Perspectives.** Appleton-Century-Crofts, 1971. .
Ashworth, William. *The Genesis of Modern British Town Planning.* New York:
    Humanities Press, 1954.
Booth, Charles. *Life and Labour of the People in London: Poverty.* 5 vols. 1902.
    Reprint. Clifton, N.J.: Augustus M. Kelley, 1969. 2nd series: *Industry.* 5
    vols. Clifton, N.J.: Augustus M. Kelley, 1970.
Brace, Charles L. *The Dangerous Classes of New York and Twenty Years' Work
    among Them.* 1880. Reprint. Montclair, N.J.: Patterson Smith, 1968.
Briggs, Asa. *Victorian Cities.** New York: Harper & Row, 1970.
Brody, Eugene B., ed. *Behavior in New Environments: Adaptation of Migrant
    Populations.* Beverly Hills, Calif.: Sage Publications, 1970.
Buer, M. C. *Health, Wealth, and Population in the Early Days of the Industrial
    Revolution.* New York: Howard Fertig, 1968.
Deane, Phyllis M. *The First Industrial Revolution.** Cambridge: Cambridge
    University Press, 1966.
Geddes, Patrick. *Cities in Evolution: An Introduction to the Town Planning
    Movement and to the Study of Civics.** New York: Harper & Row, 1971.
Green, Constance M. *American Cities in the Growth of the Nation.** New York:
    Harper & Row, 1965.
Habakkuk, H. J. *American and British Technology in the Nineteenth Century: The
    Search for Labour-Saving Inventions.** Cambridge: Cambridge University
    Press, 1967.
Hansen, Marcus, L. *The Atlantic Migration, 1607–1860.** Edited by Arthur M.
    Schlesinger. New York: Harper & Row, 1961.

Hartwell, Ronald M., ed. *The Causes of the Industrial Revolution in England.** New York: Barnes & Noble, 1967.

Jephson, Henry L. *The Sanitary Evolution of London.* 1902. Reprint. New York: Benjamin Blom, 1972.

Landes, David S. *The Unbound Prometheus: Technological Change and Industrial Development in Western Europe from 1750 to the Present.** Cambridge: Cambridge University Press, 1969.

Mandelbaum, Seymour. *Boss Tweed's New York.** New York: John Wiley & Sons, 1965.

Masur, Gerhard. *Imperial Berlin.* New York: Basic Books, 1971.

Mayhew, Henry. *London Labour and the London Poor.** 4 vols. New York: Dover Publications, 1968.

McKelvey, Blake. *The Urbanization of America, 1860–1915.* New Brunswick, N.J.: Rutgers University Press, 1969.

Morazé, Charles. *The Triumph of the Middle Classes.** New York: Doubleday, 1968.

Nef, John U. *Cultural Foundations of Industrial Civilizations.* Cambridge: Cambridge University Press, 1958.

Pinkney, David H. *Napoleon III and the Rebuilding of Paris.** Princeton: Princeton University Press, 1972.

Riis, Jacob. *How the Other Half Lives: Studies among the Tenements of New York.** 1902. Reprint. Gloucester, Mass.: Peter Smith, 1972.

Rosen, George. *A History of Public Health.* New York: MD Publications, 1958.

Rosenberg, Charles E. *The Cholera Years: The United States in 1832, 1849 and 1866.** Chicago: University of Chicago Press, 1968.

Rostow, Walt W. *The Stages of Economic Growth: A Non-Communist Manifesto.** 2nd ed. Cambridge: Cambridge University Press, 1971.

Rudé, George F. *The Crowd in History, 1730–1884.** New York: John Wiley & Sons, 1964.

Schlesinger, Arthur M. *The Rise of the City, 1878–1898.** Chicago: Quadrangle Books, 1971.

Sennett, Richard. *Families against the City: Middle Class Homes of Industrial Chicago, 1872–1890.* Cambridge, Mass.: Harvard University Press, 1970.

Sheppard, Francis H. W. *London, 1808–1870: The Infernal Wen.* Berkeley: University of California Press, 1971.

Shyrock, Richard H. *The Development of Modern Medicine.* New York: Hafner, 1969.

Simon, John. *English Sanitary Institutions, Reviewed in Their Course of Development and in Some of Their Political and Social Relations.* 1890. Reprint. New York: Johnson Reprint, 1970.

Stearns, Peter N. *European Society in Upheaval: Social History since 1800.** New York: Macmillan, 1967.

Thompson, Edward P. *The Making of the English Working Class.** New York: Random House, 1966.

Tobias, J. J. *Crime and Industrial Society in the Nineteenth Century.* New York: Schocken Books, 1968.

Tunnard, Christopher, and Reed, Henry H. *American Skyline: The Growth of Our Cities and Towns.** New York: New American Library, 1956.

Weber, Adna F. *The Growth of Cities in the Nineteenth Century: A Study in Statistics.** 1899. Reprint. Ithaca: Cornell University Press, 1963.

Wilcocks, Charles. *Medical Advance, Public Health, and Social Evolution.** Elmsford, N.Y.: Pergamon Press, 1965.

The Modern City

Adams, Bert N. *Kinship in an Urban Setting.** Chicago: Markham, 1968.

Berry, Brian J. L. *Geography of Market Centers and Retail Distribution.** Englewood Cliffs, N.J.: Prentice-Hall, 1967.

————, ed. *City Classification Handbook: Methods and Applications.* New York: John Wiley & Sons, 1972.

Bott, Elizabeth. *Family and Social Network: Roles, Norms, and External Relationships in Ordinary Urban Families.** 2nd ed. New York: Free Press, 1972.

Bracey, John H., Jr.; Meier, August; and Rudwick, Elliott, eds. *The Rise of the Ghetto.** Belmont, Calif.: Wadsworth, 1971.

Clark, Samuel D. *The Suburban Society.** Toronto: University of Toronto Press, 1966.

Coulter, Philip B., ed. *Politics of Metropolitan Areas: Selected Readings.** New York: Thomas Y. Crowell, 1967.

Doxiadis, K. A., and Douglass, Truman B. *The New World of Urban Man.** Philadelphia: United Church Press, 1965.

Duncan, Beverly, and Lieberson, Stanley. *Metropolis and Region in Transition.* Beverly Hills, Calif.: Sage Publications, 1970.

Ferman, Louis A.; Kornbluh, Joyce L.; and Haber, Alan, eds. *Poverty in America: A Book of Readings.** Rev. ed. Ann Arbor: University of Michigan Press, 1968.

Freeman, Thomas W. *The Conurbations of Great Britain.* 2nd ed. New York: Barnes & Noble, 1966.

Gans, Herbert J. *The Levittowners: Ways of Life and Politics in a New Suburban Community.** New York: Random House, 1969.

Ginger, Ray, ed. *Modern American Cities.** Chicago: Quadrangle Books, 1969.

Glaab, Charles N., and Brown, A. Theodore. *A History of Urban America.** New York: Macmillan, 1967.

Glazer, Nathan, ed. *Cities in Trouble.** Chicago: Quadrangle Books, 1970.

Gottmann, Jean. *Megalopolis: The Urbanized Northeastern Seaboard of the United States.** Cambridge, Mass.: MIT Press, 1964.

Green, Constance M. *The Rise of Urban America.** New York: Harper & Row, 1967.

Halebsky, Sandor, ed. *The Sociology of the City.* New York: Scribners, 1973.

Hatt, Paul K., and Reiss, Albert J., Jr., eds. *Cities and Society.* 2nd ed. New York: Free Press, 1957.

Hoover, Edgar M., and Vernon, Raymond. *Anatomy of a Metropolis.** New York: Doubleday, 1962.

Howard, Ebenezer, *Garden Cities of To-Morrow.** 1902. Reprint. Edited by F. J. Osborn. Cambridge, Mass.: MIT Press, 1965.

Jacobs, Paul. *Prelude to Riot: A View of America from the Bottom.** New York: Random House, 1968.

Kramer, John, comp. *North American Suburbs: Politics, Diversity, and Change.** Berkeley: Glendessary Press, 1972.

Lieberson, Stanley. *Ethnic Patterns in American Cities.* New York: Free Press, 1962.

McKelvey, Blake. *Emergence of Metropolitan America, 1915–1966.* New Brunswick, N.J.: Rutgers University Press, 1968.

Merlin, Pierre. *New Towns: Regional Planning and Development.* Translated by Margaret Sparks. London: Methuen, 1971.

Moynihan, Daniel P., ed. *On Understanding Poverty: Perspectives from the Social Sciences.** New York: Basic Books, 1969.

Mumford, Lewis. *The Highway and the City.** New York: New American Library, 1964.

———. *The Urban Prospect.** New York: Harcourt Brace Jovanovitch, 1968.

Murphy, Raymond E. *The American City: An Urban Geography.* New York: McGraw-Hill, 1966.

Pollock, F. *The Economic and Social Consequences of Automation.* Translated by W. O. Henderson and W. H. Chaloner. Oxford: Blackwell Scientific Publications, 1957.

Schnore, Leo F. *Class and Race in Cities and Suburbs.** Chicago: Markham, 1972.

Suttles, Gerald D. *The Social Construction of Communities.* Chicago: University of Chicago Press, 1972.

Tunnard, Christopher. *The City of Man: A New Approach to the Recovery of Beauty in American Cities.** 2nd ed. New York: Scribners, 1971.

Whyte, William H., Jr. *The Last Landscape.** New York: Doubleday, 1968.

———. *The Organization Man.** New York: Simon & Schuster, 1972.

Wilensky, Harold L., and Lebeaux, Charles N. *Industrial Society and Social Welfare.** New York: Free Press, 1965.

Wilson, James Q., ed. *Urban Renewal: The Record and the Controversy.* Cambridge, Mass.: MIT Press, 1967.

Yeates, Maurice H., and Garner, Barry J. *The North American City.* New York: Harper & Row, 1971.

INDEX